D1030848

HIDING
THE ELEPHANT

How Magicians

Invented the Impossible

JIM STEINMEYER

MAGICIANS' PORTRAITS BY WILLIAM STOUT

William Heinemann: London

Published in the United Kingdom in 2004 by William Heinemann

1 3 5 7 9 10 8 6 4 2

Published by arrangement with the original publishers, Carroll & Graf

William Heinemann
The Random House Group Limited
20 Vauxhall Bridge Road, London, SW1V 2SA

Random House Australia (Pty) Limited
20 Alfred Street, Milsons Point, Sydney
New South Wales 2061, Australia

Random House New Zealand Limited
18 Poland Road, Glenfield
Auckland 10, New Zealand

Random House (Pty) Limited
Endulini, 5a Jubilee Road, Parktown, 2193, South Africa

The Random House Group Limited Reg. No. 954009
www.randomhouse.co.uk

A CIP catalogue record for this book is available from the British Library

Papers used by Random House are natural, recyclable products made from
wood grown in sustainable forests. The manufacturing processes conform
to the environmental regulations of the country of origin

Printed and bound in the United Kingdom by
Mackays of Chatham Plc, Chatham, Kent

ISBN 0 434 01325 0

For Frankie

Contents

List of Illustrations

Photographs

Portraits by William Stout

Cast of Characters

THEO BAMBERG (1875–1963)
The fourth generation in a family of Dutch magicians, Bamberg performed as Okito, impersonated an Oriental conjurer, and toured in American vaudeville.

DION BOUCICAULT (1822–1890)
A popular Irish actor and playwright who authored "The Corsican Brothers" and invented the Corsican Trapdoor to produce a ghost; he offered his endorsement to the Davenport brothers.

GEORGE A. COOKE (1825–1904)
John Nevil Maskelyne's partner at Egyptian Hall in London, he started as Maskelyne's boyhood friend from Cheltenham, and worked as an assistant in many of the illusions.

IRA ERASTUS DAVENPORT (1839–1911) AND
WILLIAM HENRY HARRISON DAVENPORT (1841–1877)
Two Buffalo, New York brothers who originated the controversial cabinet séance act and presented it on stages around the world.

JOSEPH BUATIER DEKOLTA (1848–1903)
An ingenious French magician who began his career with sleight of hand magic and later invented a number of trendsetting mechanical illusions such as The Vanishing Lady.

DAVID DEVANT (1868–1941)
Respected among his peers for his mix of skill, creativity and a natural performing style on stage, this British magician became famous as Maskelyne's partner at St. George's Hall in London.

HENRY DIRCKS (1806–1873)
A British civil engineer and author who discovered an optical principle to produce transparent ghosts on a theatre stage; the idea was licensed to Professor Pepper at the London Polytechnic.

HORACE GOLDIN (1874–1939)
At the turn of the 20th century, this American illusionist and vaudeville star was best known for the whirlwind pace of his act; he later became famous for performing the illusion, Sawing a Woman in Half.

WILL GOLDSTON (1878–1943)
An author and London magic dealer who was notorious for publishing the secrets of the most popular illusions; he was a longtime friend of Harry Houdini.

ALEXANDER HERRMANN (1843–1896)
A French-born wizard, his Mephistopheles-like appearance formed the cliché of a magician; after a long run at Egyptian Hall in London, he became a popular star in America.

HARRY HOUDINI (1874–1926)
Brash, dynamic American vaudeville performer who started as a magician and achieved his greatest success as an escape artist; he made an elephant disappear at the New York Hippodrome in 1918.

HARRY KELLAR (1849–1922)
Avuncular, business-like and beloved by his audiences, this touring American magician proudly filled his program with the finest illusions from London.

GUY JARRETT (1881–1972)
Famous among magicians for his opinions and innovations, this expert behind the scenes worked as an assistant to Howard Thurston and created illusions for Broadway shows in the 1920s.

JOHN NEVIL MASKELYNE (1839–1917)
The respected chief of British magic, he began his career by imitating the Davenport brothers' cabinet act and later founded the famous Maskelyne theatre of magic at Egyptian Hall in London.

NEVIL MASKELYNE (1863–1924)
Part of the second generation of Maskelyne magicians, John Nevil's son considered himself a scientist, although he took part in the family business, writing plays, and performing onstage.

JASPER MASKELYNE (1902–1973)
One of the third generation of Maskelyne magicians, he performed during the final years at St. George's Hall in London and in British music halls.

CHARLES MORRITT (1860–1936)
A versatile British magician, impresario, and music hall hypnotist, he worked for the Maskelyne family and was renowned by his associates as an expert in optical magic.

GEORGE MÉLIÈS (1861–1938)
French magician, proprietor of the Theatre Robert-Houdin, and pioneer filmmaker; he was responsible for developing many special effect techniques for the cinema.

PROFESSOR JOHN HENRY PEPPER (1821–1900)
Popular director of London's Royal Polytechnic Institution, lecturer on science, and the first man to produce optical ghosts on the stage.

JEAN EUGENE ROBERT-HOUDIN (1805–1871)
A renowned, innovative French magician, he opened his own theatre in Paris and featured a unique mix of sleight of hand and beautiful mechanical apparatus.

P.T. SELBIT (1879–1938)
A British music hall magician who created the Sawing through a Lady illusion in 1920—this was just one of his many original inventions for the stage.

COLONEL STODARE (1832–1866)
A Liverpool-born magician and ventriloquist who surprised London audiences when he presented Tobin's latest illusion, called The Sphinx—a living head on a table.

HOWARD THURSTON (1869–1936)
The successor to Kellar and America's favorite magician from 1908 to 1936; Thurston was known for his easy rapport with children and a wonderful speaking voice.

THOMAS WILLIAM TOBIN (1844–1883)
A chemist, architectural apprentice and scientific lecturer at London's Polytechnic Institution, as a young man he discovered an optical formula for invisibility on a stage.

PAUL VALADON (1869–1913)
A German magician and sleight of hand artist who performed at Egyptian Hall in London, he stole important secrets before joining the show of the American magician Harry Kellar.

Introduction

In November 1995 I found myself standing offstage at a Los Angeles theatre with a brown Sicilian donkey named Midget, who, I was about to tell the audience, could disappear.

There was major problem with this situation.

I don't consider myself a performer. I first learned about magic the way many have, as a kid with a drawer full of magic books who made visits to the local magic shop. I might have been a bit luckier than most. I had the example of my older brother, Harry, whose love of magic was balanced with a practical emphasis on the amount of serious work involved, planning, scriptwriting, and rehearsal. My local magic shop was one of the finest in the country. Magic Incorporated, in Chicago, was an old-fashioned shop with dusty shelves in back that yielded countless long-forgotten treasures—rare books, crumbling manuscripts, and brown paper-wrapped props that had been lacquered and stacked back in the 1930s, when the enterprise was first founded as the Ireland Magic Company. In the late 1960s and into the 1970s, when I was growing up, the shop was owned by Jay and Frances Marshall, two true professionals with talent and experience. At that time, the city was the home of a number of amazing old vaudevillians and a group of innovative sleight-of-hand magicians who had perfected the fast-paced Chicago style, which was well-suited to working behind a bar, entertaining the customers, and keeping them happy as drinks were being served. Other well-known magicians passed through town and naturally stopped in to spend the afternoon with Jay and Frances.

My early performing experience consisted of children's birthday parties, fun fairs, and the occasional Blue and Gold Banquet, an annual

Cub Scout event that seemed to require after-dinner entertainment for the boys. I carried my props in a black wooden box that could be unfolded into an upright table: the Egg Bag, the Sliding Die Box, and a wooden duck that pulled individual cards out of a deck. I endured rowdy audiences of kids who hooted, hollered, and heckled—always anxious to know how the tricks were done. I performed at talent contests, Christmas parties, and ice cream socials; the last of these involved standing on a lawn on summer evenings, hoarsely reciting my patter while linking and unlinking five large steel rings. After presenting magic shows throughout my school years, I met a number of veteran professional magicians and was offered opportunities to work with their shows. I was hired to plan their acts, set-up props backstage, or work as an assistant. Humbled by my employers' performance skills, I quickly realized that I'd better stick to offstage operations, working in the wings or inventing and designing material that could be used by magicians in the spotlight. With my days as the star of the show over, I took heart in the fact that many good performers relied on others to help create their effects. I've been privileged, over the years, to work with many of illusion's most popular and successful practitioners.

Technically, of course, that makes me a magician. I've studied the techniques and immersed myself in the labor of magic. I've even written books on magic—new technical material for magicians as well as historical volumes on the great illusions of the past. But the actual process of spending months training a donkey to perform with me in a magic act, then putting on a tuxedo, listening to the music, and awaiting our cue, convinced me that I had drifted far out of my element.

Then, too, I knew that the Disappearing Donkey, the illusion I was about to perform, was from a different era. It wasn't intended to dazzle the audience. It was slower, clumsier, and more complicated than the current fashions in magic. I was hoping only to prove a point and to demonstrate the result of my speculations, the revelation of a puzzling secret that had been created, perfected, and then perfectly kept by an Edwardian British showman. Because of my work with magicians and my interest in the obscure history of the art, I've been involved in exploring a number of forgotten inventions. The Donkey had become a personal mission, a particular mystery that had teased me for many years.

During my career in magic, I have come to think of it as an art. This isn't a lofty, self-aggrandizing pose, but it sometimes seems like idealism. If you've ever browsed the practical jokes and blister-packed novelties at a magic shop, read a description of a do-it-yourself trick suitable for "idiots," or ever endured the obsessions of an amateur magic club meeting, you would realize that magicians have survived by generating notoriously sturdy constitutions, ignoring the shambling, tawdry elements that surround them, and focusing on the tiniest, most glorious achievements. The process is a lifetime of continually panning for gold. To really understand magic, you need to nudge past the tyros at the magic shop and sidle up to the old professionals standing in the corner, who aren't interested in the five-dollar plastic envelopes stuffed with instructions, but are whispering in a weird sort of shorthand—the names of past masters, the precise moment they chose to "accidentally" drop a silk handkerchief on the stage and pick it up, or the particular bend in their thumb as they cut a deck of cards in preparation for a shuffle. Audiences have seldom looked beyond the *how* of magic, rarely asking *why*, *when*, or *who*. It's not simply the tricks that are amazing, but the personalities, presentations, and psychology—the thousand careful choices surrounding any illusion and the intricacies and subtleties involved in any performance. These are the touches that can elevate magic to an art.

Generally, there have been two approaches to writing about magic. Many books appeal to the public by breathlessly promising to tell "how it's done," then marching through techniques in shorthand: It's done with a mirror, the box has a false panel, or the lady slips through a trapdoor. In this way, the secrets sound simple, crude, and uninteresting. On this level of X's and O's, they are.

Other books simply ignore the techniques of magicians or consider them too precious to discuss. They keep the secrets and focus only on the personal histories of the performers.

My experience tells me that the story of magicians can only be understood when you understand their art. And the secrets are only impressive when you understand the people responsible, the theatrics, and the history surrounding them.

So readers may be surprised to find that this story does indeed explain a number of secrets, some of the important techniques that have been used by magicians onstage. Perhaps I may be considered guilty of breaking ranks and betraying trust.

Actually, there's a long, important tradition of magic being recorded and published. As my good friend Jay Marshall, the man behind the counter at the magic shop, has said for many years, "If you want to keep something a secret, publish it." Once in print, information is often filed, forgotten, or dismissed. Publishing a secret takes away its cachet and causes it to be overlooked. Every illusion that I've discussed in this book has already been explained in books. Sometimes they were explained by the people who invented or performed them; sometimes they were described by writers who studied them or recorded the backstage gossip. If you feel the revelations in *Hiding the Elephant* are especially shocking, I'll take that as a compliment. The particular secrets that I've explained here I first found when I was a boy, in books published for the public that were in the local library. I've merely put them into context, pointing out why these principles of magic were significant and how they evolved and were sometimes mistakenly ignored or dismissed.

As an illusion designer myself, I've tried to be judicious about my explanations. I've left out plenty of technical information and a number of working details, that, quite simply, aren't necessary for the sake of this story. I've focused on particular inventions and ignored additional creations that were being used by those performers during their careers. I also haven't explained which of these historical illusions have been discarded, which are still being used, and which I've actually been using within the last few years to deceive audiences of Broadway shows, Las Vegas revues, and television specials. Based on my observations of audiences in this field, I know what you'll overlook or forget the next time you see an entertaining performance by a magician. Ultimately, the end result is part science and part showmanship. The great, creative magicians were practical men of the theatre who wrestled with their techniques to surprise their audiences with something new.

The story of *Hiding the Elephant* is a small slice of magic's history, the story of optical conjuring, and how a series of ingenious magicians and curious characters developed their art by refining, inventing, and adapting. There was also a certain amount of spying, embezzling, and back-stabbing, which belied the fairy tale images illuminated by the footlights. And, befitting a profession of mystery, many elements of this story have remained unknown, even within the small world of magicians.

My interest in magic had led me to believe that making a donkey disappear would be an important experiment, testing a secret that had been used by Houdini in the early twentieth century to hide an elephant. It's ironic that I'd spent years studying donkeys and elephants, but never ventured into the realm of political chicanery. My interests were strictly confined to the most honest type of trickery, the magician who advertises that he will deceive you and then does. Which brings us back to Midget, my donkey in Los Angeles, now impatient that the show hasn't started, puffing, pawing, and stomping at the doors of the theatre.

—Jim Steinmeyer

1
Overture

Houdini Hides an Elephant
—*Variety* headline, 1918

At the height of his career, during the longest continuous theatrical run of his lifetime, Harry Houdini boldly marched to the edge of the stage at the New York Hippodrome and propelled his voice across the footlights to an expectant crowd of 5200 people, announcing his newest headline-making innovation.

"Lay-deeahs and gintle-menh," he began, holding a finger upright. "Perhaps you have all-red-dy heard of the fame and a-comp-lish-ments of my spesh-shel guest!" The world-famous daredevil, escape artist, self-liberator, movie star, publicity genius, and mystery performer was in real life a little man. On the enormous stage of the Hippodrome, he seemed even smaller, but he compensated with an outsized energy, just as he had corrected a thick East Side of Manhattan accent by overenunciating each syllable; his words stabbed the back wall of the theatre like a knife. "Allow me to in-tro-duce Jennie! The world's only vanishing ell-ee-phant!"

Crowds expected a lot at the Hippodrome. The theatre was famous for its ambitious productions, bigger, better, more opulent, and more spectacular than any other vaudeville show. Audiences had seen entire armies invade the stage, marching bands, cavalry charges, and zeppelin attacks. They had craned their necks as the circus acts performed overhead, and they had inched forward in their red plush seats as an earthquake-like rattle seemed to dislodge the wide wooden platform. Slowly, the famous stage sank out of sight, revealing torrents of water, that bubbled up to fill a large tank. Enter the boats, the water ballet, and diving horses.

A Hippodrome show was a special treat for New Yorkers and out-of-town guests, but it was never sophisticated entertainment, with the pretensions of the Broadway revues or plays one block west on Seventh Avenue. The Hippodrome was designed to make audiences gasp, smile, and write home about. This particular show, titled "Cheer Up," predictably included a patriotic medley filled with hundreds of American soldiers. Houdini was the guest act and had been included halfway through the run of the show in order to give it a boost of publicity and attract new crowds.

It was fitting that Houdini had chosen the Hippodrome for the premiere of the largest illusion ever attempted. Even the décor of the theatre was a perfect match—Moorish filigree and white marble, and hundreds of gilt elephant heads adorning the electric wall sconces and the tops of each column.

As Houdini completed his introduction, an animal trainer dashed onto the stage, leading Jennie, a full-grown Asian elephant. The ample backstage space at the Hippodrome gave her plenty of room to make a spectacular entrance, running at full speed as she came into view, circling Houdini in wide arcs, shaking her head from side to side with each stride. Jennie was nearly eight feet tall and weighed over six thousand pounds, monstrous and graceful at the same time. The audience likely recognized her as one of Powers' Elephants, a group of performing pachyderms that were regularly featured in Hippodrome revues. For this performance she wore a gigantic baby-blue ribbon around her neck and a "wristwatch"—an alarm clock tied around her hind leg. Jennie stopped in the center of the stage; she stood on her back legs, saluted the audience by raising her trunk, and finally reached over to Houdini to give him a slobbery kiss. He rewarded her with a handful of sugar cubes and joked about how she was contributing to the sugar shortage caused by the Great War.

The curtain opened on an oversized wooden box, about the dimensions of a small garage and decorated like a brightly colored circus wagon. It was raised off the stage by large wheels. As a Sousa march rumbled from the orchestra, the trainer led Jennie stoically up a ramp, through two opened doors, and into the box. Few in the audience would notice this point: It wasn't simply the Vanishing Elephant, but the Vanishing Elephant and Trainer. The doors were then closed as a crew of Hippodrome stagehands in white uniforms and cotton gloves leaned against the corners of the box, slowly giving the circus wagon a quarter turn.

The audience might have suspected that the great beast would be lowered through the floor into the famous Hippodrome water tank, but as the box was raised on wheels, it was plain that Jennie was still inside. The apparatus was far from the curtains, isolated in the center of the vast stage.

Houdini, now little more than a black speck hovering in front of the action, signaled for the orchestra to stop. "Watch closely . . . for it happens in two sec-conds," he proclaimed. The whole operation had in fact taken several minutes to this point, but no one would quibble with his exaggeration. Drumroll. He clapped his hands, and the stagehands, taking their cue, quickly ran to the opposite ends of the circus wagon. They reached over and opened circular doors, cutout panels in the ends of the wagon so the audience could look straight through the box to the bright curtains hanging at the back of the stage. A loud crash chord, and Houdini turned to face the audience. "You can plainly see . . . the an-nee-mile is com-plete-ly gone!" Houdini was right. The box really looked empty.

The Great Houdini bowed deeply as the front curtains closed. Amazing. And then the most amazing part: The Hippodrome patrons squinted at the scene, mumbled to themselves, and let go with what seemed a collective shrug, contemplating the next feature on the busy program: a trapeze act. They'd just seen the most gigantic wonder ever presented on a stage yet greeted it with only a deflating smattering of applause.

Houdini was a terrible magician.

That's not how he's remembered, of course. But to his public, during the first decades of the twentieth century, Houdini wasn't thought of as a magician at all; he was the *escape artist*, the fellow who got out of jails, swam to the surface after being nailed in a box and thrown into the river, or wriggled out of a straitjacket while dangling upside-down from the cornice of a building. Houdini was fiercely proud of his escape specialty; it was his innovative, new act that had made his name on vaudeville and music hall stages. His sensational challenges as an escape artist had quickly given Houdini legendary status, which transcended the variety stage and make him the envy of magicians, comedians, jugglers, and singers. He was no mere amusement; he was a myth: a lone figure who challenged the system, a hero who refused to be restrained.

As far as audiences were concerned, there were other men who were great magicians, like Howard Thurston, who toured American cities every year with his big show and covered the sides of buildings with his colorful posters. In London there was David Devant, of the famous Maskelyne and Devant Theatre of magic, who produced solid ivory billiard balls between his fingertips or performed in dramatic plays featuring stage illusions. In one of his most memorable effects, he made a lady disappear in the middle of a well-lit stage; as he attempted to embrace her, she seemed to dissolve into thin air. In vaudeville you could see T. Nelson Downs, whose specialty was sleight of hand with hundreds of silver dollars, or P.T. Selbit, who toured with famous mysteries like Sawing through a Woman or Crushing a Lady.

Houdini was about something altogether different. He was not especially graceful or elegant, as magicians were expected to be, but was a restless collection of shapes: slightly bowlegged, with muscular shoulders and a triangular face. He'd found his calling with the escape act, which complemented his brash, rough-around-the-edges appearance. But Houdini desperately wanted to be a magician, a real magician.

Houdini's Vanishing Elephant was the result of over fifty years of careful experiments by stage magicians in France, England, and the United States; it was also a secret that had been purchased by Houdini and the latest flourish in his spectacular career, spanning a lifetime of theatrical mysteries. The man behind the trick remains a puzzle. Harry Houdini was a famously complicated personality, and much of his life seemed to consist of dares, challenges and denouncements, which were played out in his vaudeville act. He had been born Erich Weiss in 1874, and his early inspiration was the romantic, adventurous autobiography of Jean Robert-Houdin, the Parisian magician of the mid-1800s. *The Memoirs of Robert-Houdin* so influenced him that he took a stage name derived from Robert-Houdin's as an homage.

Robert-Houdin's book was filled with his picaresque adventures, brushes with royalty, and dramatic triumphs over superstitious tribes in Algeria, who deeply believed in magic and were cowed by the French master. Renowned as the "Father of Modern Magic," Robert-Houdin had a short but spectacular career. In 1845 he opened his own theatre in Paris and performed elegant, sophisticated conjuring. His illusions were ingeniously combined with mechanical figures, called *automata*, which he constructed.

Such a world must have seemed like a wonderful dream to young Erich. He quickly learned the rudiments of the craft, endlessly practicing the maneuvers in Robert-Houdin's own guide to sleight of hand and swapping the latest secrets at the local magic shop. Robert-Houdin had written of his overnight success in magic, instant acceptance into the world of Parisian society, and his glittering career. He was celebrated in the capitals of Europe for his ingenious deceptions and inventions. Houdini found work in grimy dime museums, the big-city versions of sideshows, where the magic act was given a few short minutes to impress the crowd as they paraded past a row of human oddities. Houdini's first successes consisted of the usual handkerchief and card tricks; for a while he billed himself as the "King of Cards," trying to impress audiences with his newly mastered manipulations and flourishes. He worked on the midway at the Chicago Columbian Exposition in 1893; in a burlesque show in Manchester, New Hampshire; on the platform of a medicine show in Kansas; and in a small tent circus through Pennsylvania, where he presented a magic act, performed as a singing clown, and then muddied his face and climbed into a cage to appear as the "wild man." Show business for him was not very much like the world of Robert-Houdin.

Houdini's beloved innovations, the escape tricks that set him apart and gradually became the staple of his act, were derived from traditional magic. The Davenport brothers, New York performers in the 1860s, had presented an act in which they were tied securely inside a large wooden cabinet. When the cabinet was closed, a series of chilling, ghostly manifestations was produced from the cabinet. The brothers secretly escaped from the ropes to orchestrate the illusions, and then retied themselves before the cabinet was opened again. Houdini's act emphasized the *freedom* rather than the *spirits*, challenging his audience to restrain him with ropes, chains, or handcuffs. John Nevil Maskelyne of London had introduced the escape from a sealed trunk around the time Erich was born. Maskelyne's escape required several minutes as the trunk was concealed inside a cabinet. Houdini increased the pace of the trunk escape, calling it Metamorphosis. He would be locked inside the trunk, which was then hidden by a curtain. Houdini's brother, outside the trunk, clapped his hands three times, signaling three seconds. When the curtain was pulled open, they'd changed places. Houdini was outside the trunk. His brother was now securely locked inside.

His escapes, not the card tricks or handkerchief tricks, made Houdini a success. Vaudeville theatres and music halls were always anxious for the latest novelty. Houdini's remarkable iconography—the little man taking on the bonds of society—was evidenced in the elaborate challenges that he proudly accepted. In London in 1904, early in his career, Houdini was dared to escape from a special pair of handcuffs that had taken a proud British workman five years to make; they were designed using the famous "pick-proof" Bramah lock, the pride of English machining. Houdini hesitated. The *Daily Illustrated Mirror* formalized the contest, wondering if the smart-talking Yank was worthy of his reputation. The next day, thousands crowded into a London theatre to watch Houdini take on the *Mirror*'s cuffs. They were clamped on his wrists, the key turned, and he retired inside a small curtained cabinet to begin his work in secret.

The following seventy minutes are legendary. After working diligently in his cabinet for over half an hour, Houdini emerged perspiring, with his collar pulled away. The audience was ready to applaud but was disappointed to see the cuffs still firmly in place. Houdini asked that the lock be opened so he could remove his coat. The audience groaned. The representative of the paper demurred. After all, this was an obvious ruse to see how the lock operated. No, he refused to open the cuffs unless Houdini admitted defeat. The audience must have shared in this opinion. The wily American was trapped, suggesting a transparent excuse to gain his advantage.

Houdini shrugged, pulled a penknife from his pocket, opened it, and held it in his teeth. He gathered his frock coat over his arms so that it hung at his wrists, and dramatically shredded the coat with the knife, bit by bit, until he could pull the pieces away from the handcuffs: dared, defied, defiant. The audience whooped and cheered. Houdini disappeared back into his cabinet.

The band played on for almost 30 minutes longer. Houdini readjusted the curtains to get a better look at the lock; he called for a glass of water. Suddenly, he bounded from the cabinet, free of the impenetrable cuffs.

The audience nearly rioted. Houdini sobbed in relief; the committee onstage hoisted him to their shoulders and carried him around the theatre as handkerchiefs were waved and the crowd shouted their approval. It took one hour and ten minutes for Houdini to play all the parts: outsider, bounder, conniver, then victim, gentleman, hero.

The current opinion, based on experts who have examined the *Mirror* handcuffs and the records of the event, is that Houdini had staged it all. He had the cuffs made and then entrusted them to a man who would deceptively step forward to "challenge" him, and this careful preparation seems consistent with the way he went about all of his escapes. Houdini took bold challenges for his publicity; he seldom took real chances with his escapes. Ultimately, well-reported episodes like the escape from the *Mirror* cuffs made Houdini's reputation as a determined, mysterious master of locks. There wasn't anything magical about it, even if the performance was a glorious deception.

His most famous escapes, like being locked inside a giant-sized milk can or shoved upside-down into the tall, narrow aquarium of water he called the Chinese Water Torture Cell, were thrilling examples of showmanship and sensational features in vaudeville. Houdini portrayed himself as the little man and delicately cast the proceedings as a cross between a sporting event, a noble acceptance of a dare, and an execution. The audience seemed to sense that they were watching something extraordinary, and more than a few have commented on the odd sensation of being in the audience when—those in attendance suddenly remind themselves—something might go wrong.

Despite the myths that have filled out Hollywood screenplays, Houdini never failed in an escape. He was too much a perfectionist, too careful in his planning. He also never disappointed an audience. For example, twice a night, as he performed the Chinese Water Torture Cell, which he featured for thirteen years in his career, he was locked in the tank of water and surrounded by a curtained cabinet.

The audience waited patiently, calculating how long they could hold their own breaths. Sometimes Houdini escaped in as little as thirty seconds. Sometimes he extended the suspense, taking over two minutes before showing that he was free. During these longer acts, the spectators shifted uncomfortably in their seats, calculating that he must have run out of air. With the anxiety at a fever pitch—and there is no question that Houdini had a supernatural ability to calculate this moment—he would burst through the curtains, dripping with water, gasping for breath. His specialty was convincing each person that they had witnessed a near catastrophe.

All his life, Harry Houdini proudly associated with magicians. He was president of the Society of American Magicians and the Magicians' Club of London. His fellow performers seemed to tolerate Houdini as one would a spoiled child, indulging his monstrous ego, nodding politely through his arguments, and congratulating him lavishly on any successes. Mostly, they stayed out of his way, as he tended to view any performing magician as a rival.

Sometimes, strangely, even dead magicians seemed to be rivals. Houdini had long collected materials on the history of magic, with an aim toward writing a book on the subject. During his years of research, his focus changed, and he began collecting facts that challenged the importance of his idol, Robert-Houdin, and in particular the truth of the French master's famous memoirs. The finished volume was titled *The Unmasking of Robert-Houdin*, with the surprising premise that his onetime inspiration and current namesake was actually a fraud. Houdini picked apart many of the showman's exaggerations and quickly labeled him a self-promoter. Where Robert-Houdin wrote modestly, underplaying his abilities, Houdini accused him of ignorance and ineptitude. Houdini even lambasted him for using a ghostwriter.

The Unmasking of Robert-Houdin was indicative of Houdini's mercurial personality and his love of challenges, but the vengeful tone of the book made it an embarrassment. Houdini seemed to forget how inspiring and literary the French magician's memoirs had been; he put it under a microscope and analyzed every phrase as history. A generation later it became apparent just how shortsighted Houdini had been.

Robert-Houdin, researchers now know, was a clever writer who authored his own books. Houdini, on the other hand, regularly employed ghostwriters to clean up his ragged prose, including *The Unmasking of Robert-Houdin*. When his peculiar history was released, magicians thought the accusations were rich coming from Houdini—a man renowned for shameless self-promotion and a tin ear for the fine points of conventional magic. According to his friend the well-known illusionist Servais LeRoy, Houdini

> had a pleasing stage presence but was in no sense a finished magician, although this detail never seemed to trouble him. As an illusionist he never left the commonplace. His escapes were incomparable. I frequently wondered at the indifference of the one and the perfection of the other and finally was forced to the conclusion that his want of originality was the answer.

The very best Houdini mysteries, like his wonderful escapes, were neither elegant nor sophisticated but hinted at supernatural power. At one engagement he appeared to walk through a brick wall, disappearing in a three-fold screen that had been set up on one side of the wall and quickly emerging from another screen on the opposite side. It was a perfect complement to the Houdini myth. Another favorite effect, the East Indian Needle Mystery, consisted of supposedly swallowing a packet of loose needles and a length of thread, then regurgitating them perfectly strung together. It was an old sideshow feat, but it suited Houdini's showmanship.

These successes led him, several times in his career, to deemphasize the straitjackets and water tanks, presenting "Houdini's Grand Magical Revue." In his last tour, Houdini decided to include an extended section of magic. He caused gold coins to appear in a small glass chest (an invention of the reviled Robert-Houdin). He made a bouquet of feather roses grow in a pot. A girl entered a box and disappeared. Another lady was turned into an orange tree. Alarm clocks disappeared on one side of the stage and appeared, loudly ringing, on the other.

"It was awful stuff," in the opinion of Orson Welles, who was taken by his father to see Houdini's last tour in Chicago. The 1926 program consisted of three acts of Houdini: magic, escapes, and exposures of spirit mediums. According to most reviews, Welles's opinion was typical. The escapes, including his upside-down escape in a tank of water, were "thrilling"; the exposures and accompanying lecture on spiritualism were "riveting, like a perverse sort of revival meeting." But the magic merely filled out the evening.

"He was a squat little man in evening clothes," remembered Welles. "The first thing he did was march to the front of the stage and rip off his sleeves; he pulled them right off, showing his bare arms. Can you imagine? A short-sleeved tailcoat? Even as a kid, I realized the coarseness of it. It was supposed to be a sort of 'nothing up my sleeve' thing. Then, of course, he proceeded to perform a bunch of silly mechanical tricks that couldn't have involved his sleeves at all."

Typical was his opening trick, in which a metal lamp supposedly disappeared from one table and reappeared, with a wave of a wand, on another. It was a magic shop item manufactured by the Conradi company, and a touch of a spring telescoped the clanking, mechanical lamps into tabletops. "Houdini's magic was just a bunch of junk," according to Vic Torsberg, a longtime Chicago magician. "You know, that push-button German crap. That's what he performed." At one of Houdini's performances, when fellow magician David Bamberg was in the audience, the lamp trick spectacularly misfired. Bamberg was horrified to see the misshapen metal lamp clearly pop from the tabletop as the audience snickered. Houdini seethed. He stopped the music and promptly informed the audience, "The cause of the failure of this trick is due to the poor workmanship of Conradi-Horster of Berlin."

After years of publicity stunts and dares, Houdini could add little finesse to these illusions; it just wasn't in his nature. Audiences had come to expect genuine thrills from Houdini, and he couldn't make mere tricks worthy of his reputation. Houdini compensated by attempting to portray his performance of magic as a challenge, force-feeding the mechanical wonders to the audience with great dollops of his personality. Watching him play the part of an elegant conjurer was a bit like watching a wrestler play the violin.

The true violinist was Howard Thurston.

"You have to realize that, in their day, Howard Thurston was every bit as well known as Harry Houdini," Walter Gibson once told me. Gibson, the prolific author of *The Shadow* stories and numerous books on magic, had ghostwritten for both Houdini and Thurston and knew them well as friends. Howard Thurston was born in Columbus, Ohio, in 1869 and was America's most successful magician from 1908 to 1936. He toured with an enormous show, featuring a cast of beautiful chorines, an appearing lion, a disappearing horse, Sawing a Woman in Halves, and the Indian Rope Trick—one spectacle after another. "In fact," Gibson believed, "Thurston was probably better known than Houdini. Still, every bit of Thurston's publicity was about getting you into the theatre to see the show. And Houdini's publicity was about creating a legend. As each year passes, Houdini becomes more and more famous, and Thurston is forgotten."

By most accounts, it was Thurston who was the great magician and Houdini who envied his status. Orson Welles, as a boy, idolized Thurston for his captivating voice; the magician was, in many ways, everything that Houdini was not. A small man (Thurston was still some four inches taller than the five-foot, two-inch Houdini), he had a straight back, aquiline nose, high forehead, and dark eyes; he was perfectly suited to evening clothes and not prone to tear them away. Thurston was said to have studied at Moody Bible Institute, and his oratory was worthy of any pulpit. "I wouldn't deceive you for the world," he proclaimed from the stage. There couldn't be a more preposterous statement from a professional magician, but Thurston could make the claim because of his warm rapport with his audiences. He stood behind the curtain during each overture, hidden from the audience but whispering to them his pre-show mantra, "I love you all. . . . I love you all. . . ." He realized that his success was expressing that love on the stage.

Typically, he would linger over the tricks that used children from the audience. A standard effect, in which cards rose from a deck, was enhanced when a little boy in the audience was urged to stand on his theatre seat and pull his father's hair to make the cards rise. The boy, suddenly convinced of his own magic, became the focus of the effect. His father, wishing to indulge him, winced stoically, and Thurston, casting the spell over the proceedings, temporarily turned his audience into the center ring of his magic circus.

Another favorite effect involved a little girl who was, Thurston explained, to be awarded a live rabbit as a pet. She was invited onstage, and the rabbit was wrapped in paper. But checking the parcel, Thurston found that the animal had turned into a box of candy. Sensing the girl's disappointment, Thurston followed her into the audience, and then reached down her father's collar, pulling out another live rabbit. The little girl left the theatre with the candy and the rabbit.

How was it done? On one level it's possible to explain the secret very simply. Thurston swiftly switched the rabbit for a box of candy using a tricked tray; he introduced the final bunny into the father's coat using sleight of hand. But those simple deceptions were secondary to the emotions that played on the face of the little girl: her belief in magic as she seemed to win, then lose, then triumph, after all. Playing out this drama with a child from the audience required the deft touch of a master.

Throughout Thurston's career, his most famous illusion was the Levitation, which he included in every performance. When Thurston spoke of discovering the secrets of levitation from an Indian fakir, his wonderful sermon-trained baritone took command, modulating from a ripple to a wave, slowly casting a spell.

> *In all our lives there are certain events that stand out that cannot be forgotten. I am going to show you something now, ladies and gentlemen, you will remember as long as you live.*

His audience knew instinctively that Thurston had searched the world for such wonders. (He really had toured the Indian subcontinent early in his career as a magician, although his marvelous, invisible lev-

itation device was perfected in London, Cincinnati, and Yonkers.)
When he mumbled the mystic hypnotic incantation that held the
princess aloft, the children in his audience watched, dumbfounded,
convinced of real magic. (His spell was actually a genuine string of
Hindi profanities.) Finally, as the beautiful princess, draped in sweeps
of white and pink silk, floated high over the stage, lying as if asleep in
midair, Thurston passed a seamless metal hoop over her, twice.

> Round your form I cast the mystic spell. Rest and sleep.
> Sleep, Fernanda. Safely, securely, as you did at the temples
> of love in India.

He invited a small boy from the audience onto the stage. Taking the
boy by the hand, Thurston walked him completely around the floating
lady, then lifted him so that he could touch the golden ring on her
finger for good luck.

> It is said, in those parts of the Himalayan Mountains, that
> if you make a wish, a sincere wish, and touch the ring of the
> floating princess, that wish will be granted. True in India.
> True here.

It was more than a trick; it was theatrical magic.

Houdini would have been ridiculous had he attempted this sort of illusion. Still, he was technically a magician, even if he had difficulty convincing the public of this. The secrets of his escapes were hardly the
work of superhuman strength, supernatural flexibility, or supersensi-
tive lock-picking. Much of his work was dependent on the basic
secrets of magic, ingenious and dependable. He didn't take those
secrets to the grave. His brother inherited his apparatus, and Houdini's
particular escape secrets, even his famous Water Torture Cell, have
been studied and copied by other magicians.

Ironically, he did leave the world with one spectacular mystery, a
single feat that has been hotly debated since his death in 1926. It

wasn't one of his daredevil escapes or his headline-making challenges. Instead, it was the lackluster moment of pure illusion in the Hippo-drome: No one really knew where or how he hid that elephant.

This famous illusion, a typical Houdini feat promising more than it delivered, has enthralled generations who have sought to solve it. It presents a real puzzle. How could Houdini's accomplishment, in which a live elephant disappeared in the bright glare of spotlights, have failed to impress an audience? His brief turn on the Hippodrome stage touched upon the essence of the magician's art and the subtle differences between wonder and deception.

In fact, it probably was a great illusion, not for its ability to dazzle his audience but for the backstage intrigue and ingenious thinking that it represented. Houdini's Vanishing Elephant hinted at fifty years of carefully evolved optical illusions for the stage, the work of many past masters at deception, and the particular achievement of one little-known showman, who had been laboring to change the tech-niques of magic. It had started a half-century earlier, on a small stage in London when a British civil engineer discovered that he could create ghosts. It was evolved, in spurts, by a series of ingenious magi-cians and showmen who were anxious to use the latest creations in their performances. They devised marvelous, dreamlike deceptions, which were guarded like backstage treasures or stolen in meticulous acts of espionage. Like any great illusion, Houdini's Vanishing Ele-phant was the result of equal measures of mathematics, optics, psy-chology, and blustery showmanship—a secret perfectly hidden in plain sight.

Magicians guard an empty safe.

In fact, there are few secrets that they possess that are beyond the capacity of a high-school science class, little technology more com-plex than a rubber band, a square of mirrored glass, or a length of thread. When an audience learns how it's done, they quickly dismiss the art: "Is that all it is?"

The real art is how the rubber band is handled with the finesse of a jewel cutter, how a mirror is used or concealed precisely, how a mas-

terful performer can hint at impossibilities that are consummated
with only a piece of thread. Magicians understand the careful inter-
actions of secret and performance and have learned to appreciate the
art for these subtleties. But casual observers, eager to diagnose the
gimmick or solve the deception, focus on the uninteresting part and
are quickly disappointed, the same way one can always turn to the
final pages of a mystery novel.

The success of a magician lies in making a human connection to the
magic, the precise focus that creates a fully realized illusion in
the minds of the audience. The simple explanation is that seldom
do the crude gimmicks in a magic show—those mirrors, threads, or
rubber bands—deceive people. The audience is taken by the hand and
led to deceive themselves.

Jean Robert-Houdin was famous for the opinion that a magician is
actually just "an actor playing the part of a magician." It was an especially important distinction in separating the loud mountebanks on
the street corner making balls appear and disappear beneath three
metal cups from Robert-Houdin's elegant Parisian deceptions. Today
it serves to remind us that a magic show is a piece of theatre, and the
Frenchman's analogy can be extended: A magic effect is a short play
that simulates a supernatural occurrence. Like any real play, there are
characters and a developing plot. There is a progression, or an *arc*, to
the action. There is a surprise and a resolution, which not only com-
pletes the audience's expectations but builds upon them.

Just as no actor would attempt to walk on a stage, instantly begin
crying, and expect to move the audience to tears, no real magician
thinks that a performance consists of flapping an Inverness cape and—
poof!—causing a lady to disappear. It only works that way in comic
books. A great magic performance consists of a collection of tiny lies,
in words and deeds, that are stacked and arranged ingeniously to form
the battlement for an illusion. It's a delicate battle of wits—an audience that welcomes being deceived, then dares to be fooled, alternately questioning, prodding, and surrendering. A great magician
seems always to play catch-up to their thoughts but secretly must stay
two steps ahead—not only solicitous and anticipating, but suggesting.

In order to understand how Houdini hid his elephant, we're

going to have to explain a few secrets. We'll have to violate that sacred magician's oath. In the process, I promise that there will be a few disappointments and more than a few astonishments. But to appreciate magic as an art, you'll have to understand not only the baldest deceptions but also the subtlest techniques.

You'll have to learn to think like a magician.

2
The Ghost

*That apparition was far beyond anything
I could have hoped for.*
—Professor J.H. Pepper

hen I was a boy growing up in the Midwest, I was mystified by the colors of the autumn leaves. The maple leaves in particular seemed unreal, a strange shade of magenta. How could a green leaf take on this color? I remember walking home from school and picking up these leaves from the sidewalk as treasures. I had no idea what to do with them. Certainly, adults weren't interested in them; to them they were things that needed to be raked into piles and burned.

Sometime around the fourth grade, I was told in science class that the reason the leaves turned red was that the chlorophyll in the leaf had died in the autumn, revealing a bright color. I appreciated that the mystery had been completely solved and I could stop wondering about it.

Unfortunately, science often serves the purpose of actively teaching us to stop wondering about things, of causing us to lose interest. Of course, it's good that we take things for granted. The world would be impossible to bear if we were constantly curious about all things, if we woke up each morning wondering if gravity were still in effect. Still, trying to recall the leaves and fourth-grade science, I now have to admit that I don't quite understand why leaves turn red. If I'm really objective about it, it still doesn't make sense to me. I was simply told that it makes sense to scientists, who have figured it all out. I learned to stop being intrigued about the leaves. But do red leaves "make sense"? Or is sense assigned in retrospect? Are leaves red because science says leaves will turn red, or does science say they will turn red because they do turn red? In fourth grade I was given the impression that I had been given a bit of sophisticated scientific information. I now realize that, in the process, something was also being taken from me.

Every once in a while, a simple scientific discovery has been utilized to accomplish the opposite, to captivate people by hinting at some larger intrigue. That's the value of a great bit of magic. It offers the pleasure of something plain and ordinary unexpectedly elevated to a marvel. It's a redemptive feeling, a reminder of many potential wonders. When a magician places a coin in his hand and makes it disappear, it is a reminder that there's something about coins and hands that we've failed to appreciate. Unlike a mere deception or a simple secret, which gives the impression that something's been taken away, a great magician makes you feel like something's been given to you.

The best ghosts have always been theatrical ghosts.

"Real ghosts," whatever they may be, the weird apparitions reported in stately homes or creaky hallways, seem to arrive unexpectedly, function independently of the world around them, and never manage to convey a message or even suggest the reason for their extraordinary appearances. They don't make sense. When photographed, they are hardly there. When questioned, they have nothing to say. Mediums are necessary to interpret for them, and they generally do a bad job. As P.T. Barnum wrote of such ghosts, they are "utterly useless. In fact, none of the ghosts that haunt houses are of the least possible use. They plague people but do no good. They act like the spirits of departed monkeys."

But onstage, ghosts are always important. They're characters that inject meaning into a story by haunting it; they can presage a disaster or mysteriously direct a plot. Often they have a lot to say. Shakespeare was an expert at writing for ghosts. Hamlet's deceased father drifted across the stage, uttered eighty-four lines in blank verse, and efficiently initiated a great and tragic story, still being analyzed for the logical motivations of its characters and the realistic progression of its action.

Of course, if playwrights benefited from the efficiencies of all-knowing spirits, the ghosts themselves also benefited from theatrical conventions. Samuel Taylor Coleridge described the situation as the "willing suspension of disbelief." In a good, captivating story, the audience will happily play along with such fantasies or illusions. In various stage plays throughout the nineteenth century, a ghost's entrance would be announced with a rumble of tympani. The gaslights were dimmed with dark blue glass. An actor draped in white gauze might be greeted with openmouthed stares or screams by other characters. The audience knew he was a ghost because for centuries the tricks and machinery of the stage had made it all clear. Real people entered from the right or left. Gods and angels descended from above. Devils and spirits were pushed through a trapdoor in the floor.

Theatre managers loved these spirits because they made any story seem exotic and dangerous. Playwrights relied upon them to electrify any plot, providing shortcuts to the motivation of characters or infusing a scene with urgency. Victorian audiences found the ghosts in their favorite melodramas provided emphatic sensations, supernatural thrills, and cliff-hanging action. Considered to be on the borderline with reality, the spirits could be cloying and sentimental or irrational and terrifying. Half a century later, these surreal elements would be highly prized in moving picture melodramas.

One of these theatrical ghosts was featured in the play "The Corsican Brothers," first produced in 1852 in London and based on the Dumas novel of the same title. The story concerned twin brothers Fabien and Louis de Franchi, who have a psychic link at dramatic moments in each other's lives. Dion Boucicault wrote his show as a tour de force for the leading actor, Britain's famous Charles Kean, who played the parts of both twin brothers when the show opened at the Princess's Theatre in London. Well aware of the tricks and effects required to enchant an audience, the playwright skillfully planned his script with doubles, trapdoors, and false panels, allowing Kean to weave his way in and out of scenes so that he could duck out, make a quick change of costume, and reappear as the other twin.

The most remarkable of these devices was Boucicault's Corsican Trap, or gliding trap, which he created especially for this play. At the conclusion of an onstage duel, the close of the first act, one brother had a vision of his twin's fate. The stage darkened to moonlight as the orchestra played an eerie, whispering theme, which became famous as the "Ghost Melody." From one side of the stage, the twin's bloodied ghost appeared through the floor. It was moving in an indistinct, surreal manner: standing still, gliding silently across the stage, and ascending at the same time.

Boucicault's ghost was state-of-the-art stagecraft. A wide slot, about twenty feet from right to left, was cut across the stage, and this was covered with a strip of narrow wooden slats, like the flexible surface

of a rolltop desk. A small, oval wooden frame—an oval just large
enough to push a person through—could be pulled along this slot as
the slats were rolled or unrolled on either side of it. The center of the
oval was closed with the bristles of stiff brushes, completing the trap.
In this way the darkened stage floor seemed to be solid.

The other secret was a platform on wheels, beneath the
stage, which moved up an
inclined ramp as it rolled
from side to side with the
trap. As the trap was pulled
right to left across the stage,
the actor, standing on the
platform, rolled with it.

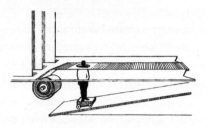

*The Corsican Trap, for the
appearance of the ghost*

Because of the incline, he would gradually ascend through the oval
hole. The trap was operated slowly, allowing the audience to appreciate the strange appearance of the ghost. Concluding his scene by
skillfully finding the small oval trapdoor and standing inside of it, the
ghost disappeared by gliding across the stage as he descended. Not
only was "The Corsican Brothers" an enormous success, but the ghost's
weird appearance was one of the most famous entrances in the history
of the theatre. Queen Victoria saw the production five times,
sketching scenes in her journal and writing of the "alarming" ghost.
When the play was restaged over the next thirty years, with actors
Charles Fechter or Henry Irving, the Corsican Trap and the "Ghost
Melody" were always included; they formed a sort of trademark for
the production. Many leading theatres installed the wide slot for the
Corsican Trap, awaiting the next revival, and until recent years the
platforms and supports for the mechanism could still be seen under a
number of English wooden stages.

Ultimately, the ghost from "The Corsican Brothers," and theatrical
ghosts like it, required the artifice of sliding trapdoors or trick panels
because flesh-and-blood actors played their roles. Ghosts could appear
to melt through walls or the floor only if there were trapdoors that
allowed them to pass. No one could actually make a misty, glowing
ghost materialize on a stage, haunt the scene, then dissolve through

walls or disappear in front of your eyes. Before 1862 those sorts of ghosts could only be imagined.

Henry Dircks was neither a magician nor a medium. He was born in 1806 in Liverpool and worked as a civil engineer, author, patent examiner, and part-time inventor. By 1850 he had "saved some property and was an independent man," according to an associate, and Dircks's patented inventions showed a number of solid industrial pursuits: a variation in locomotive steam engines and wheels, a way of preparing vegetable extracts, gas burners, a sewing machine, a vent for steam boilers, a fire escape. He had contributed an essay on the fallacy of perpetual motion for a book titled *Perpetuum Mobile* and written a book on electrometallurgy and a biography of the second Marquess of Worcester, who invented a model steam engine.

But his strangest and most famous invention was his discovery of how to put a ghost on the stage, which he called the Dircksian Phantasmagoria. Dircks never explained how he came to discover his ghost. He hadn't expressed a particular interest in drama or stagecraft, but he was clearly familiar with optical principles and had studied the standard texts on lenses and mirrors. His proposition involved reflectors, lighting, and some careful geometry. The necessary apparatus could be obtained in any large city, and once a theatre was equipped to show Dircks's ghosts, there would be a wide variety of effects that could be staged.

Perhaps because his ghost was far from his usual area of interest, Dircks seemed unsure of what to do with his invention. He built a small model of his idea and presented it at the 1858 meeting of the British Association for the Advancement of Science in Leeds. His paper was summarized in the *Transactions for the Association* and in journals like *The Engineer, The Mining Journal, Mechanics Magazine,* and *The Athenaeum.* Not surprisingly for the formal and scholarly event, his presentation offered the proper scientific dignity and an array of dry references, and—sandwiched between presentations on natural phenomena, chemical experiments, and mechanical devices—Dircks's invention attracted little interest. Still, he suspected that the idea could revolutionize the stage, making possible a wide range of special effects, materializations, and manifestations, entirely new optical illusions and magical transformations. It would, he believed, change dramatic traditions forever, allowing playwrights to let loose their imaginations. He took his paperwork and an expensive new model to the Coliseum and the Crystal Palace in London, where he expected the theatre owners to welcome him with open arms.

Like many inventors, Dircks saw only the advantages of his plan and ignored its inconveniences. In fact, his invention would have not only revolutionized stage productions, but it would have demanded that theatres be rebuilt. London playhouses recognized that Dircks's proposal was for a brand new construction, with the stage lying below the audience and all the seats in a raised balcony. Dircks also called for special windows installed into the ceiling and walls, insisting that it would take sunlight—and daytime performances—to witness the effect. And yet, matinees were not in favor, and London has never been able to bank on bright sunshine.

Dircks was surprised to see producers assigning little value to his astonishing spectral wonders, calculating them on a balance sheet as calmly as one would account for a new set of costumes. After all, the producers reasoned, Shakespeare had done pretty well without the Dircksian Phantasmagoria. Did Banquo's ghost really necessitate rebuilding their theatres? Dircks's invention was greeted with cursory interest and quickly ignored.

In 1862, with the Christmas theatre season approaching, the instrument makers who manufactured Dircks's model contacted the Royal Polytechnic Institution, asking if they'd be interested in displaying the idea. The Royal Polytechnic was an imposing structure with white columns, on Regent Street opposite Langham Place. When it first opened in 1838, it was intended as a sort of permanent science fair; it supported the latest inventions by displaying them before the public and arranged a series of programs and lectures on scientific topics. Originally, these lectures consisted of training for teachers in chemistry and physics, and classes in navigation for naval officers. But lectures for the public soon became the focus of the institution, and the Polytechnic achieved fame as a popular storehouse of entertaining exhibits and demonstrations more or less related to science.

Visitors to the Great Hall, or the Hall of Manufacturers, could see model steam engines, astronomical clocks, a hydrostatic bed, and manufacturing machinery like printing presses, lathes, looms, and a brick-making machine. A popular feature for many years was a three-ton diving bell, which would be lowered into a tank of water several times a day, accommodating five or six curiosity seekers, who paid a shilling for the experience. An audience in the Hall watched from above. Prince Albert himself tried out the famous diving bell shortly after the Polytechnic opened. Other exhibits—something for everyone—offered a stuffed pig and a wax tableau of the Resurrection.

There was plenty of flashy theatre at the Polytechnic. The Polytechnic was the originator of Dissolving Views lantern shows, which invariably inspired gasps of appreciation from the audience. Painted glass slides of exotic localities were projected on a screen, then overlapped and faded, from one image to another, using six large lantern projectors. The institution also introduced the oxyhydrogen projecting microscope, which could display the contents of a glass slide on a 425-square-foot screen. Crowds were horrified to see the gigantic microbes that merrily swam across the screen as the lecturer casually explained the contents of a drop of London tap water.

One of those lecturers was John Henry Pepper, who joined the Polytechnic in 1848 and attracted crowds with lectures on fermentation, detection of poison, and the process of how coal went from mines to the home. Once, as he was demonstrating one of his chemical experiments before Queen Victoria, Pepper remarked with delicate propriety, "The oxygen and hydrogen will now have the honor of combining before your Majesty." A distinguished gentleman with gray hair, a waxed mustache, and the vocal tone of an earnest, enthusiastic lecturer, he could say something like that with all seriousness. He was a genuine man of science, with a degree in chemistry, but the title "Professor" was awarded by the Polytechnic itself. Pepper's real value to the institution was as a showman, and there was a little bit of Barnum in everything he did. When he assumed the management role as director and sole lessee of the Polytechnic in 1854, those qualities were put to the test, as the Polytechnic depended on a string of novel features to attract the fickle Victorian crowds. Pepper's new programs emphasized diversions: travelogues; model theatres; harps that seemed to play by themselves; readings from Shakespeare; and the "Italian Salamander," Signor Buono Core, who walked through flames.

By 1862 the Polytechnic had survived on a series of crowd-pleasing shows that, despite their tangential ties to science, were every bit as dependent on sensations and wonders as any London theatre. The esteemed John Henry Pepper had no illusions about what was needed to draw the public. When Dircks walked through the door with his model in the autumn of 1862 and promised that he knew how to make a ghost, he found an interested customer in Professor Pepper.

Pepper examined the model carefully. It was a wedge-shaped box that sat on a table near a window in his office. The Professor peeked into a slot at the top, which simulated the experience of the audience looking down at the stage. A number of small, white plaster figures, arranged in the scene, took the place of the actors. "I can see all the characters on the stage," Pepper reported. "What should I be looking for?" "Just keep watching. The play is progressing," Dircks told him.

With Pepper's eyes pressed against the slot, Dircks twisted flaps open on the sides of the model. The light inside shifted slightly. Suddenly, with a flicker, extra figurines appeared magically on the stage. "Oh, I see," said Pepper. As he examined the figures, he realized that they were oddly transparent. He could definitely see the walls and the floor through the little white figures, as if they were made of glass or smoke. "What are they made from?" he asked Dircks. "They're transparent in some strange way."

Dircks twisted the flaps again, and the figures disappeared. "They're supposed to be like that. They're ghosts, remember. Just spirits. They come and go. They can walk, or float, or pass through walls. . . ." Dircks quickly promised a long string of wonders. The characters would appear from nowhere, multiply into other characters or change completely, a man becoming a woman.

Pepper looked up from the model, blinking in the sunlight, and realized that he had seen enough. Ghosts. If he could really produce a spirit on the stage, a real human shape that looked and acted like any specter that had ever been described in fiction, that would surely be enough to bring in audiences. He was anxious to use Dircks's invention but, like any other theatre operator, he was in no position to rebuild the auditorium at the Polytechnic as Dircks was suggesting.

Professor Pepper was determined, and as he came to understand the secret of Dircks's device, he recognized that the invention could be altered to fit in a regular lecture hall. It was something the other theatre managers had missed. Dircks himself had missed it. Pepper arranged for the modified apparatus to be built. The oxyhydrogen lamp, previously used with the projecting microscope, illuminated the effect in place of sunlight streaming through windows. The necessary traps and pits were installed in the stage of the small lecture room.

The ghosts at the Polytechnic first materialized on December 24, 1862, to enhance a dramatic scene from one of Charles Dickens's Christmas stories, "The Haunted Man." That Christmas Eve, audiences entered the dark, narrow lecture room, never suspecting what was in store for them. It wasn't much of a theatre, with a tiny proscenium at the end of the room, more of a large doorway, and a small stage reached by several steps. The curtain opened on a simple story in pantomime. A student toiled at his desk, studying by candlelight. Suddenly a ghostly image appeared in front of him, a glowing skeleton draped in gauze and seated cross-legged on the stage floor. Perhaps the most alarming part of the demonstration was the way the skeleton materialized from thin air—hazy at first, then brighter and brighter, until it seemed to glow in a transparent, unearthly way. The skeleton reached out, flailing its arms menacingly. The student lunged from his chair, grabbed a sword, and swung it at the ghost, which suddenly disappeared to avoid the blow. The student looked around, rubbed his eyes, and then returned to the desk. Slowly, the hazy image appeared again to torment him.

The scene was a short one, and the quality of the effects was severely limited by the size of the stage. For example, in that first demonstration in the lecture hall, the ghost could neither stand nor walk but appeared sitting on the stage. It wasn't great drama. There wasn't much of a story except to establish the scene and accommodate the special effect. But the audience response was instantaneous and electric. The Ghost, from its very first appearance, delivered everything that was promised.

Professor Pepper, in keeping with the scientific tone of the Polytechnic shows, had intended to introduce the play, then return to the stage at the conclusion and explain how the optical device had accomplished it. However, when the curtain closed on the scene and the lights came up on the redoubtable Professor, he was greeted with silent stares, then an unexpected torrent of applause. He couldn't deprive his audience of the marvel. He had never pretended to be a magician, but at that moment he seemed to know instinctively what to do. He thanked them all and bade them good evening. The Ghost would remain his secret.

The public never heard the name Dircksian Phantasmagoria. Dircks happily accepted five hundred pounds for the idea and waived any future royalties, merely asking that his name be attached to the invention. Somehow, that proved to be the most difficult part of the operation. Even the first review in the *Times* bungled the credit, misreporting that a Mr. Rose of Glasgow was responsible for the invention. Pepper made sporadic attempts to include Dircks's name in the advertising, but the illusion quickly became known as Pepper's Ghost, and it was this title that became famous, emblazoned across posters and advertised in the daily papers.

This slight on Dircks is one of the most puzzling parts of the story. Dircks wrote his own book exposing the mystery and complaining of his treatment. His revenge was to fill 102 pages without ever mentioning the name Pepper. The omission worked against him; by avoiding the popular title, he limited interest in the book. Pepper, writing years later, made a simple, logical case that he had done his best to credit the inventor. Still, something went wrong, and it's easy to imagine that the managing director, flush with success and flattered by the public's attention, conveniently edged his way into the spotlight. Unfortunately, this ostensibly greedy billing made Pepper, who had long been suspected of being more of a showman than a scientist, look like nothing more than a sideshow barker.

Later writers, noticing this slight on Dircks, questioned whether Pepper had anything to do with the invention at all. The lack of credit is a shame, because it's clear that Pepper came to the project last but made an otherwise unattractive idea suitable for the stage and, with his suggestions, made a questionable idea worthy of a patent. Even Dircks admitted as much the following year in his book. Reading both sides of the arguments, it's easy to conclude that Dircks entered into the agreement by offering generous terms but came to resent Pepper's control over the invention and became a prickly partner. For better or worse, Pepper simply grew tired of dealing with his complaints and ignored him.

Inspired by his first-night audience, Pepper moved the Ghost illusion to the large theatre at the Polytechnic, where the gauzy phantoms could walk or glide across the stage. When "The Haunted Man" was shown there, audiences were surprised by additional effects: The student rose from his chair and seemed to leave his own glowing, transparent soul behind, still seated and watching the action. At the conclusion, having vanquished a different ghost that had threatened him, the actor seemed to walk through the walls and disappear. Other short plays followed, including "Scrooge and Marley's Ghost," inspired by Dickens's *A Christmas Carol*; "The Ghost of Napoleon at St. Helena," and "The Ghost of Hamlet." The Polytechnic attracted substantial crowds. Performances were initially offered three days a week—afternoon and evening shows. Soon the illusion was being shown daily. The Ghost drew crowds for a full fifteen months, and in a very short period of time, the illusion earned 12,000 pounds ($60,000) for the institution, which means that nearly a quarter of a million visitors queued up at the Polytechnic's lecture hall.

Pepper also licensed the effect to various theatres and music halls. He introduced it during a lecture in Manchester, then again in Bath. He arranged for the Ghost to appear at the Britannia Theatre, Hoxton, and in a play specially written for it, "Widows and Orphans," at the Haymarket in London. The Ghost also appeared at the Adelphi, Merchant's Hall in Glasgow, the Crystal Palace, and at Drury Lane for Byron's choral tragedy, "Manfred." It made its first, brief appearance in America at Wallack's Theatre in New York, as a special effect in a forgotten melodrama entitled "True at Last." A decade after its premiere in London, Pepper brought his Ghost to performances at the Tremont Theatre in Boston, where he enhanced his scientific lecture with several amazing images, including a lady who held her hand in a flame without any damage and a person who slowly seemed to pass through the body of another.

The ultimate compliment paid to Pepper might have come from Spiritualists. Their movement was based on a belief that the dearly departed could be contacted in a darkened room during a séance where they would communicate with the living. Pepper claimed to have collected a trunkful of letters from those who had seen his Ghost, many of whom insisted that he had found a way to exhibit real spirits. Pepper, embarrassed to be drawn into these arguments, found that by ignoring the claims, he had only fueled the debate. A percentage of his audience wouldn't have it any other way. There were ghosts on stage.

Special guests were invited backstage by Professor Pepper and shown the secrets of the Ghost. That is how the Prince of Wales witnessed the famous illusion. After Pepper's performance at the Polytechnic, members of the royal party missed the finer points of the optical principles but were happy to crawl into a dark alcove and amuse themselves by temporarily becoming ghosts. When Michael Faraday visited the Polytechnic to witness the latest sensation, Pepper welcomed the renowned electrical scientist. After the performance, he enthusiastically escorted Faraday onto the darkened stage, pointing out the apparatus for the ghost and the concealed lighting, explaining the details of the sightlines and the optical principles involved. Faraday interrupted him to admit, "Do you know, Mr. Pepper, I really don't understand it." Pepper took Faraday's hand and put it against an enormous sheet of clear glass, which had been suspended on the stage. As the scientist's knuckles bumped against the invisible glass, a smile of recognition came over his face. "Ah, now I comprehend it!"

When you look through a window into a dark night, you can see your hazy image reflected in the glass and superimposed on the setting just outside. The figure staring back at you is Pepper's Ghost. The window is transparent, but with the proper lighting it can also reflect as a mirror. Most important, as Henry Dircks realized, it can be transparent and reflective at the same time.

Dircks might not have been the first to put these pieces together. In his 1558 book *Natural Magic*, the Italian author Baptista Porta described a similar effect. Porta wrote of creating an illusion of "How We May See in a Chamber Things That Are Not," a simple arrangement in which, if a spectator were looking through a polished glass window into a room, objects could be arranged on a sort of balcony above and behind the spectator, hidden from his direct view. These would reflect as if they were actually in the room. Porta's book was translated into English in 1658, and Dircks was familiar with this work.

A French provisional patent, filed in 1852 by Pierre Séguin, an artist, showed a small viewing box with moveable flaps to allow the light to enter. A rectangle of glass, fixed at a 45-degree angle, was concealed inside the box. When the viewer peeked inside the box and operated the flaps, the glass would start out transparent and then reflect a painted image beneath the mirror. Séguin, who experimented with optical devices and pre-cinema moving images, intended his box to be used to change one picture into another. When it was finally sold, it was as an illusionary toy, a box that contained small, ghostly figurines. Children reached into the box to grasp the figures but found their fingers grasping at air. Boys and girls must have quickly become bored with this deception, and the toy was not a success. Séguin allowed the patent papers to lapse.

Coincidentally, Dircks's model was shown to the British Association exactly three centuries to the year after Porta's book was pub-

lished, and six years to the day after Séguin's patent was filed. The proposed Dircksian Phantasmagoria was a theatre in which the audience was confined to a balcony, looking slightly down at the action on the flat stage. Beneath the

Dircks's suggested stage to produce ghosts

balcony, unknown to the audience, was a matching stage, carpeted and draped in dead black fabric. Between the two stages was a large, upright sheet of transparent glass. The glass would need to be fault-less and clean so that it was effectively invisible to the spectators.

The main stage could be moderately lit, showing the actors engaged in their scene. An additional light source was concealed in the black area with the actors playing ghosts. If this bright light were directed at an actor on the hidden stage, he would be reflected in the glass. Anything draped in black would not reflect. As the glass was perfectly clear, not silvered like a mirror, the reflection would be transparent and ghostly and would appear at a distance behind the glass equal to the actor's distance from the front of the glass. That's the most important point about the success of the illu-sion and one that has often been misunderstood. Some accounts have suggested that the image is projected *on* glass. But the audi-ence didn't perceive the plane of the glass and, because the ghost was a reflection, the image always appeared behind the glass, moving in the same space with the actors and the scenery. If all the players were perfectly synchronized, the ghost could interact with the characters on stage, avoiding sword thrusts or walking through walls. Dimming the light on the ghost would cause it to fade away; brightening the light made it seem more substantial.

Pepper's suggestion, which made the Ghost practical for a small theatre, was to angle the glass slightly toward the audi-ence, which meant that they no longer had to be seated in a raised balcony. It was an inspired idea. Just as someone in a submarine twists the tiny mirror in the periscope, giving a wide range of views with a

Pepper's Ghost at the London Polytechnic

slight movement, Pepper realized that the reflective piece of glass could perform a double duty. Not only would it reflect the image, but it could also be tilted slightly to "reach down" and find the image, effectively changing the axis of the reflection and "lifting" the reflection until it seemed to be on the stage. Pepper called his system a double stage, referring to the two distinct levels of stage that made it possible.

Pepper's changes added a number of mechanical complications. First, a sort of oversized orchestra pit would need to be recessed at the front of the stage, lined with dark fabric and hidden from the audience's view. This is where the live actor who played the ghost would be concealed. Second, this actor would need to be tipped at the perfect angle so that his image would appear to be standing upright on the stage. This required a dark slant board behind the actor to support him. The angled support made it impossible for the ghost to walk. A rolling trolley on a track allowed him to be pushed or pulled across the scene. By pumping his feet as he glided across the stage, the ghost could give the rough appearance of walking, or—better still—he could simply glide from side to side. Pepper also suggested using the brilliant oxyhydrogen spotlight within the pit to efficiently illuminate the ghost.

This allowed the apparatus to be fit into existing theatres—provided that the theatre was small enough (glass was available only in sheets of about nine by fifteen feet) and had enough room beneath the stage to accommodate the trolley and lights for the ghost.

The large sheet of glass across the stage meant that the actors in the production would sound muffled if they attempted to speak. Each of Pepper's short, ghostly plays was performed in pantomime, to musical accompaniment.

The stagehands who worked alongside the ghost in the darkened pit had their own name for their workplace: the oven. The hissing, smoking oxyhydrogen lamp made the oven unbearable; even worse, assistants operating the lamp or trolley would be completely wrapped in black velvet clothing to prevent any stray reflections in the glass. The work in the sweltering oven called for amazing precision. The ghost could not see the actors above; the actors could not see the ghost. So, all took their cues from the music, the stagehands rolling the trolley to precise marks as the actors on stage mimed their reactions to the spirit.

• • •

The day after the Ghost's premiere at the Polytechnic and still reeling from the audience's enthusiastic response, Pepper went to a patent attorney recommended by Dircks and filed the invention in the names of Dircks and Pepper. It was patent number 326 for the year 1863, "Improvements in Apparatus to be used in the Exhibition of Dramatic and other Like Performances." The weird suggestion that a ghost could be patented wasn't lost on the public. One music hall song, titled "Patent Ghosts" and written at the height of Pepper's Ghost's fame, explained:

> At Music Halls, Theatres, too,
> This Patent Ghost they show;
> The goblin novelty to view,
> Some thousands nightly go;
> For such a sight they gladly pay,
> In order just to boast
> To all their "country cousins" they
> Have seen a perfect ghost.

Patents are notoriously dense and confusing documents, and the patents of more than a century ago can seem especially odd by modern standards. The patent papers for the Ghost, which were filed on February 5, 1863, suggest the twists and turns that were necessary to solidify the claims of the inventors.

> The arrangement of the theatre requires in addition to the ordinary stage a second stage at a lower level than the ordinary one, hidden from the audience as far as direct vision is concerned. A large glass screen is placed on the ordinary stage in front of the hidden one. . . . The glass screen is set in a frame so that it can be readily moved to the place required and is to be set at an inclination to enable the spectators . . . to see the reflected image.

During most of the show, the large, framed sheet of glass was safely hidden in a long, deep slot through the stage. While the ghost effect was being set, behind the curtains, ropes were used to pull the glass straight up and to tip it at the proper angle. The cover of the oven was then removed, and when the curtains opened again the elements of the illusion were in place and ready to perform.

Other details were oddly lacking and seem to indicate that the patent was hurriedly prepared, or deliberately unhelpful to discourage anyone from trying to build the invention. For example, Pepper and Dircks wrote:

> *The proper angle of inclination of the glass is ascertained experimentally by having persons in different parts of the house to say when the image is shewn to them correctly. . . . The phantom actor leans against the screen which is inclined so as to be parallel with the glass screen and is covered with black velvet or other dark material. . . .*

But that's all wrong. For an optical effect like Pepper's ghost, the angles and sightlines of the audience's vision can be carefully calcu-

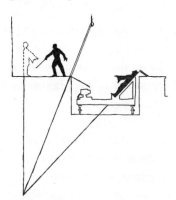

The angles to calculate
Pepper's Ghost

lated. Imagine the line on stage where the ghost is to appear. The glass is suspended at an angle in front of this. By extending the imaginary lines of the ghost and the glass down through the stage, there is a point where they intersect. If this point is plotted as the center of a circle, then the actor portraying the ghost must be the same distance from the glass as the desired image, at an angle corresponding to the radius of the circle. In this way it's easy to diagram the variations as the angle of the glass changes or the glass's distance from the actor in the oven

increases. Perhaps Pepper and Dircks had arrived at these positions for
the Polytechnic by trial and error, and their patent contained only
rough approximations.

The Professor had the misfortune of filing the patent at the same
time that the invention was creating a sensation in his theatre. Music
hall proprietors fought the patent so that the Ghost would become
public property. A number of affidavits from producers, actors, and
even one from a minstrel performer contended that the Ghost show
had been seen years before or that Dircks and Pepper had acquired the
idea from a previous source. These vague recollections were countered
with letters from scientists Michael Faraday, Sir David Brewster, and
Professor Wheatstone, great men who enthusiastically endorsed the
invention.

Pepper later claimed that during the patent process "the Solicitor-
General, Sir Roundell Palmer, declined to grant a patent of Dircks's
crude idea, as it was only when he understood the great improvement
made by the use of the double stage and the employment of the electric light that he granted the ghost patent." The evidence of the patent
bears this out. Then, as now, inventors sought to protect every possible element of their inventions, and Pepper and Dircks would have
sought to protect Dircks's original scheme with a balcony. But their
patent records only the specific system—the slanted glass and dark
pit—originated at the Polytechnic.

Henry Dircks was bitter about the patent. He credited Pepper with
the idea of the angled glass but never understood its importance to the
workability of the invention. In fact, he became convinced that it had
ruined his creation. He wrote,

> *A sloping or inclined mirror is, as an invention, one of the*
> *inverse ratio of improvements; it is improving backwards . . .*
> *to simplify the idea of the more elaborate . . . a sketch as*
> *compared to a finished painting. . . . The patent adds nothing*
> *to the original invention, besides the power of rendering the*
> *specters "cabined, cribbed, confined" with the necessity of*
> *placing them on a railway to effect locomotion.*

Similarly, the patent process gave Pepper reasons to doubt Dircks's intentions. First, it's puzzling why Dircks, a patent examiner and patented inventor, hadn't taken early steps to secure his own idea. On the contrary, Pepper discovered that the disclosure of the idea years before—the descriptions from the British Association for the Advancement of Science—complicated the process and jeopardized their claim. Once an invention had been publicly disclosed, it could not be protected, and Dircks's demonstration of his model was described in various publications.

Then there were the previous inventions. Dircks had dismissed Porta's three-hundred-year-old version as an unsophisticated idea, but the essence of the idea had clearly been recorded in the Italian's book. Was this the inspiration for Dircks's idea? Professor Pepper was also horrified to hear of the French toy for the first time during the patent hearing. Lord Westbury commented:

> I well remember being taken to the house of Belzoni, the distinguished traveler, and seeing an effect no doubt somewhat similar to that produced by the Defendant's apparatus, but I could not for one moment compare the toy of Belzoni with the refined and complete contrivances used by the Defendant at the Royal Polytechnic.

Pepper must have held his breath through the above statement. After months defending his and Dircks's patent, Pierre Séguin's Polyoscope toy almost unraveled their claim. Fortunately, the patent was granted (sealed) on October 31, 1863, but Pepper was left with an obvious question:

> Had Mr. Dircks's [original] patent agent, in his searches after patents, ever come across the toy invented in Paris? Because it is substantially [the same as] the ghost apparatus and produced that illusion.

Pepper never received an answer to these questions, but the

difficulty in obtaining their patent had convinced him that if Dircks didn't know of the previous inventions, he should have.

It certainly seems that Dircks did not get the idea from Séguin, as the Polyoscope, with a 45-degree glass, shows a sophistication and efficiency that Dircks never actually understood. A decade after the original Pepper's Ghost, unauthorized copies of the illusion appeared in American sideshows and British fairgrounds, using the 45-degree glass so it could easily be set up or taken on tour. With the glass at 45 degrees and the actor lying flat in the oven (concealed from the audience's view by the scenery), the angles could be easily calculated. The result was very similar to Séguin's original Polyoscope toy. Pepper and Dircks had not sought a patent in the United States, and it was a 45-degree version of the Ghost that was first patented in the States in 1877 by Charles and Olive McGlennen of Ohio.

American actor David Lano described one of his early roles in a touring melodrama, the ghostly child in a production called "The Death of Little Jim." The show used a 45-degree glass. The story concerned a little boy caught in a mine cave-in who had wedged himself between the rocks, making it possible for his friends to escape. The boy died a hero, and the Ghost illusion was used to portray him ascending to heaven, "in the best Little Eva tradition."

One night Lano fell asleep during the performance, lulled by the warmth in the dark pit beneath the stage. When his image appeared in the reflection at the climax of the show, he was still dozing peacefully, unfortunately pointed head-down as if headed "to the nether world." The audience howled with laughter, and Lano reported that he ended up "with a trouncing" from the company manager.

Pepper attempted to stop these unauthorized copies in Britain. A Mr. King was forced to withdraw his illusion from the British music halls, but not every showman respected Pepper's claim. Poole and Young offered the Phantascope, and Gompertz toured with the Spectrascope, slight variations on the Ghost that they claimed were independent inventions. Dircks recalled the months when imitation Ghosts were the rage in theatres:

> *A gentleman connected with a large institution, calling at*
> *the Thames Plate Glass Company, was met at once, before*
> *naming the object of his visit, with the observation, "It's no*
> *use your coming to us, we cannot supply you." "What do*
> *you mean?" enquired the unconscious customer, adding, "I*
> *only want some large plate glass." To which business-like*
> *reply he received the ready rejoinder, "Well, Sir I knew it the*
> *moment you entered. It's 'The Ghost,' and we are quite out*
> *of large plates; it is true you see three, which we are now*
> *packing, but they are ordered for Belgium. We have, how-*
> *ever, written to several of our agents, and may shortly be*
> *able to supply orders.*

In 1863 Pepper began the process to obtain a French patent for his idea, and in July of that year, he was engaged to bring his Ghost to the Theatre Chatelet. It was to be incorporated into an elaborate play, "Le Secret de Miss Aurore," and the producers paid 20,000 francs for the secret. Three large sheets of glass, each five square yards, were placed side by side on the stage, and two Drummond limelights were installed in the oven.

However, Pepper arrived in Paris to find that a magician named Henri Robin had already installed a copy of the Ghost in his own Paris theatre, and drew large crowds. Robin's real name was Henri Donckele, and he was a popular magician and exhibitor of scientific curiosities. Robin used an enormous piece of glass, five by four meters, suspended at the front of his stage. There's no question that his ghost effects were especially magical and dramatic. One terrifying scene portrayed a cemetery. As a man walked among the gravestones, a vision of his fiancée, as a spirit bride, materialized. He reached to embrace the glowing bride, but his arms passed through her. Slowly, she disappeared, leaving him desolate.

Even more popular was "The Demon of Paganini," a parody of the famously dramatic Italian violinist. A tall actor with a wig of long, lank hair portrayed Paganini. As he reclined on a couch, a devil dressed in bright red and green slowly appeared, climbed atop the sleeping man, and terrorized him with a frantic violin solo. Paganini fought off the devil, reaching for the violin, but the specter appeared and disappeared, playing on and cavorting atop his host. The real Paganini, who had died just over twenty years earlier, had been famous for his frenzied, demonic violin solos. The image of him being inspired and tormented by the devil matched the public's caricature of his image. In Robin's illusion an actor played the devil and cavorted in the oven. A second violinist, hidden in the darkness beneath the glass, provided the real music, synchronized with the action on stage.

Robin claimed that he had actually invented the Ghost illusion between the years of 1845 and 1847 and exhibited it in Lyon and Saint-Etienne under the name the Living Phantasmagoria. According to Robin, it met with little effect, but he persisted, later perfecting it in Venice, Rome, Munich, Vienna, and Brussels. Pierre Séguin, he claimed, had worked for him as a painter of magic lantern slides and based his patented Polyoscope on Robin's ghost effect.

The French magician could offer no more than a playbill from the 1840s advertising the Living Phantasmagoria as proof. The title was certainly not conclusive. Many phantasmagoria shows, billed with assorted adjectives, had been exhibited throughout Europe, and *phantasmagoria* was a generic term for a performance of projected lantern images on smoke or gauze curtains. It was hard to believe that Robin had toured with such large pieces of glass. In fact, throughout his career Robin had earned his reputation by copying more successful and innovative performers, and the ghost effect at his theatre was a slavish copy of the Dircks and Pepper Ghost; it looked nothing like Séguin's Polyoscope. Overall, Robin's claim might not have been convincing, but by offering the playbill and citing Séguin, he managed to muddy the waters for his competition. Regardless of the situation, Pepper was disappointed to learn of the Séguin patent and how it had lapsed. According to the French law at the time, "all improvements of a patent fell to the original patentee." According to Pepper, "Under that law I lost the patent in France," and as Séguin's patent had lapsed, the ghost became public property in that country.

• • •

Robin's use of the Ghost may have been an annoyance to Pepper, but it also signaled the incorporation of the invention into the performances of magicians. Before that time magicians had specialized in sleight of hand, presented mechanical apparatus, or mind-reading effects. Robin, a magician, had also exhibited projections from magic lanterns. But to magicians, the Ghost represented an entirely new category of illusion: optical conjuring. The use of reflections to create illusions on stage quickly suggested a wide range of possibilities.

Just as several innovative magicians were beginning to analyze the Ghost in Europe and America, they were faced with a new ghostly sensation that captivated the public and provided serious competition. It was a show by Ira and William Davenport, two American brothers who didn't bother with sheets of glass or velvet curtains or spotlights. Audiences insisted that the brothers, like Pepper, could materialize spirits on an empty stage—but their ghosts were the real thing.

3
A New Type of Magic

Strange how people imagine things in the dark!
—Ira Davenport

You're in Las Vegas watching a magic act. Hunched over the narrow little table, sipping the last of your two-drink minimum, you look up to notice the wide curtains sweep open. A tuxedo-clad magician steps to the center of the stage, rolling up his sleeves as the spotlight finds him. The audience responds with a smattering of applause. This must be the star of the show.

"Legends tell us," he begins with a smile, quickly scanning the audience, "that every person has a double, whether we know it or not. A mysterious Doppelgänger, a perfect match who is out there . . . somewhere." A feather-clad showgirl steps onto the stage, gracefully handing the magician a sheet of white paper. "Tonight, I'd like to demonstrate that even inanimate objects have perfect doubles. All it takes is a little magic." He carries the paper into the audience, twisting it with a flourish at his fingertips, and asks someone—anyone at all—to sign their name across the paper. The people at the surrounding tables crane their necks to watch. Yes, he's found a woman who is signing the paper with a large magic marker.

Whatever he's about to do, the build-up certainly seems impressive. This is going to be good.

The orchestra starts a waltz, and the spotlight swings across stage, illuminating a large office copy machine.

The magician places the signed paper on the glass surface of the copier, deftly closes the cover and, flexing his hands to display that they're empty, extends a finger and pushes the start button. There's a flash of light from the top of the copier and, to a sustained drum roll, a piece of paper rolls out of the side of the device. The magician picks up the paper in one hand and slides the original signed paper off the glass with the other hand. Holding them up in the spotlight, he takes a step forward so the entire audience can appreciate the marvel. . . .

"The signatures match exactly!"

You're not applauding. Why not?

It's just an office copier, you say. There's nothing impressive about that.

47

But as far as magic tricks go, it's a pretty good one: It has audience participation and mysterious apparatus, and it ends in a surprise finish. Besides, you were fooled, weren't you? You don't work for Xerox or Minolta. Do you actually have any idea how the copier works?

Of course, it's not enough just to be fooled; simply being fooled is not entertaining. The magician reaches his goal by presenting a marvel, making you intrigued. For better or worse, we stopped marveling at copy machines long ago, even though they seem to be fooling us every day.

A more difficult problem has always been topicality. Imagine, instead, a modern, topical illusion involving a copy machine. A standard photocopier is shown and plugged in. Someone in the audience thinks of a name and calls it out: Chester. A blank piece of paper is fed into the machine and emerges from the other side with the name printed boldly on the paper: Chester.

It's a bad trick because it's still so confused with a mysterious technology. Perhaps the machine is some sort of fax machine, perhaps there is a way, using a hidden keyboard, that the magician can surreptitiously input the name. People in the audience are quickly reminded that they don't quite understand how a copy machine works, so no one can quite appreciate just how wonderful a "mind-reading" copy machine really is.

Here's a much better trick. The paper is folded and sealed in another piece of paper, then suspended from a ribbon so that it dangles over the middle of the stage. A name is selected. The paper is plucked from the ribbon, unfolded, and shows the name emblazoned across it. The same trick, which would impress you today, is one that entertained your grandparents or great-great-grandparents. In fact, a version of this paper trick was described in a 1584 book on conjuring.

When brothers Ira and William Davenport offered to produce ghosts on stages throughout America and Europe, they had hit upon one of the most original, topical, and successful performances in the history of the theatre. They created a new sort of magic that is still popular today. They inspired imitators, exposures, and converts. They started riots in many of the cities where they appeared. They were booed from the stage as fakes, hailed in the press as mediums, threatened, bloodied, cheered. At a time when the Victorians prided themselves on science and rationality, the two quiet young men from Buffalo, New York began a confusing debate about just how honest a magician needed to be or could afford to be.

Most important of all, these magicians—who spent their careers denying that they were magicians—inspired the careers of a generation of important magicians who followed them. Though there were no actual supernatural phenomena involved in a Davenport séance, the bizarre, tumultuous story of the Davenport brothers was nothing short of phenomenal.

In 1864 Dion Boucicault, the popular Irish actor and playwright who had given the world "The Corsican Brothers," lived in a fashionable apartment at 326 Regent Street in London. On September 28 of that year, Boucicault hosted a séance orchestrated by two strangers for twenty-two of his good friends. The playwright was not a particularly religious man, nor was he a follower of Spiritualism, the popular movement which had started over a decade earlier in the United States and promised the opportunity to communicate with the dead. Yet Boucicault had been told that his special guests could summon ghosts, and the theatricality of the situation greatly appealed to him. It was a strange coincidence. As the playwright's guests arrived for the séance that afternoon, they must have noticed that London's Royal Polytechnic, where Pepper's famous optical ghosts had been drawing crowds just months earlier, was across the street.

The Davenport brothers, William and Ira, were convincingly serious and taciturn, two slight, dark-eyed young men from Buffalo, New York with handlebar mustaches, goatees, and dramatic long locks combed back from their foreheads. Like any "phenomenon" of the day, they employed people who did the business of explaining for them. A man named William Marion Fay, another Spiritualist from Buffalo, managed their tour, handling the physical elements of the act, and served as an assistant. A Reverend Ferguson introduced the act with an impressive lecture related to Spiritualism.

The London society audience at Boucicault's watched the strange performance with only a rough idea of the Davenports' career and achievements. The young men seemed to be prodigies who had an ability to attract ghostly manifestations, but who seemed oddly calm and disinterested in the procedure. Ira was twenty-five years old, William only twenty-three. But by the time they'd come to London, the brothers had been performing this exact séance—virtually move for move—professionally on stages across America for nine years, since 1855.

At one end of the room sat their cabinet, which was raised off the floor on simple sawhorses. The cabinet was like an oversized wardrobe, about six feet tall and six feet across, only thirty inches deep and closed on the front by three vertical doors. The center door had a small oval hole cut at the top; the hole was backed by a loose curtain. The wooden walls of the cabinet were of simple construction, and the interior was empty except for two plank seats, behind the right and left doors, which allowed the brothers to sit inside facing each other.

The Davenports stripped off their frock coats, and their remaining garments were searched for concealed devices. Then guests were invited to securely tie the brothers' wrists behind their backs using thin, strong ropes. Ira and William then took their seats in the cabinet. The ropes from their wrists were passed through holes in the plank seats, tied around their ankles, then extended across the floor of the cabinet and knotted to the ropes tying the other brother. Other ropes were used to tie their knees and upper arms. After ten minutes of careful work, they were pinioned against the wooden seats of the cabinet.

Fay closed the side doors, then the center door. Seconds later there was an odd ripple of movement at the curtain behind the center door's oval hole. An arm was quickly thrust through the window and withdrawn. Then a flutter of ghostly hands. The guests leaned forward in disbelief. Fay invited several of them to place their own hands through the oval opening, so that they could feel the spirits brushing against them. The cabinet doors swung open and the brothers emerged smiling, completely free of their bonds, which were now lying coiled at their feet. The doors of the cabinet had been closed scarcely a minute.

The process was reversed. They sat on their benches, and the cabinet doors were closed. Spectators heard the sounds of the ropes sliding. A minute or two later the doors were opened, showing the two mysterious brothers impossibly tied up with their wrists behind their backs. Guests examined the knots and the ropes, which were secure, exactly as they had been tied before.

Now that they were tied in the cabinet once more, the Davenports began a series of tests. A guitar, violin, tambourine, and trumpet were hung on hooks against the back wall of the cabinet and the doors closed. Instantly a "hell's bells" of rattling, pounding, and thumping began. Instruments were strummed or blown, tossed against the walls of the box or pushed through the opening to tumble on the floor in front. An arm, bared to the shoulder, emerged from the window in the cabinet, violently ringing the bell, and then withdrew. Fay quickly dashed to open the doors, catching the instruments almost airborne as the two brothers were revealed, sitting quietly and tied up tightly. The procedure was repeated, but this time, still tied up with their hands bound behind their backs, their fists were filled with spoonfuls of flour and their mouths with water. Again the guitar was strummed and the horn blown in a devilish discord. On opening the doors, the brothers displayed that their fists were still filled with dry flour and their mouths with water.

The juxtaposition of violent activity and the Davenports' calm, unruffled demeanor seemed superhuman. It definitely suggested another presence, a personality or a force which was sharing the wooden box with the young men. This was clear in the climax of the cabinet séance, as one of Boucicault's guests, Sir Charles Wyke, was invited to take a seat in the center section of the cabinet, between the two brothers. One of Wyke's hands was roped to the shoulder of the first Davenport, and his other hand was tied to the knee of the second brother. The doors were closed and instantly the instruments rattled and screeched. In an instant, the racket stopped. The doors were opened and the three men were found still tied in place. But now Sir Charles, slightly dazed by the brief experience, wore his handkerchief on his head, with the tambourine serving as a fedora. His cravat was wrapped around the neck of one Davenport, while his glasses were on the nose of the other. Released from the cabinet, he could only explain that, in the darkness, he felt a flurry of hands brushing against him or pulling his hair.

With the doors closed again, the brothers were miraculously released from their bonds and stepped free, unruffled by the experience.

For the second part of the afternoon séance, the cabinet was pushed to one side of the room and the two young Americans were seated at a small table, just several feet from the front row of guests. The lights in the room were completely extinguished for about two minutes, and the audience sat in uncomfortable silence, listening to the breaths of the people seated next to them or the creak of a chair. Fay called for the lights, and the spectators gasped. The brothers had now been tied completely in their chairs, their arms, legs, and bodies covered with a network of ropes and tight knots, their wrists pulled behind their backs. The séance proceeded using the musical instruments, which had been smeared with streaks of phosphorescent oil so they would glow in the dark. The lights were completely extinguished again.

One spectator recalled that the viewer:

> Begins to experience an indescribable sensation of 'all-over-ishness.' There is very little applause. A performance of this kind is not calculated to produce a feeling of exaltation. On the contrary, it rather tends to make one feel a kind of nervous depression.

In the darkness, the glowing streaks of light were seen to rise in the air and move through the room in weird, luminous curves. As the instruments moved past the spectators they ruffled their hair, bumped their noses, or created a sudden draft.

> The situation is rather painful than pleasant. One experiences a sort of indefinable feeling of dread, which for the time being paralyses the reflective faculties.

A sort of controlled bedlam haunted the dark room. Hats and coats were pulled away from guests; glowing instruments were deposited in their laps. When the lights were turned up for the last time, the Davenports were sitting quietly in their chairs, as before. But now, one of them was wearing a spectator's coat, with his wrists still knotted behind his back. The séance was over.

The author of "The Corsican Brothers" clearly appreciated a good ghost story. As the inventor of effects for his plays, Boucicault also knew his way around theatrical trickery. Still, after the two-hour lecture and séance were concluded, Boucicault, like the rest of his guests, contemplated the flashes of light, puffs of wind, rattles, and knocks which had sent chills down his spine and could come up with no explanation save the supernatural. He had detected no trickery. He had discovered no special apparatus or collusion from others in the room. He and his party unanimously decided to endorse the Davenports.

The English press reacted with scorn, suggesting that Dion Boucicault's guests had been badly fooled by these bold Americans. After all, how much deception could they have detected in a perfectly dark room? Boucicault offered a letter defending his opinion.

> Some persons think that the requirement of darkness seems to [imply] trickery. Is not a dark chamber essential in the process of photography? And what would we reply to him who would say, "I believe photography to be humbug—do it in the light, and we will believe otherwise!"

• • •

The Davenport brothers were quiet by nature, but early in their career they must have realized that the secret of their success was to say absolutely nothing. It's interesting to read accounts of their performances in Paris, where a lecturer introduced them by graciously apologizing that the brothers were unable to speak French. Even in England, the Davenports sat Sphinx-like through the various manifestations, realizing that others, more fanatical on the subject, would fill the vacuum, making sensational claims for their wonders. They invited debate, then silently sidestepped the most controversial opinions of their audience. Their lack of showmanship turned out to be a masterful touch of showmanship. Were they simply modest? Or unwilling subjects controlled by a higher power? Technically, they never claimed to be mediums. They didn't have to. Others came to that conclusion.

Ira Erastus Davenport was born in Buffalo, New York, on September 17, 1839; his younger brother, William Henry Harrison Davenport, was born on February 1, 1841. According to one account, their father, Ira D. Davenport, was a police detective and invented or improved the rope-tie escape used by his sons after seeing a similar feat demonstrated by a Native American medicine man. Simple escape tricks had also been included in the programs of some early nineteenth-century magicians.

Although there's no account of their first contact with Spiritualism, the timing suggests that the young brothers saw a demonstration by the founders of the movement, which began on May 31, 1848, in the small town of Hydesville, New York, at the farmhouse of John D. Fox and his wife. The Foxes were plagued by a series of strange rapping noises inside the house. The raps excited the family, particularly Mrs. Fox, who was gullible and excitable; she in turn told neighbors, who visited the house on following evenings to hear for themselves. Two of the Fox daughters, Margaret, age 8, and Kate, 6, seemed to be at the center of the phenomenon, although no one suggested the duplicity of these little girls. The noises seemed random and mysterious until someone suggested a simple code, which allowed the raps to answer questions. Slowly the family and visitors to the house were made to understand that a disembodied spirit was generating the sound; the girls called the presence "Mr. Splitfoot." "Was there a murder committed in this house?" one visitor asked anxiously. There was a pause, then one loud, clear rap, signaling yes.

A much older married sister, Leah, returned to Hydesville for a visit and discovered the local interest in the strange raps. She quickly organized a Society of Spiritualists and took charge of her young sisters, promoting their occult powers. Leah took Margaret and Kate to nearby Rochester, where the mysterious raps seemed to follow the girls. For a hefty fee, audiences could commune with the spirits and ask their own questions. In Rochester, the Fox sisters earned as much as $100 to $150 a night in profit.

The citizens of Rochester were fascinated with the new "spiritual telegraph." Three University of Buffalo physicians examined the Fox sisters and decided that the noises were caused by the young girls, perhaps by clicking bones in their knees. Other investigators—businessmen, doctors, attorneys, and even a local judge—disagreed, and could find no physical explanation for the raps.

Margaret, Kate, and Leah Fox went to New York, Philadelphia, and then on a grand tour of cities as interest in Spiritualism boomed. The raps of the Fox sisters—the most primitive communications from the spirits—were quickly imitated by a number of psychics, and the procedure evolved into the standard séance. A medium would take her place at a table in a darkened room, surrounded by believers. Hymns were sung. Questions were asked. The spirits made their presence known by taps or raps, by speaking in low whispers or materializing messages on slates.

On October 21, 1888, Margaret Fox Kane, now long past her career as a medium, wrote a confession for the *New York World*, explaining the raps had all been a fraud, originally intended to terrify their superstitious mother. They started by tying an apple to a string; when the girls went to bed at night they tugged on the string, causing the apple to bump on the floor. As neighbors became intrigued by the raps, the girls discovered a new way of making the sounds, by surreptitiously snapping their toe joints against the wall or floor, creating a loud, resonant knock. Margaret became adept at these raps, but insisted that this peculiar ability was the sum total of their mysterious talents. "I think, when I reflect about it, that it was a most wonderful discovery, a very wonderful thing that children should make such a discovery, and all through our desire to do mischief only," she wrote in her confession.

If the deceptions were truly this simple, the girls must have been thunderstruck by the movement they inspired. The opportunistic Leah clearly understood that the public was anxious to make the connection between this world and the next, and the attractive notion of the Spiritualism movement she created soon inspired a life of its own, in addition to (or in spite of) the silly Fox raps and knocks. It became not only a Victorian fad, but also a religious cause. The new religion attracted celebrities like Horace Greeley, Elizabeth Barrett Browning, Mary Todd Lincoln, Cornelius Vanderbilt, and even Sir Arthur Conan

Doyle, the British creator of the supremely logical character, Sherlock Holmes. There were eight million Spiritualists in the United States, we are told, by the time of Margaret's confession in 1888.

The night her confession was published, Margaret Fox was scheduled to lecture at the Academy of Music in New York. The hall was packed with curious spectators. Margaret had endured a tumultuous life in the public eye. At that point in her life, she was widowed, poverty stricken, and alcoholic. Margaret was living in fear of the Spiritualists, who had a great deal at stake and were threatened by her confession, and especially her older sister, the domineering force in the family. As Margaret stepped to the platform, she faced more than two thousand people, including a good number of devoted Spiritualists who greeted her with hostility. As she attempted to speak, she found that the words were rambling and disjointed; the strain was too great, and Margaret was completely unable to continue. The expectant crowd realized that she had lost her nerve. Perhaps the entire confession had been a hoax. As the crowd began to murmur and hiss, someone on the lecture platform offered Margaret a chair and then positioned a wide wooden plank in front of her. Margaret removed her shoe, carefully placing her right foot on the plank. As the audience realized what was happening, they grew breathlessly silent.

Almost instantly, a series of short, sharp little raps sounded through the room. The effect on the crowd was electrifying, and the next day the *New York World* described how the curious audience had been rewarded with "those mysterious sounds, which have for forty years frightened and bewildered hundreds of thousands of people in this country and in Europe." A committee of physicians was invited onto the stage that night to make an examination. They assured the audience that the sound was made by a nearly invisible action of a joint of Margaret Fox's large toe.

But the confession gave Margaret no peace. Shortly before her death in 1895, it is said that she publicly recanted her confession, once again associating herself with the Spiritualist cause that she had accidentally created as a little girl.

•   •   •

Around 1850, during the early days of Spiritualism, the Davenport family also happened to move to Rochester, where the Fox sisters were giving demonstrations. They must have been fascinated by the local controversy, which was quickly becoming a worldwide movement. Ira and William Davenport were about nine and ten years old, roughly the same ages as Margaret and Kate Fox. The quiet brothers had the same potential for mischief as the Fox girls and must have been tempted by the fame and fortune of such simple dishonesty. P. T. Barnum, in his 1866 book, *The Humbugs of the World,* gave an intriguing early history of the Davenports. He claimed that they began giving private séances in Rochester in 1852, around the time of the Fox sisters' success there, and were brought to New York City in 1855 by John F. Coles, a Spiritualist, who organized spiritual "circles" with the Davenport boys in the afternoon and evening at 195 Bowery. The séances were simple and crude, with the Davenports sitting in the center of a room, opposite a row of spectators who had paid to witness the new phenomenon. The Davenports were not tied in their chairs, and on a nearby table were several musical instruments. When the room lights were extinguished, the spectators heard the tambourine rattle and the guitar being strummed. It seems that, at those early séances, the deception relied upon the Davenports' boyish innocence. During one of the dark séances, a policeman's lamp suddenly exposed the boys wandering around the room with the musical instruments in their hands. Their father took them back to Rochester where they attempted to rebuild their reputations as mediums, "by being not more honest," according to Barnum, "but more cautious." In Rochester the Davenports then perfected the cabinet séance.

The famous Davenport cabinet was just a large wooden box of a specific size, but it meant the performers could standardize the rope tying, control the sequences, and carry the "darkness" with them— the headline-making subject of Spiritualism could take the stage and be exhibited before hundreds of people at a time. Over the years their various cabinets were pawned, lost, or broken to bits by angry mobs. The Davenports would appear in the next city with a sketch for a local carpenter and would quickly be back in business.

They still concluded their performances with a dark séance, for an extra charge, in which both young men were tied to their chairs. The act was presented from 1855 to 1864 throughout the eastern part of the United States, in public rooms and small theatres. It was always treated as a lecture or demonstration, not really a performance, and journalists—at a loss to describe the marvelous abilities—eagerly endorsed the brothers. During the Civil War, the Davenports found their opportunities limited and took their cabinet to Europe.

The reception from Dion Boucicault splashed their name across the British papers, and their performances filled theatres in London. The magazine *Punch* joked about the "tie-fuss fever" and appointed the two mediums "Ministers of the Interior, with a seat in the Cabinet." Still, British audiences greeted them with open suspicion. The introductory lecture, delivered by Reverend Ferguson, was filled with extravagant claims, including stories of how the brothers had levitated during séances in Rochester or actually floated across the Niagara River— these naturally put the audience on guard. In later years, Ira remembered how, in some towns in England, they could not appear on the street without hearing taunts of "Yankee Doodle," "Barnum's Humbug," "and many other nice things too numerous to mention," and that Britain's support of the Confederacy during the Civil War contributed to its citizens' icy reception of the Northern boys.

It all blew up in Liverpool, Huddersfield, and Leeds in February of 1865. The Davenports were challenged by two men in the audience, who sadistically tied them with their own specialty, something called a "tom fool knot." Reverend Ferguson protested, asking for other volunteers. The audience, proud of the local challengers, insisted that the men proceed, but Ferguson cut the ropes, William held his arm up to show the bloody injuries he had endured from the knots, and the brothers stalked off the platform. The triumphant crowd stormed the stage, upended the cabinet atop Ferguson and smashed it to pieces. At the next engagement in Huddersfield, the Americans arrived with a new cabinet, and The Philosophical Hall was filled with an expectant audience. But the unconventional technique for tying the brothers had already preceded them from Liverpool. Just minutes into the demonstration, as the spectators cinched the ropes extra tightly, one of the brothers complained that the rope was hurting him. Ferguson quickly cut the ropes, and he and the brothers disappeared from the stage. The audience cheered the local knot tiers and, after some confusion, the ticket receipts were refunded. The Huddersfield gentlemen followed the Davenports to Hull on the next day, announcing their intention to repeat their knot tying. The performance was postponed, and the American mediums were considered exposed.

More than likely, it wasn't a special knot that defeated the Davenports. From what we know about their method, they could have escaped from any particular knot. But they were fearful of the intensity of the audience and the painful ferocity applied to the bonds.

The appeal of the Davenports' act, its mix of religion, agnosticism, science, superstition, and fraud, was a magnet for controversy. A number of European audiences, filled with chauvinistic pride, were content to disrupt a performance and congratulate themselves for having exposed the American impostures. Just days before they opened in Paris, in September of 1865, an article in *Opinion Nationale* gave an indication of the hissing fuse that brought audiences to see them.

> *Do you come and show us mere stock marvels, after having in America worked miracles which a god might envy! Do you take Paris for one of those two-penny-half-penny country villages whither used-up, unappreciated, and out-of-date performers come and try to scrape up some scanty remnant of success! Is it not passing strange that in the year of 1865, when the whole of the human race is pressing with rapid strides in the direction of progress—an attempt should be made to revive these supernatural tomfooleries! Come, deal openly with us; new ideas have no terrors for us. A good sound truth makes its own way in the world, without any accompaniment of luminous guitars or phosphorescent fiddles.*

By trading in the unknown, the Davenports had raised their audiences' expectations to an impossible degree. If the performance were genuine, it would be terrifying. If it were a fraud, it would be insulting.

Not surprisingly, only two days after their premiere at the Salle Herz in Paris, the performance exploded. A French engineer volunteered to tie the brothers, but with the first manifestations, he was outraged to see how easily they had escaped his knots. "They are making fools of us! It is a shameful hoax," he shouted. Leaping to the platform, he suggested that the seats in the cabinet were hinged to allow them to escape. He pounded on the planks of the cabinet, breaking one seat away and tumbling a Davenport to the floor. The audience rushed the stage, and the management called for the police to clear the hall.

An audience member wrote of the evening:

> *Everyone is on his feet in a moment, the storm spreads throughout the assembly; everyone leaves his seat and goes to examine for himself. Everybody is on the platform at once. At this point the constables make a sharp and energetic entry and the performance comes to an end of the preemptory order of the commissary of police. Even at the late hour at which I write these lines (midnight), the Boulevards are still in a high state of excitement and nothing is spoken of but the Davenports.*

Riots, arguments, smashed cabinets, or exposures never really affected the Davenports' success, which was measured in nothing but ticket sales. The next day in Paris, the press examined the cabinet and announced that the engineer had been wrong and the cabinet had not been rigged. The screws and hinges that the engineer had seen were merely there so the cabinet could be taken apart for transportation.

The Davenports quietly ignored these controversies and continued their tour through Europe, appearing before the emperor of France, Czar of Russia, the King of Belgium, the King of Holland, and the King of Prussia. In 1868 they circled back through London, appearing before Queen Victoria and performing across the road from the Polytechnic at St. George's Hall, a small theatre behind All Soul's Church. In the summer of 1868 they toured back through the United States, then followed with tours through the West Indies, India, New Zealand, and Australia. William, the younger brother, died in Sydney in 1877. Ira returned to America and attempted to revive the act with Fay in the 1890s, but by then the cabinet séance had been widely copied and presented with variations. Without the riots, accusations, and press speculations, the famous Davenport manifestations seemed slow and repetitive.

There's an old joke about the ventriloquist who decides to give up show business and use his skills as a fake spirit medium. When his first customer, a grieving widow, arrives for a séance, he explains his prices. "For ten dollars your departed husband will speak to you. For fifteen dollars, I drink a glass of water while he's talking."

Despite their innovations and contributions to the world of conjuring, the Davenports indulged in a typical mistake of many amateur magicians, by doing "too much" simply because they could, inadvertently violating the illusion they wished to create. This was seen when, after being tied securely by the audience and demonstrating a brief burst of manifestations, the cabinet was opened to show that they were completely free and the ropes were lying, unknotted, on the floor of the cabinet. Then, after several minutes more in the closed cabinet and another burst of manifestations, they appeared tied securely again. By clearly demonstrating that they could free themselves, they were no better than the ventriloquist who offered to drink a glass of water just because he could. A good magician would have realized that the entire performance was being undermined by this unnecessary display.

Perhaps the reason for their escape from the ropes was a simple effort to control the act as much as possible. Barnum pointed out something missed by many accounts, that "the principal part of the show is after the tying has been done in their own way," which is to say, after the brothers had retied themselves in the preferred manner, in preparation for the more action-packed portion of the show.

Of course, the integral skill of the Davenport brothers was to escape from their ropes and then retie themselves, or quickly slip back into the bonds. There are many guesses about the Davenports' specific methods. Based on the accounts of people who knew them, and the eyewitness recollections of their act, it now seems that they used two basic secrets to obtain their results.

As the first rope was knotted around the first wrist, each of the brothers brought their hands together behind their back and caught a twist of the thin, smooth cord, holding a loop of rope as the second wrist was tied. This allowed them the necessary slack to make their escape, regardless of the complexity of the knot tied in the rope.

The second secret, which was explained by Ira to Harry Houdini, involved the way that the Davenports had been linked together by the ropes inside the cabinet. Ira and William faced each other in the cabinet, with their knees several feet apart. Under Fay's supervision, the ropes from their wrists, behind their backs, passed through holes in the wooden seats, then were pulled down to be tied around their ankles, then pulled straight forward and tied together between the two brothers. In the darkness of the cabinet, if Ira pushed his ankles forward, he was able to slacken the ropes around William's wrists, giving him a chance to untie the knots. By reversing the process, Ira could gain enough slack to escape. It's a simple plan, as the leg muscles can efficiently move the necessary slack in this long system of rope. Once the Davenports had used these techniques to escape from the audience's knots, the rest of the act was much simpler. Their "to and fro" motion was particularly useful in the next phase of the routine, when the Davenports quickly retied themselves by using slip knots in the ropes.

Some romantic descriptions of the Davenport brothers suggest that they were masters of improvisation, and that their séances made the most of seat-of-their-pants opportunities or quick thinking. But their show changed very little over the years. They depended upon a carefully organized performance, with control over every element and insurance against every unknown. When faced with a challenge or a perplexing situation, the brothers gave a signal and the lecturer quickly and quietly terminated the show without further explanation and the money was returned to the crowd. Ira later insisted that the men who presented their lectures, Reverend Ferguson or later Dr. Nichols, were innocent of the fraud, but this is hard to believe, as he also claimed to have employed a number of confederates in the audience, as many as ten, to guarantee certain results in the dark séance.

Fay was definitely in-the-know and sometimes filled in for William when he was unable to perform; the younger brother's health was always delicate. Fay carried a duplicate length of rope in the mandolin, prepared for any emergency. He boasted to his partners his plan for such a crisis: "I'll not chaw the ropes like you fellows, I'll cut!" Ira also claimed that their parents were never aware of their fraud, but this also seems an exaggeration considering their father's early interest in the act. Because their father had taught them the rope trick and was there for the exposure with the policeman's lantern, it's safe to assume that their very first lecturer was part of the deception. We know that their later road manager, Harry Kellar, was initiated into a number of secrets. It seems as if the Davenports were always surrounded by a group of protectors who not only were aware of their tricks, but helped to refine them.

Several memorable elements of the séance had been devised in order to control the audience and guard against exposure. The audience was asked to hold hands, securing a front row of Davenport confederates who could effectively block the spectators from interfering in the darkness. Even better, a cord passed through the buttonholes of everyone present was explained as a way to prevent collusion from the audience; in fact, it guaranteed that the Davenport brothers could work in the dark without worrying about someone jumping to their feet and lunging for a ghost.

Fay invited local celebrities to tie the brothers; he told the audience that this would guarantee that the knots were genuine. In fact, the use of a local mayor or businessman was insurance against the aggressive sailor or tradesman who was out to embarrass the American performers. Few businessmen knew how to properly tie a prisoner. Of course, the use of the large cabinet was, itself, a way of controlling the light in the room and any unexpected threats from the audience, like the policeman's lamp. As they were first tied and enclosed in the cabinet, Fay closed the three doors one by one. The sound of the bolt being thrown from the inside was clearly heard, locking the center door. It was an odd touch, happening instantaneously and, hence, so "unghostlike." It probably indicated the brothers' meticulous concerns with safely locking audience members out.

Even with their precautions, the Davenports were always on guard against threats, sometimes to a perilous extent. They once heard that the Pinkerton Detective Agency had been hired to expose their act as a fraud, and in an effort to prevent this they had a confederate smuggle a bear trap into the darkened room, setting it in the aisle in the midst of the audience. There is no record of it snapping shut on anyone.

For all these precautions, they were still exposed with regularity. Many accounts of their act gleefully mentioned their supposed mistake with the flour test, in which they held handfuls of flour during the manifestations. One night, as the audience watched, a quick-thinking spectator, standing behind one brother, opened his snuff pouch, filling Davenport's tied hands with dark snuff instead of white flour. At the end of the séance, the brother opened his hand, disclosing pure, clean flour. The explanation inferred was that the brothers had simply been depositing the damp lumps of flour in their pants pockets, then re-filling their hands with a new supply at the end.

Ira Davenport later claimed that the incident never happened. In fact, the brothers could easily hold a fistful of flour and still manipulate the instruments, cause raps or pick up objects by using just their thumb and forefinger.

But it was another pocketful of flour that led to an exposure. A Mr. Addison, a London stockbroker, took a cold-blooded approach to discerning the secrets. Addison and a long-legged friend took front row seats, and during the dark séance the two men extended their legs, stretching as far as possible. As the instruments were conveyed around the room, the two men "soon had the satisfaction of feeling someone falling over them." As further proof, they waited until the next time the lights went out, then each took a mouthful of dry flour and blew into the center of the perceived "manifestations." When the lights came up, Fay's back was covered in white powder. Addison and his friend convulsed with laughter.

The Davenport brothers' most famous imitator was Henry Irving, who was at that time a popular actor on the British stage and would, within a generation, be revered as England's leading actor and theatre manager, Sir Henry Irving of The Lyceum. When the Davenports appeared in Manchester early in 1865, Irving decided to expose the "shameful imposture" and organized a performance at a private club in imitation of the brothers. Two fellow actors, Fredrick Maccabe and Edward A. Sothern, the famous American comedian, took the parts of Ira and William Davenport. Irving gave an accurate impression of Ferguson, the "talker," and in a long, witty introduction, ridiculed the performance and Boucicault's defense of the brothers.

> *Many really sensible and intelligent individuals seem to think that the requirement of darkness seems to infer trickery. So it does. But I will strive to convince you that it does not. Is not a dark chamber essential to the process of photography? [If] scientific men will subject these phenomena to analysis, they will find why darkness is essential to our manifestations. But we don't want them to find out. . . . We want them to be blinded by our puzzle, and to believe with implicit faith in the greatest humbug in the nineteenth century.*

Most insulting of all, Irving, Maccabe, and Sothern then proceeded to duplicate the séance accurately, escaping from the bonds, retying themselves, and producing the mysterious phenomena. The appearance was so successful that it was repeated for the public several nights later, in a large Manchester theatre.

The Davenports must have rankled at these jokes, but they realized that exposures inspired defenders, and debate sold tickets. Audiences wanted to see for themselves. Then, as now, any publicity was good publicity.

Of course, many magicians imitated the Davenports. A few, like Hamilton and Rhys in Paris, or Alexander Herrmann in the United States, admitted that they were puzzled by the brothers' act—or, at least, exhibited the professional courtesy to say so. Some, like the Scottish "Wizard of the North," John Henry Anderson, or the Frenchman Henri Robin, insisted that it was merely a trick and turned their own performances into crusades against the Americans, which put them in the unusual position of criticizing other magicians—the Davenports—for not being honest about their deceptions. The brothers had successfully painted a "grey area" between superstition and conjuring and deftly straddled it through their career. Fifty years earlier it wouldn't have been unusual to appear before an audience and claim a "spirit connection" or supernatural skills during a performance of magic. The surprise was that the Davenports had managed to do this in the sophisticated, scientific Victorian age. This was their real innovation, a much rawer and more elemental magic, not the pleasant society conjuring which was then the fashion.

Magicians took notice. Harry Kellar and William Fay started in the employ of the Davenports and set out on their own careers utilizing their secrets. John Nevil Maskelyne and George Cooke were amateur magicians in Cheltenham, England, when they saw the Davenports on their first European tour. Perceiving the brothers' secret, Maskelyne and Cooke had soon copied the famous cabinet séance. Charles Morritt, a young Yorkshire magician, was first attracted to the art by the Davenport tour of England, and his first experiment was his own version of their ghost cabinet.

Though born a generation after the Davenports, in 1874, Harry Houdini once worked as a "spirit medium," admired the Davenport brothers, and was familiar with the then-standard séance act. But Houdini found a specialty in escapes, taking elements of the Davenport act—specifically escaping and resuming the bonds—and boldly refocused it on his ability to free himself from ropes, locks, and cabinets, a personal triumph rather than a psychic mystery.

Later in his career, as a successful vaudeville artist, Houdini became a collector of magic memorabilia and a historian of the art. In 1908, through Harry Kellar, Houdini was surprised to learn that Ira Davenport was still alive, living in retirement in Mayville, New York. Houdini was busy with a two-year tour of Europe and Australia when his letters located the old showman. "You must not fail to do me the honor of a visit when you return to America," Davenport wrote to Houdini, "although two years is a long time."

Houdini must have been nervous about delaying a meeting with the great Ira Davenport. Years earlier, in 1903, he had tried to meet a

retired master of magic, Wilajalba Frikell, who was living outside of
Dresden, Germany. Long forgotten by the public, Frikell was initially
uneasy about meeting with the young magician. Houdini plied him by
sending imported tea, telegrams, and press clippings of Houdini's successes. The attention flattered the old man, and a meeting was finally
arranged. Houdini arrived that afternoon and was ushered inside by
Frikell's tearful wife. Herr Frikell's parlor had been laid out with the
mementos of his career. He had polished his medals and framed his
photographs. At one end of the room, the body of Frikell, dressed in
his best suit, his moustache waxed and hair neatly trimmed, was
slumped in a chair. Houdini was told that just two hours before his
arrival at Frikell's home, the old man had collapsed of a heart attack.
His face was still wet with the cologne that his wife had used to try
to revive him.

Shortly after Houdini's return to New York City in the summer of
1910, he boarded a train and traveled to upstate New York to meet Ira
Davenport. Mayville was a tiny community on the edge of Lake Chau-
tauqua, near Buffalo and just down the road from the famous Spiritualist camp of Lily Dale, where Davenport was revered as an elder
statesman of the movement.

Houdini bounded from the train and was surprised to find a tiny,
stoop-shouldered man, with a walrus moustache and sleepy eyes,
standing on the platform and anxiously awaiting his guest. Ira Davenport displayed none of the mysterious intensity that had captivated
audiences during the Davenport séances. It was hard to believe he had
been one of the Sphinx-like brothers who carried Spiritualism on their
backs for nearly a generation. Davenport was suffering from throat
cancer, but he was anxious to talk about the good old days, explain his
part in the famous controversies, and tell the truth about the secrets
of the famous Davenport cabinet.

It was a curious pilgrimage for Houdini. Just several years later,
Houdini became a crusading anti-Spiritualist, condemning the fraud
of the séance room and loudly challenging the mediums who preyed
on their victims. But that July afternoon in Mayville, Davenport
charmed and flattered the young escape artist. Sitting on the porch of
the Davenport house, enjoying the cool lake breezes and sipping

lemonade, the two tricksters swapped gossip about the old show business and the new show business. Ira suggested that he might be tempted to come out of retirement to tour with Houdini; he whispered stories about their tours and warmly complimented Houdini on his knowledge of entertainment history, telling him, "You positively know more about the real facts than I, who was the principal actor." In the twilight, Davenport picked up a piece of sash cord, hitched his chair close to Houdini and smiled conspiratorially. Houdini realized that he was watching history. He reached for his notebook and wrote furiously, which was difficult because he didn't want to take his eyes from the old man. Davenport deliberately opened his wrists to display the proper way to catch an extra loop of rope, the precise way he would pause before putting his hands behind his back to have them tied, and the technique for pushing slack in the rope as he was seated on the bench inside the cabinet. He spoke in whispers, pausing before each revelation, leading Houdini to the edge of each secret: "Now, if they pull on this end, you simply. . . . Like this. You understand, don't you?" Both men would nod quietly.

Zellie, Davenport's daughter, later told Houdini that as the two men were absorbed in the secrets, she and her mother hid behind the drapery of an open window, astonished to watch the demonstration, straining to hear bits of the conversation. When Houdini had been taken through all of the Davenport secrets, Ira told him with a smile, "Houdini, we started it, you finish it."

The flattery worked. In his 1924 book, *A Magician Among the Spirits*, Houdini attacked all fraudulent Spiritualists, including the Fox sisters, and ridiculed the credulous people who defended them, like his former friend Sir Arthur Conan Doyle. Still, he included an awkward chapter on the Davenport brothers, which sought to draw a line placing them outside the boundaries of criticism in his book. Houdini honored Ira Davenport, who had died in 1911, the year after the meeting in Mayville, and defended the Davenports' career. In Houdini's typed manuscript for the book, he included the incredible sentence, in capital letters, "THEY DID NOT POSE AS SPIRITUALISTS." In the finished book, Houdini's editor reworked this statement to read,

The brothers have always been, and are still, pointed to as being indisputable proof of the reality and genuineness of mediumistic phenomena . . . yet an interesting train of circumstances put me in possession of facts more than sufficient to disprove their having, or even claiming, spiritualistic power.

Throughout *A Magician Among the Spirits*, Houdini was a moralist. In the Davenport chapter he became a pragmatist. Ferguson and Nichols' preposterous claims for the brothers were dismissed by Houdini with the explanation, "publicity was part of the game," an indulgence he did not afford his other subjects. The magician also approved of the Davenports' twenty-year indifference to what was being said about them. Ira had told Houdini,

We never affirmed our belief in Spiritualism . . . nor did we offer our entertainment as the result of sleight of hand . . . we let our friends and foes settle that as best they could between themselves, but unfortunately we were often the victims of their disagreements.

Appealing to Houdini's love for his own mother, Ira insisted that the brothers were fearful to admit the truth, as it might have caused their parents to commit suicide. Considering how Ira Davenport so successfully wheedled the younger showman, it's curious just what he meant by the remark, "Houdini, we started it, you finish it." Although Houdini was besotted with the pronouncement, was Davenport referring to the fact that they had originated the rope-tie act, which Houdini then exploited? Or was he admitting that the Davenports had popularized Spiritualism, and he was now entrusting Houdini with stamping it out?

Professor Pepper, who viewed illusions as demonstrations of scientific principles, must have been puzzled by the success of the Davenports and their crude deceptions. Then, too, he was probably disappointed to watch the two bold American performers wrestle away his franchise for ghosts. Pepper later wrote,

> . . . *Friends and the public all know how steadily [I have]
> opposed the so-called Spiritual deceptions, which generally
> are not a half nor a quarter as clever as the tricks of a first
> rate conjurer.*

He responded, just months after the Davenports' successes in London, with his very own magic cabinet, designed to show up the Spiritualists. It was an astonishing discovery, and a secret that offered unlimited potential for deception.

4
The Formula for Invisibility

The conjurer demonstrates that things are not always what they seem. Therein lies his philosophy.
—Colonel Stodare

The first time I was ever invisible, actually invisible, was at the Palmer House in Chicago in 1980. I was attending Loyola University at the time, but I couldn't resist taking this job. It was a special act being designed by my good friend Bob Higa, a skillful magician who specialized in performing magic for sales meetings. Bob had been asked to present an early morning show for a company that—if I remember correctly—manufactured display tables, racks, and signs for retail stores. Bob was supposed to introduce the new line of products by demonstrating that they would be "magical" for the company's sales force.

I usually hate this kind of show. It's tough to make magic work in these situations. It's seldom appreciated by the people who produce business meetings; they tend to stand in the back of the room and fret over every detail, as if they'll be fired because a projected slide was backwards or a microphone crackled when the president of the company was about to speak into it. Still, I knew that Bob was professional in his approach to these shows, and he had a surprisingly artistic touch at tailoring his magic to suit a company message.

Besides, I realized this was my chance to be invisible. It turned out to be a great experience. I don't know what I was expecting, but the sensation was strangely different from performing. When I was a performer standing on stage, I always had the impression of being supremely, uncomfortably, surreally visible—the most illuminated person in the room, being watched by hundreds of people who are sitting in the darkness; I could not see them. I was aware that my every gesture and expression was magnified. But that morning in Chicago, as I was standing on the stage, invisible, it was the exact opposite. The lights in the room made the audience visible to me. I was watching their eyes, but they couldn't see me. When I first stepped onto the sales meeting stage, there was a temptation to do something silly, to wave my hands in a broad gesture or weave from side to side to see if any eyes were following me. But no one noticed me. The crowd's eyes followed Higa, they nodded appreciatively to each other as their products magically appeared (that was me secretly handing them to Higa) and laughed when the products floated through the air (me again, holding them aloft). No one saw me. Applause, fulsome thanks from the president of the company, and as the salesmen stumbled out for their morning coffee, I quietly crept back onto the stage. Now that the show was over, I was visible once again, just a stagehand who had wandered out to look at the stage as the last people left the room.

The particular secret for my invisibility that morning was first used on stage in the 1880s. A number of magicians have understood the basic principle, but the dozens of fine points of an illusion—the important touches that really made it work—are really known only by magicians who refined the illusion through their own experiments.

Just a few years earlier, in 1977, I had first learned about invisibility from a magician named Vic Torsberg. Vic had first used the principle in the 1930s, then developed it into an act which he performed in the 1950s. When I knew him, he was the demonstrator behind the counter at Chicago's Magic Inc. Vic was a heavyset man with thinning white hair who wore shiny black suits and thin black ties. He had a clear tenor speaking voice that carried perfectly from the stage. Like every real magic demonstrator, he knew how to pick up almost any trick and make it look great. He loved magic, but he had a no-nonsense approach to it all. If I asked him about a trick that Magic Inc. advertised in their catalog, he might scowl and shake his head. "You couldn't really use it." The first couple of times, this sort of advice would shatter me. But sooner or later, I learned that Vic was always right.

In the 1970s, when I was a high-school student and aspiring magician, hanging around in a magic shop on Saturday afternoons was a substitute for actually being a magician. I bought many more tricks than I could ever really use, many more than I'd dare to perform. A lot of junk just didn't work or never fooled anyone. Mostly, my friends and I hung around the shop to spend time with Vic or our idols, Jay and Frances Marshall, who owned and operated Magic Inc. I'd pretend to be an important customer with a need for the latest trick.

Starting out in magic I was attracted to those new tricks, but as I spent enough time in the shop, I began to realize that the best secrets were those that had been worked out years before. I could benefit from the experience of old timers. Tim Felix was a friend of mine who worked at the magic shop on weekends. Tim and I were the same age, and we liked to engage Vic in conversation, asking him about the magicians of the past. Tim had discovered that Vic liked to eat. One night Tim and I picked him up and drove him to a Japanese steak house on the north side of town, calculating that Vic would have fun, and he might impart a few secrets on a full stomach. Over dinner, he started talking about his old act. At first he was reluctant to say much, but we evidently asked the right questions, because soon there was a pause in the conversation and then a slight "what-the-hell" shrug from Vic. He suddenly offered, "I'll show you *exactly* how I did it." Vic reached for a pen and scribbled on a napkin between bursts of fire and flying shrimp. He explained the way most magicians overused the lighting, told us the perfect materials for the backdrop, and the best way to place the props on stage. We were learning how to be invisible. Tim and I were amazed. The clatter of the knives and spatulas faded into the background as we focused on every word. We were nervous about looking too interested and we tried to avoid glancing at each other, worried that we might break the spell and Vic, coming to his senses, would stop talking. "A lot of the books are wrong about this," he said, picking up a slice of beef with his chopsticks and pointing to the sketches on his napkin. "This is exactly the way to do it. Believe me, this works perfectly."

Three years later, with Vic's help, I was invisible on stage at the Palmer House. That's the real way to learn about the art.

Everything in magic changed with the ghosts, who quickly rapped and rattled apart the great traditions of Victorian conjuring. Just as magicians found an entirely new type of presentation based on the Davenport séance, they were presented with an entirely new range of secrets based on Pepper's Ghost. The fact that Pepper's Ghost was protected by a patent meant that it was a badly kept secret; anyone who was curious about it, and diligent enough to visit the patent office or patient enough to send off for a copy of the paperwork, could see a diagram of the illusion and an efficient explanation of how it worked. Patents protect inventions by memorializing them in words and

diagrams, then making them part of the public record. It's a good
system for most inventors but an inefficient one for magicians, who
would prefer to hide the details of their inventions, not publish them.

The success of the Ghost at the Polytechnic only inspired other
inventors, who quickly filed patents detailing their variations; many
of these inventors were never heard from again. Some of the ideas, like
the patent of Alfred Silvester, a lecturer at the Polytechnic, were designed as improvements to the original invention. Others were clearly
designed to sidestep the specifics of the original patent and secure pro-
tection for a similar invention. So, a mysterious showman by the
name of H. N. King filed a patent that suggested setting up the glass
on the stage floor at an angle pointing toward the wings at the side,
like a door opened at a 45-degree angle, so that the lower pit was not
necessary. A man named J. Munro suggested adding tinted glasses,
multiple mirrors, or the illumination of smaller parts of the scene.
J. W. Hoffman filed a provisional patent adding synchronized traps or
gauze curtains to increase the effects. C. Bolton suggested hiding the
ghost to the side or above the scene, not below. J. H. Weston and
C. Morton suggested moving the glass to give the effect that the ghost
was rising or falling. Various patents suggested using the glass to produce rain, fountains, fire, waterfalls, or miraculous transformations.

The string of patents serves to demonstrate how the principle was
being tweaked and twisted in a heated effort to find something new—
tracing a clear evolution to the next important discovery. However, as
a practical matter, these inventions all made the same mistake: they
assumed that the Ghost was a versatile, practical, and important
invention for the theatre. It wasn't.

First, there were mechanical concerns. The installation of the glass
was expensive and complicated, and far too much trouble for a simple
effect like a flame or fountain. The angles were dependent on the size
and shape of the theatre; for many stages it was completely impossible. Even worse were the sensory limitations to the plays themselves: The glass prevented anyone on stage from being heard, and
the short scenes featuring the Ghost were performed, of necessity, in
pantomime.

There was also an optical limitation. Henry Dircks had always promised that a wide variety of effects would be made possible by his invention: the appearance or disappearance of people or objects changing color. But the invention was really only good at creating light colored, glowing, transparent images—ghosts. Even then, it required intense lights to illuminate the figure in the oven. The clear sheet of glass made a poor reflector, and it certainly wasn't up to reflecting solid-looking people or colored objects.

For this reason, several patents suggested the use of completely silvered mirrors in conjunction with the Ghost illusion.

The most interesting of these patents, filed by a Joseph Maurice of Langham Place in London, was a typical grab bag of ideas. But Maurice had hit upon a wonderful notion, an invention of an entirely new category.

> *It has hitherto been the practice in producing spectral illu-*
> *sions to place the real actor or object out of sight, and to*
> *throw a representation or image of such living actor or real*
> *object upon a sheet of glass placed on the stage, but [I reflect*
> *in the] plate of glass the duplicate scene, which may be wall,*
> *forest, or wainscoting*

On a practical level, Maurice had simply reversed the equation. Stand the actor on the stage. On top of him, reflect the image of a portion of an empty room. The actor disappears.

But on the level of marvels, it was an astonishing idea. After all, for centuries, mirrors had been used to reflect *something*, to place a face over a blank space on the wall. On stage, the reflection could place an object in a location where it was not expected—which had been the formula for the Ghost. The object of the illusion was the object of the reflection.

Far less logical was that a mirror could reflect *nothing* (or, more precisely, an open space bounded by some scenery or curtains): a wall at a great distance could be reflected over a face! In other words, something could be hidden by the use of a reflection. It was, very simply, an optical formula for invisibility. We don't know if Maurice's patent was the inspiration for the inventions of a lecturer at the Polytechnic and an associate of Professor Pepper's, Thomas W. Tobin. But more than anyone else, Tobin understood the importance of this basic formula. He applied it, in quick succession, to three amazing illusions.

On April 10, 1865, four days before President Lincoln's assassination in Washington, D.C., while the Davenport brothers were still touring in Great Britain, a new illusion was introduced on the small stage of London's Polytechnic Institution. Newspapers listed it as the joint invention of John Henry Pepper and Thomas Tobin, titling it "Proteus, or We are Here but not Here."

The latest of Pepper's illusions was his own version of the magic cabinet. The small upright closet, about three feet square and six feet tall, was wheeled to the center of the stage. It was on tall legs with casters, which made it easy to maneuver and also demonstrated that no one could enter or exit the cabinet through a trapdoor in the stage. Professor Pepper introduced the cabinet with a quick reference to Proteus, the old sailor of Greek mythology, who could instantly assume any form. As an assistant revolved the cabinet, slowly showing each panel, Pepper rapped on the walls with a long stick. With the cabinet facing the audience, the two doors were opened in front. Pepper pointed out that the cabinet was completely empty except for a narrow vertical post, mounted roughly in the center of the box. The post supported a gas lantern that brightly illuminated the inside walls of the cabinet, which were covered with a white and gold figured paper. With the front doors opened, the audience could see that the cabinet was empty. Pepper entered the cabinet, standing in the opening.

Stepping down from the cabinet, Professor Pepper used his stick to push the front doors closed again. They were sealed, and instantly a knock was heard from the inside. Upon opening the doors, the boy who handed out the theatre's programs was found inside. He stepped from the cabinet and received his applause. Pepper had the cabinet revolved and shown again, and the boy re-entered it. As the piano player accompanied the action, the cabinet doors were closed. "Watch closely," Pepper warned, waving his stick in the air dramatically. "There he goes!" The doors had been closed for only a few seconds, but when they were opened, the cabinet was empty again. The audience was shown every side of the cabinet and every inch of the interior, but the boy had disappeared.

Proteus was not only the first magician's cabinet trick, but the first trick "all done with mirrors." There were two tall, narrow, rectangular glass mirrors—real mirrors with silvered backs, not just clear sheets of glass as in the Ghost illusion—hinged to the inside walls of the cabinet. The mirrors could be pushed flat against the sides, where they were unnoticed because their backs were covered with the same wallpaper as the inside of the cabinet. With the doors closed, the program boy could hinge the mirrors in toward the center of the cabinet, where they would stop against the vertical post.

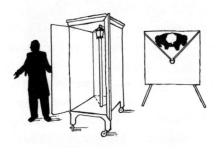

The Proteus cabinet, and the view from the top

The careful geometry of the box ensured that the boy standing in the wedge shape behind the mirrors would seem to disappear; as the audience looked into the cabinet, each mirror reflected a side wall in place of the back wall. It was a perfect optical illusion.

The nature of mirror viewing is that, unless the mirror is cracked or dirty, the viewer never focuses on the surface of the mirror but focuses through it, to an object that's being reflected. In Proteus, even though the mirrors were in front of the hidden assistant, the reflections seemed to be of the wall at the back of the cabinet—just as if one were looking right through the mysterious program boy.

Proteus was a fascinating curiosity at the Polytechnic. It never matched the Ghost for public appeal and was treated only as an optical curiosity. It wasn't a sensational illusion, but it led to a great number of important ideas.

Thomas William Tobin was the inventor of Proteus, despite the patent and the advertising offering joint credit with Pepper. Tobin was a prodigy; he had been trained as an architect when he was fourteen, and first came to Pepper's attention several years later, when he was working as a chemist, experimenting with the mixture of gases in the oxyhydrogen lamp. When Tobin was only twenty, he was not only inventing the Proteus illusion, but also serving as secretary of the Polytechnic and lecturing on scientific subjects. Considering his early training, it's not surprising that Tobin's patent for Proteus shows an architectural understanding of dimensions and angles. Proteus was designed to fit perfectly in the right-angle world of square cabinets, walls, and ceilings.

It's worth looking at the simple geometry involved in the illusion: what could be seen and what shouldn't have been seen inside of Tobin's wonderful cabinet. Sightlines are the imaginary extreme lines of vision, the boundaries of what an audience will see or what they will be prevented from seeing. They've always been a standard part of the design for theatre stages and can be neatly calculated on a blueprint for the front seats, or the back seats, or the audience at the far sides of the theatre. The scenery must be arranged so that all the important elements are clearly seen by the audience, but the audience must be prevented from seeing the stagehands working in the wings.

For magicians, the sightlines for a piece of apparatus take on a special significance. They are the battle plans for an illusion, the mathematical proof of a principle, and the formula to make an illusion deceptive. Proteus is a neat example of just how sightlines work with a mirror.

From the top, the "safe zone" inside the cabinet

Within the 90-degree walls of the cabinet, the mirrors are hinged in place at exactly 45 degrees—bisecting the angle formed by the back and side walls. It's a case of one plus one equaling two; more precisely, the actual 45-degree angle plus the reflected 45-degree angle equal a 90-degree angle. The reflection in the mirror, giving the illusion of a 90-degree angle, makes the cabinet appear empty.

Looking down on the floor plan of the cabinet, there is an imaginary "safe zone," a roughly triangular area in front of the mirrors. If the mirrors have been closed so that the audience is looking into them, and the magician outside of the cabinet can step up and stand within this "safe zone" (as Pepper did, waving his stick in front of Proteus), he won't cause any reflections in the mirror. But should the magician carelessly drift out of this area, moving closer to the mirrors, or even wave his arms outside this area, stray reflections of feet or arms will appear in the mirror for spectators sitting at the sides. This would betray the illusion.

This "safe zone" is not strictly an extension of the diagonals of the mirrors. The sightlines defining this space are actually the perpendicular lines drawn from the very front edges of the mirror. Notice how, if the center post is widened, the "safe zone" changes in shape.

Similarly, the safe sightlines for the audience lie along these lines. They might be imagined as extending out from the front of the cabinet. As long as the audience is viewing the cabinet from within these angles, the interior of the cabinet appears perfectly empty. This is part of the wonderful efficiency of Tobin's idea. If these angles are trapped by the dimensions of the cabinet, then the doors can be opened and the cabinet turned completely around, displaying that it's empty.

However, if the dimensions are altered slightly, by making the cabinet shallower and the front edges of the mirror closer to the front, the illusion won't work. The audience can view the interior from angles

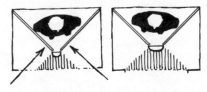

From the top, the angles inside the Proteus cabinet

wider than the "safe zone." As the cabinet is turned, or seen from the extreme sides, some spectators will find they are looking at themselves in the mirror.

There are formulas for correcting the situation. The perfect angles can be captured again by widening the center post or increasing the framing around the front doors of the cabinet. The goal, of course, is to show the audience as much of the interior as possible, giving the impression that every corner of the cabinet is visible.

Proteus was a wonderful illusion, but it suffered from the clinical, scientific atmosphere at the Polytechnic, where it wouldn't receive any of the tweaks and touches of showmanship that have always been part of a first-class magic show. It could have been a miracle in the hands of a magician, rather than being demonstrated by a lecturer. Tobin must have realized this, because he made sure that his next creation had the advantage of a great performer.

Professor John Henry Anderson, a Scottish magician who billed himself as "The Wizard of the North," later regretted that he didn't buy the new Thomas Tobin illusion. Tobin had asked for 80 pounds. Anderson, a practical old showman, couldn't bring himself to pay the price.

So Tobin approached Colonel Stodare, a young English magician who was renting the small theatre at Egyptian Hall in London—a former museum adorned with Egyptian sculpture and hieroglyphics. Stodare had come to London in 1865 and found himself working in opposition to Anderson, a strange irony as a later rumor suggested that Stodare was actually Anderson's illegitimate son.

The title "Colonel" was a showman's prerogative, suggesting an adventurer or explorer of foreign mysteries. Stodare's real name was probably Joseph Stoddart, born in Liverpool in 1831. He was a ventriloquist and magician whose posters promised "Indian Magic" and "Two Hours in Wonder World," explaining that he performed "without the aid of any apparatus." This recent fashion eliminated the elaborate, exotic vases and mechanical automata which had been popular in the mid 1800s; instead, Stodare used objects borrowed from the audience or ordinary looking apparatus like baskets and tables. One of his original effects, and a good example of his simplistic approach, was the Instantaneous Growth of Flowers. Stodare showed two pots of soil and placed a seed into each one. These were covered with empty pasteboard cylinders. When the cylinder was removed from one pot, a small sprout was seen emerging from the earth. The pot was covered again. Both cylinders were then lifted from the pots, revealing two beautiful rosebushes in full bloom.

Stodare's Indian conjuring was his version of the famous Basket Trick. He placed a young lady in a rectangular basket, then repeatedly plunged a sword through the wicker sides. The audience heard her scream and gasp for breath; the screams grew quieter and more desperate as the sword was pulled from the basket, dripping with blood. Finally Stodare tipped the basket forward and opened it, showing that the lady had disappeared. She was discovered, unharmed, at the back of the theatre.

A dashing performer, Stodare dressed in a tail coat and had long dark hair and a narrow mustache. Equally adept with a graceful illusion like the roses, then a horrific one with the lady in the basket, he could be skillful, funny, or dangerously exotic. He was the perfect choice to present Tobin's latest wonder.

For weeks in the fall of 1865, cryptic notices were run on the front page of the *Times* teasing readers that "The Sphinx has left Egypt." Then, in October, the message changed. "The Sphinx has arrived and will soon appear." The premiere of The Sphinx was October 16, to mark Stodare's 200th performance at Egyptian Hall. The small theatre held only a couple hundred people; for Stodare's well-advertised feature, the room was filled, shoulder-to-shoulder, with curious Londoners.

The curtain rose on a simple setting with a square alcove, about ten feet across, lined with drapery. In the center of this alcove sat a small, round, three-legged table, about the size of a card table. It had a thin wooden top and slender, turned wooden legs. There was no tablecloth. Stodare appeared on stage carrying a small fabric-covered traveling case, roughly a twelve-inch cube, and placed it in the center of the table. The front of the box was hinged open, revealing a human head adorned with an Egyptian headdress. The head seemed remarkably realistic, a sculpture of a placid Egyptian oracle with his eyes shut. Stodare retired to a side of the stage and waved his wand. "Sphinx, awake!" The head opened its eyes, looked from side to side, and gradually seemed to become conscious of its surroundings. He asked it to smile. The corners of its mouth turned up slightly. Stodare posed questions and suggested that it make a speech. The head responded with some twenty lines of dramatic verse. There was a rolling, building gasp of recognition through the audience. It appeared to be a real head. As Stodare was well-known as a capable ventriloquist, his presence at the far side of the stage tantalized the audience, which was searching for a secret. They turned from Stodare to the head on the table, convincing themselves that the voice was emanating from the box. The Sphinx concluded its talk, the powers faded, and it closed its eyes. Stodare approached the box, shutting the front lid. He reflected on the mysterious, mythical nature of the Sphinx, then re-opened the box to find that the head had disappeared, leaving only a pile of ashes.

Carrying the mysterious box to the footlights, Stodare looked out over his audience and was greeted with a momentary, stunned silence. His audience was still thinking, marveling at what they had just seen. Slowly, one person began to applaud, then another, and another. The sound of handclapping jarred the spectators from their reverie—like a domino effect, the applause increased until the walls of Egyptian Hall vibrated with the ovation.

"This is certainly one of the most extraordinary illusions ever presented to the public," the *Times* mused several days later. "That the speech is spoken by a human voice there is no doubt, but how is a head to be . . . detached from anything like a body . . . confined in a case . . . and placed on a bare-legged table?"

The *Morning Post* called it "A mystery, a miracle of art."

The *Daily News* wrote, "The Sphinx is the most remarkable deception ever included in a conjurer's programme," and the *Dispatch* confessed complete bewilderment: "We give the enigma up. The astonishment it created was universal, the applause which greeted Colonel Stodare deafening." Queen Victoria summoned Stodare and the Sphinx to Windsor Castle the following month for a command performance of the illusion that had perplexed London.

The magician's fame was brief. Less than a year after the premiere of the Sphinx, Colonel Stodare was dead. He was thirty-five years old, at the height of his success, and was packing for an engagement in Paris when he suffered a sudden, fatal hemorrhage of the lungs. His older brother, Alfred, who had also worked as a magician, continued Stodare's show and performed several variations on the Sphinx illu-

sion, and other performers soon copied the effect. But the famous
Egyptian head was never more successful than under the supervision
of this dashing and dramatic originator.

Proteus was perceived as a trick cabinet. It was introduced as a novel
invention by a scientific lecturer. The apparatus was prominent and
unusual. An inexperienced assistant—the fellow who had handed you
the program—appeared inside, awkwardly stepping out for his bow. As
there was nothing special about the boy, the audience must have been
convinced that there was *something* special about the cabinet. The
illusion offered a momentary surprise: somehow the boy made his
entrance and then escaped.

But the Sphinx was received as a perfect mystery. It was the work
of a skilled magician, who had proven himself adept at a wide
variety of deceptions. There was virtually no apparatus at all, just a
table and an ornate box. The head inside was mysterious and
exotic—it might be a puppet or an automaton, ventriloquism or
machinery, mesmerism or optical illusion. Stodare arranged the
presentation upon building surprises: the opening eyes, the moving
mouth, then words and expressions until finally, with the audience
anxious to glimpse the head one last time, it had turned to dust.
The illusion created a haunting memory for audiences, reminding
them of tales of decapitated heads, Egyptian mummies, the terrifying images of life and death.

Audiences would have never suspected that Proteus and the Sphinx
were the same trick.

Tobin and Stodare had filed a provisional patent on August 1, 1865:

> *A table consisting of an ordinary top or slab supported on*
> *legs, consoles or other appliances, under, over and on each*
> *side of which table curtains, scenery or other objects are*
> *clearly perceptible. A mirror or mirrors are arranged under*
> *this table at certain angles so as to reflect portions of such*
> *scenery or other objects, which appear to be the actual*
> *scenery or other objects observed, while in reality they only*

are reflections of such. . . . Behind these mirrors real persons
or objects may be concealed. . . .

The curtained alcove around the Sphinx's table took the place of
the walls of the cabinet. The two mirrors were disguised between the
three legs of the table; the center leg of the table served the same purpose as the center post of the Proteus cabinet.

At the start of the illusion,
the actor playing the Sphinx
was crouching between the
table legs, hidden behind
the two mirrors. As Stodare
placed the box on the table,
the actor raised his head
through a trapdoor in the
table and into the box. As
long as his body remained
behind the mirrors, it gave

Tobin and Stodare's Sphinx illusion

the illusion of a disembodied head. At the conclusion, as Stodare
closed the front lid, the actor playing the Sphinx pulled his head back
through the table, reached up to deposit a handful of ashes, and closed
the trap in the bottom of the box.

Tobin and Stodare's patent papers suggested that different angles
could be used for the scenery and the mirrors—the important part of
the formula was that each mirror bisected the angle of the identical
surrounding walls. Still, the Sphinx, like Proteus, was built around 90-
degree angles. The side walls of the alcove reflected as the back wall.
Most stable three-legged tables have legs set at 60 degrees, but the table
for the Sphinx had its three legs set at 90 degrees; it was actually a four-
legged table with one leg sawed off. The mirrors were permanently
mounted between the table legs, and throughout the presentation Stodare had to approach the table from the "safe zone," the triangle at the
front of the table, so that his legs did not reflect in the mirrors.

Proteus and The Sphinx called for a good deal of finesse and attention. First, of course, the mirrors needed to be scrupulously clean. A
theatrical manager named Alfred Thompson later wrote that when he

watched Stodare's living head at Egyptian Hall, he chanced to see two fingerprint smudges on the glass, which instantly allowed him to perceive the secret. He quietly left the theatre understanding exactly where the mirrors were placed and how the man was concealed. Using mirrors on stage always required careful lighting. With too little illumination the mirrors might appear dark or hazy on stage; with too much, they might cause weird, rectangular flares—bright patches of light—on the walls or floor. The smooth edges of the glass required endless adjustment. They might sparkle in the stage light, betraying their presence. Beneath the table, edges of the glass were visible against the carpet. Looking into a mirror, you see the silver, or reflective, surface just behind the thickness of the glass; by nature the mirror appears to be twice as deep as it really is. In other words, a quarter-inch thick glass mirror seems to be half an inch thick at its edge. This wide line needed to be camouflaged. A simple solution was to extend the V of the glass into an X of painted dark lines beneath the Sphinx, or on the ceiling and floor of the Proteus cabinet. The center of the X fell at the center leg of the table or the vertical post. Alert spectators began watching for the telltale X on the carpeting beneath the Sphinx table, which literally marked the spot where the mirrors were used.

Curious spectators could cause a variety of problems. When the Sphinx was produced in a Parisian wax museum, just months after its premiere in London, it wasn't performed on a stage but merely exhibited like a sideshow. The scene was a dark dungeon, supposedly displaying a bloody, recently decapitated head, which rolled its eyes and whispered horrifically. The public was charged an exorbitant fee to see the sensation, and some who shuffled past it couldn't resist the temptation of being left alone with the head. Perhaps they felt compelled to get the most show for their money. Leaning across a rail that separated the audience from the illusion, a group of wags took aim with paper pellets, pelting the poor actor crouched behind the mirrors in order to test his reactions. This target practice had terrible consequences. When the shot was accurate, the head would explode in a volley of abuse, ruining the melodramatic scene and sending the spectators from the exhibit laughing. But far worse was an unskillful aim, which landed the pellets against the mirror. The pellets bounced, fell to the floor and were doubled by the reflections in the glass, exposing the secret of the illusion.

Tobin's third creation was the strangest of all. It was premiered just months after Stodare's Sphinx, in December of 1865, at the Royal Polytechnic, under the auspices of Professor Pepper. The newspapers advertised it as The Modern Delphic Oracle.

As the curtain rose, the audience saw an entrance to a Greek temple, a small entrance porch about ten or twelve feet wide and about six feet tall. An "ancient Athenian nobleman" entered the stage through this porch before a curtain closed across it. After incense was burned in a brazier and the spirits of sages invoked, the curtains were pulled back again, showing the head and shoulders of Socrates floating in space over the temple porch.

Socrates uttered a series of profundities, convincing the audience that this talking head was that of a real person. The curtain was drawn, and another spirit was sum-
moned. As the curtains were pulled open, another legendary philosopher—or at least his head—was seen floating on the stage. After several of these appearances the curtain was pulled away, showing the empty setting of the porch. The nobleman exited the stage through this space, showing that there was no special apparatus on the stage.

The Oracle of Delphi, the view from the side

The secret, as explained in patent papers filed by Tobin and Pepper, was a sort of cross between two successful illusions, the Sphinx and the Ghost. It was a large mirror on a small stage. The inner temple was a raised, box-like porch on the main stage. A silvered mirror was mounted diagonally across this porch. Once again, the mirror was fixed at 45 degrees. The mirror reflected the ceiling as the wall of the temple.

The mirror was mounted on a track so that it could be completely withdrawn under cover of the curtain. This left an empty temple setting, which could be shown at the beginning and end of the demonstration.

In the center of the mirror was an oval hole, which allowed the actor to pass his head and shoulders up through the glass. Thus the effect of an empty room and a head floating in space.

The sight lines were critical. First, when the enormous mirror was in place, the inner porch appeared to have no floor. For this reason the illusion was presented on a raised platform, so the audience was gazing up at it. The actor who introduced the illusion was confined to the steps in front of the porch; if he stepped too close to the illusion, he would be reflected within the set.

Even more critical, a head pushed up through a hole in a mirror would give the weird impression of two conjoined heads, one upright and one extending straight back at a 90-degree angle. Only if the audience was directly in front of the illusion, and slightly below it, could this reflected head be concealed. More than likely, the built-up costume shoulders of the Oracle or other pieces of wardrobe were used to help with this problem.

By accident, the employees at the Polytechnic discovered that the illusion could be perfectly illuminated by a diffuse spotlight from the front. Thanks to the mirror, the circular light cast a shadow of the head on the ceiling of the chamber, which was then reflected as if it were on the back wall. The illusion created was that the isolated head cast a perfect shadow, just as if it were floating in space.

Pepper must have felt that, like his famous Ghost, the new illusion would lend itself to different settings and scenes. Just a month after its premiere, a second effect was added: The Cherubs Floating in the Air, a re-creation of Joshua Reynolds' painting in which five small cherubs with tiny wings and real heads were seen levitating over the stage. By April, the effect had been redressed as Shakespeare and His Creations, a brief weird scene in which the floating heads of Hamlet, Macbeth, and other creations of the Bard delivered nuggets from their famous soliloquies. The large, flat Elizabethan collars around each head must have been useful to hide unwanted reflections, but the combination of levitation, decapitation, and Shakespeare never found an audience. Although variations of these effects played for many months at the Polytechnic, the illusion was neither as versatile as the Ghost, nor as strikingly presented as Stodare's Sphinx.

Proteus, The Sphinx, and the Oracle of Delphi followed each other in quick succession, occupying the London papers for just over nine months in 1865. The response to each illusion—the strange appeal of the disembodied Egyptian head but the unappealing strangeness of the floating Cherubs—was merely due to choices in presentation. The overall importance of these effects was that Tobin, an architect, scientific lecturer, and part-time wizard, had defined a revolutionary category of secrets: optical conjuring.

It's easy to imagine how magicians of 1865, watching Tobin's experiments with a silvered mirror on stage, must have felt flush with the possibilities. Conjuring has always been based on techniques of concealment. That's why sleight of hand was built on a foundation of "palming," the technical term for concealing a small object in the hand, and stage magic was based on containers with false bottoms, tables with false tops, trapdoors, thin wires or threads. Invisibility was the ultimate concealment, and here was the simple geometric formula: 45 degrees plus 45 degrees equals 90 degrees, or the angle of incidence equals the angle of reflection. Objects could be made invisible, rescued from invisibility or made partly invisible. Extending the idea, a source of support holding up an object could be made invisible, or even a source of power or intelligence could be concealed. For magicians, suddenly anything seemed possible.

5
The Chief

Mirrors are practically useless to me.
—John Nevil Maskelyne

agicians tend to focus on deception, as if it's the essence of their skills. It's an attitude often reinforced by audiences, who have learned to expect very little from magic acts. If a magician manages to fool his audience, most accept that he's done his job—just as if a juggling act is great because the performer didn't drop any balls or a singer is wonderful because she didn't hit any clinkers. With the expectations set so low, most magicians are perfectly happy to descend to them.

Like many other kids, I probably became interested in magic for misguided reasons, wanting to learn various tricks because they imparted secrets, and hoping these secrets might award me a special status among my friends. In books of tricks, the recipe is specific— here's the effect and here's the method—implying that executing and concealing the secret is always the ultimate goal of the exercise.

The magician David Devant wrote:

> At the risk of offending many very proficient conjurers, both amateurs and professionals, I make bold to state that magic does not consist in a few so-called secrets, which can be mastered by any intelligent person in a few hours. To say a man who can show a few tricks is a conjurer is about as absurd as to say that a man who can recite "The Merchant of Venice" by heart is an actor.
>
> I regard a conjurer as a man who can hold the attention of his audience by telling them the most impossible fairy tales, and by persuading them into believing that those stories are true by illustrating them with his hands, or with any object that may be suitable for the purpose.

If magicians have unfortunately come to view their art as deception, they must recognize that used car salesmen, advertising executives, and politicians are also artists of deception. In fact, there's not very much art in a pure deception, the big lie, or the exaggeration. It's true that, at times, magicians might require something just this simple or bold. But usually the deception in a magic show is a negative element, the hole in the middle of the performance. The performance is a sort of inadvertent dance around this hole, with the hope that each spectator will be coaxed to slip through it.

The English landscape painter John Constable once insisted that his art "pleases by reminding, not deceiving." It's the same with magicians. The real art is in the subtle touches of reassurance that surround any deception and disguise it as a positive thing. With a gesture, a suggestion, a feint or contrivance, the audience is convinced that they are watching a genuine wonder. Great magicians aspire to creating this temporary fantasy.

The end result becomes a little work of theatre, a play with a simple plot that exists on a fairy tale level. The fantasies of a magic show can often be appreciated in everyday life: causing someone to disappear, becoming someone else, acquiring the ability to escape or walk through a wall. The play might be seconds long or be elaborately written to include a full story.

Maskelyne was once the greatest brand name in magic. The family produced three generations of popular magicians. For over five decades there was a Maskelyne theatre of magic in London—at Egyptian Hall and, later, St. George's Hall—where shows were offered, the posters boasted, "Daily at 3 and 8." It was a popular tourist destination and a treat for countless British children, who would be escorted to a Maskelyne matinee for special occasions. For magicians it was the laboratory of invention, the shrine of great conjurers, their Mecca.

John Nevil Maskelyne's contemporaries reverently endorsed him as a "showman to his fingertips," but photos of Maskelyne seem distinctly nontheatrical. He was a little man with narrow eyes and an enormous brush mustache, sober, and grandly dignified. From the earliest years of his career in the early 1870s, he was renowned as one of the world's greatest magicians. Still, it was difficult to classify Maskelyne strictly as a magician—just as Barnum was a great man of the circus although he never walked a tightrope or put on clown makeup. In fact, there was a lot of Barnum in Maskelyne, a dogged innovator and a master of publicity. Part of Maskelyne's mysterious, esteemed status among his fellow magicians—as the doyen of British magic, he was always "the Guv'nor," "Mr. Maskelyne" or "the Chief"—was due to the fact that most magicians were completely dependent upon him for their careers. They knew it and he knew it.

John Nevil Maskelyne was born in 1839 in Cheltenham, Gloucestershire. The family liked to imply that they were direct descendants of Nevil Maskelyne, the famous royal astronomer under George III, but they were not. John Nevil's father was a saddler, and young J. N. worked as a clockmaker. He was also a cornet player in a local band, a choir member in his church, and an amateur magician.

As a young man in Cheltenham, J. N. Maskelyne learned to be distrustful of Spiritualists. A local couple worked as mediums and professed to make cures through mesmerism. One day the woman medium came into Maskelyne's shop with an odd metal device, a leather leg strap with a swinging metal arm, asking that this "surgical device," as she called it, be repaired. Maskelyne found that the problem was a broken spring, replaced it, then experimented with the odd "surgical device" to determine how it was used. He found that, strapped on his leg and adjusted so the trigger fell beneath his heel, it could be used to produce mysterious raps on the bottom of a table.

Delighted with his detective work, he considered it "very sharp" to send in the bill, "Repairs to table rapping apparatus, 1s 6d." (One shilling, six pence was about 75 cents.) But Maskelyne found that this prevented any further business with the local Spiritualists, and ended his investigations and exposures. Embarrassed by his discovery, local mediums simply omitted table rapping from their future séances.

His most important bit of detective work came, he always claimed, in a flash. On March 7, 1865, when he was twenty-six years old, the famous Davenport brothers appeared at the Cheltenham Town Hall. They had just made headlines in London and were beginning their tour of Britain. It was an afternoon performance, and the windows of the hall had been covered with curtains to give the proper ghostly effect. J. N., known in the town as a conjurer, was encouraged to volunteer to be one of the committee on the stage, responsible for supervising each step of the séance.

In the dimly lit hall, the brothers were tied in place and enclosed in their cabinet. The raps, ringing, and strumming had just begun when the center door was pushed open and the instruments tumbled out onto the stage. By chance, the drapery fell away from a theatre window at that precise moment, sending a quick ray of light into the Davenports' famous cabinet. From his angle on stage, Maskelyne was lucky enough to see Ira Davenport, leaning forward to toss the instruments with one free arm. Ira glared at J. N., swung his arm behind his back, and wriggled into the ropes. The vision lasted just a fraction of a second, but it was suddenly all clear to Maskelyne.

The young, audacious magician stopped the performance with an admirable burst of Victorian propriety: "Ladies and Gentlemen, by a slight accident I have been able to discover this trick." Such local skirmishes were typical for the Davenports, but Maskelyne went farther, making a bold promise to perfect the necessary skills and, at the earliest opportunity, duplicate the séance for his fellow citizens of Cheltenham. He did this just over three months later, on June 19, at Jessop's Aviary Gardens in Cheltenham. The fellow who played the horn next to Maskelyne in the local band, an amateur conjurer and cabinetmaker, George A. Cooke, was recruited to serve as his partner in the séance.

Unlike many Davenport imitations or exposures, which explained the secrets, Maskelyne's was clever enough to improve upon them. He began with the cabinet séance, insisting that his performance would be accomplished by trickery, not spirits. After the usual bell ringing, horn playing, ropes, and handfuls of flour, J. N. introduced an original finale. He crouched inside a small, plain pine trunk, about three feet long by two feet wide and a foot and a half deep. The lid was locked and the trunk roped shut by members of the audience. The trunk, with J. N. inside, was carefully lifted into the cabinet and the doors closed. Minutes later, the doors swung open to show John Nevil Maskelyne seated atop the trunk, which was still securely roped and locked.

It was a sensational premiere of a new cabinet mystery. A Birmingham paper marveled over Maskelyne and Cooke's accomplishment by quoting Barnum: "It must be seen to be believed."

As Maskelyne and Cooke began a tour of British cities and the furor over the Davenports waned, they expanded the cabinet séance into a weird sort of skit titled "La Dame et la Gorilla." Gorillas had only recently been exhibited to Londoners, and were still mysterious creatures. Maskelyne included a gorilla in his sketch, but his anatomically incorrect costume included a long tail. Now the magicians not only escaped but also appeared in comical disguises, Maskelyne in a dress and bonnet, Cooke in the ape suit. A little over a year later, this simple routine had evolved into a short play titled "The Mystic Freaks of Gyges."

By treating his performance as a story, Maskelyne could extract the maximum effect from his illusion. Characters could enter, unexpectedly disappear or reappear, or even secretly change costumes while concealed, to later magically reappear as new characters. The action was pure nonsense, even if the magician did manage to write lines of dialogue to tie the effects together. The situations and characters guaranteed one surprise after another.

The most important element of "Mystic Freaks" was something Maskelyne called the Enchanted Gorilla Den, a cross between the Davenport spirit cabinet and Tobin's optical illusions.

Maskelyne's Gorilla Den, and the view from the side

The cabinet had two doors in the front. Inside, a wide horizontal shelf was suspended about two and a half feet from the ceiling of the cabinet. During the course of the act, the cabinet could be used for spirit effects if Maskelyne and Cooke were seated beneath the shelf. Later, one of them would enter the cabinet and the doors would be closed. When the doors were reopened, the cabinet was completely empty.

The secret was a mirror mounted against the ceiling of the cabinet that could be released so it would hinge down. It stopped at a 45-degree angle with the edge of the mirror touching the front edge of the shelf. The ceiling of the cabinet looked exactly like the back wall, so anyone lying on the shelf and concealed behind the mirror seemed to disappear.

The advantage was one of practicality. When the mirrors were in position, Tobin's Proteus cabinet left only a small area of available floor space, a small triangle at the front of the cabinet, which formed the "safe area." By lifting the illusion onto a high shelf, the floor inside Maskelyne's cabinet was free for his magic trunk or crouching actors during the course of the action.

But as a first experiment with these principles, the cabinet had a serious fault. For spectators seated in the balcony, a curious illusion was created when the mirror was lowered to the edge of the shelf. The shelf, from above, seemed to disappear completely, leaving just the narrow strip of its edge. Maskelyne attempted to improve this by angling the shelf slightly, correcting the sight lines for the balcony. But this could not have completely corrected the illusion for every possible theatre.

Despite their billing as Maskelyne and Cooke, George A. Cooke, fourteen years older than Maskelyne, was not a full partner in the enterprise. Cooke was an assistant on stage, an actor in the play, or the technician in the wings. Maskelyne, the Chief, was the featured performer, and his specialty was plate spinning, an elaborate routine in which large plates and basins were kept revolving on a large tabletop or sent wobbling and dancing up and down a spiral ramp. He was no longer a conjurer in the strict sense, and he had given up the sleight of hand from his Cheltenham days to concentrate on new mechanical effects.

In 1873 Maskelyne and Cooke brought their collection of wonders to London, ambitiously agreeing to a three-month lease at the tiny, fusty theatre at Egyptian Hall in Piccadilly. Adorned with hiero-glyphics and papyrus leaf columns, the theatre seated only about two hundred people, but its narrow stage had become a perfect showplace for magic. This was where Stodare scored his success with the Sphinx, where Pepper and Tobin continued their illusions after their success at the Polytechnic. Alexander Herrmann, a tall, deft, satanic-looking magician with an amusing Parisian accent, performed for a thousand nights at this theatre, from 1871 to 1873, before taking his show to America. Under Maskelyne and Cooke, Egyptian Hall became "Eng-land's Home of Mystery," and they extended their lease season after season as their fame spread.

Having started his career as an anti-Spiritualist, Maskelyne was still eager to expose the frauds of the séance room. Spiritualism not only gave his performances currency but also provided him with a cause and attracted audiences. Perhaps that's why he and Cooke accepted an invitation to George Sexton's long lecture on "Spirit Mediums and Conjurers," delivered on Sunday evening, June 15, 1873, at the Cavendish Rooms. Sexton was a well-known writer on the subject. Also present in the audience was Dr. Lynn, a rival conjurer who was performing at the other theatre in Egyptian Hall.

The magicians might have been expecting the usual Spiritual mumbo-jumbo, which could serve as fodder for their performances, but Sexton blindsided them. Conjurers, he began, had ridiculed Spir-itualism by offering silly exposures that were nothing like the original manifestations:

> We have in London at this moment several conjurers who night after night attempt by mere trickery to show phe-nomena something like those that take place in the presence of spirit mediums, and to burlesque and ridicule the whole subject of spirit communication. If I deal severely with these men—several of whom are present—I do it not out of any ill-will that I bear them, but simply to defend the glorious truths of Spiritualism against their miserable burlesque imitations.

The Chief fixed a grin on his face, aware that he was being watched by everyone in the audience, and listened closely. When Sexton demonstrated the "Maskelyne knot," the secret of the escape necessary in the Maskelyne and Cooke séance, J. N. was one of the spectators who rushed to the platform to examine it. "Oh, you've seen it often, Mr. Maskelyne," Sexton said, dismissing him and drawing gales of laughter.

Sexton was an intelligent and perceptive spectator, but he had been badly fooled by the Davenports several years earlier. He made the mistake of many who are predisposed to such mysteries, misremembering the Davenport séance by eliminating the faults and expanding on the wonders. Eight years later, as he watched magicians like Maskelyne, Cooke, and Lynn perform similar effects, he was quick to point out how they fell short of his memories. He did this with a long, withering account of Maskelyne's secrets, which, like all magic, seemed silly and simple when explained so efficiently:

> *The performance of Maskelyne and Cooke on the first occasion that I saw it was something like the following: A sailor comes on the stage with a bundle in his hands, in which there are probably two gorilla masks and two pairs of fur gloves. The sailor is put inside the cabinet and his hands and feet are placed into stocks . . . the door of the cabinet is closed and the sailor gets out of the stocks and up behind the looking glass. . . .*

It was a point-by-point account of "The Mystic Freaks of Gyges," explaining every costume change and the exact movements of the mirror inside of Maskelyne's Enchanted Gorilla Den. Maskelyne was now trapped in the crowded room, and as he listened he slowly became "white with rage."

Sexton offered a diagram of the cabinet, pointing out the mistake of how the shelf seemed to disappear for certain spectators in the balcony. He also noted that the reflections made illumination inside the cabinet uneven, causing a *striking contrast between the brightness of the glass when it is down and the dull appearance of the felt [walls] when it is up. A little model of this wonderful cabinet may be easily made by any of you at home, and if you do this you will see in an instant how the whole thing is arranged. When Mr. Maskelyne talks about no one having ever found out the principle upon which this illusion is accomplished, he displays an amount of effrontery that is really amusing. . . . It is exactly the same thing as the Proteus of Professor Pepper, excepting that the glass is differently arranged.*

It's hard to imagine just how this affected the great John Nevil Maskelyne, one of the most inscrutable figures in magic, a master of keeping secrets and keeping his own counsel. But when battling in the courts, in newsprint, or from the stage, The Chief was at his very best. So, the Monday after the lecture, he returned to the crusade, complaining to his Egyptian Hall audience how he had been unfairly treated at the Cavendish Rooms and not allowed a hearing. He insisted that Sexton had sent someone backstage to break his Enchanted Gorilla Den—utterly untrue but all sensational claims. Most important of all, he secretly began fixing his magic cabinet.

His new apparatus was another deep wooden cabinet with two vertical doors in front. It was now decorated as the town lock-up, a portable jail, so the interior contained a zigzag wall of vertical jail bars to contain the prisoner.

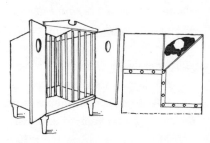

Maskelyne's cabinet, and the view from the top

As in the original Proteus, Maskelyne used two mirrors that could be hinged flat against the inside walls of the cabinet. If swung out so the mirrors formed a wedge, one of the vertical jail bars covered the edge where the mirrors touched. But Maskelyne used one mirror hinged at 45 degrees and one hinged at 90 degrees, forming a much smaller wedge to conceal the assistant.

Maybe it was inspired by his experiments with his Gorilla Den; the wedge does resemble the shape of the shelf and mirror that were suspended in his original cabinet. It's an obvious improvement if you consider the "safe zone" inside the cabinet. Now an actor seen by the audience could occupy a large area in the cabinet, moving around from the front corner to the back corner while the mirrors were in position and still not causing reflections in the glass. There was space on the floor to place his locked trunk. It made an important difference to the action of the play, making the illusion even more deceptive.

By introducing a 90-degree mirror, Maskelyne found an efficient optical secret. This mirror reflected a small section of the back wall and used that reflection to conceal an adjoining section of the back wall.

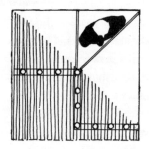

"The Mystic Freaks of Gyges" was evolved into an improved play titled "Will, the Witch and the Watchman." After years of experiments with the apparatus, costumes, and characters,

From the top, the "safe zone" in Maskelyne's cabinet

Maskelyne had found an ideal formula—a farce set on a village green in a small town. He invited a committee of men to examine the cabinet and sit on stage, in chairs at the sides, to watch the action closely. This holdover from the Davenport séance gave the play an unconventional and appealing sense of challenge.

Now the characters entered. The witch cast a spell to allow the sailor, Will, to escape from the jail. But her magic seemed to have inadvertently created an enormous ape, which appeared and disappeared from the cabinet. At one point the ape grabbed the village butcher, pulled him into the cabinet, and locked the doors. When the cabinet was opened, the ape was sitting alone, suggesting that he'd swallowed the butcher whole. Seconds later the butcher reappeared sitting in the back of the auditorium with the audience. Two characters hatched a plot to lock the ape in a trunk and sell him to the

Zoological Gardens, and the spectators on stage were asked to help examine the trunk and lock the ape inside. But after being placed in the cabinet, the trunk was found empty and the ape had disappeared. The witch returned to cast another spell. Will, the sailor, who had disappeared at the start of the action, reappeared. Tableaux and curtain.

Every element of the illusion was sharpened and accentuated by the situation comedy. The final script, which played out in just over thirty minutes on stage, received a polish in the 1880s by Nevil Maskelyne, the Chief's oldest son. Nevil was then in his twenties and had joined the family business at Egyptian Hall. As Nevil grew older, he sometimes appeared as the head watchman. Cooke either took the role of the sailor or the monkey. John Nevil Maskelyne often appeared as the cackling witch, wearing a tall pointed cap and a dark cloak. It was the star turn. The witch was the magical character, responsible for the spells and enchantments that put the entire story into motion. At the finish, Mr. Maskelyne could dramatically pull away his mask and cloak to take his bow: the producer, author, inventor, actor, and wizard.

Shortly after Maskelyne and Cooke's 1873 premiere at Egyptian Hall, Maskelyne began work on a mysterious invention. It was an automaton, or mechanical man, who seemed to actually think, could answer questions, and could even play a hand of cards.

It had been suggested to him by John Algernon Clarke, a resident of Lincolnshire, who lived much of his life in London. Clarke had some renown as a "writer on agricultural subjects," an editor of several journals, and a frequent contributor to the *Times*. He also had a number of inventions to his name, patents related to farming devices and a strange device that assembled lines of verse using wheelwork. Clarke's idea was the ultimate attempt at invisibility: rather than concealing a person, he would use air pressure as the invisible force to start and stop an automaton. In this way the mechanical man could give the illusion of thinking on its own, because a distant operator, manipulating the air pressure, was actually responsible for animating it.

Maskelyne and Clarke filed patent papers for the idea, and Maskelyne retired to his workshop to create Psycho, his name for the automaton that was first shown to his audience in January of 1875. Psycho was a miniature man, dressed in Hindu garb with an elaborate turban, seated cross-legged on a wooden chest. Beneath his hand was a curved metal rack, which held thirteen playing cards. The wooden chest beneath Psycho was opened and shown to the audience; it was much too small to conceal a person inside. Maskelyne further isolated it by placing the chest atop a clear glass cylinder, about eight inches in diameter and two feet tall, which stood upright on the stage. In this way his audience could see that there were no strings or electrical wires connected to Psycho.

Still, Psycho managed to give an impressive performance, slowly moving his hand along the rack of playing cards with a "click, click, click," then pausing to lift one card, his choice, which was handed to Maskelyne to play on the whist table.

Psycho filled the theatre at Egyptian Hall and was hotly debated in the press. His game of whist was analyzed and various scientific methods proposed for his mysterious motive power. In the days before radio waves, Psycho's reputation inspired a great deal of speculation: Could it be magnetism, electricity, or rays of heat? Others thought that a dwarf or a small boy must be concealed inside, or that a dog was inside the machine, playing the cards—which presumed that a whist-playing dog was less astonishing than a whist-playing machine.

Psycho was much simpler than many suspected. With the aid of a small bellows, air was pushed up through the stage and into the glass cylinder. This affected corresponding bellows concealed inside the wooden chest beneath the figure. George Cooke, concealed backstage, could see Psycho's playing cards. By blowing or drawing through the bellows, he moved the automaton's hand and selected the proper card. It was an almost perfect deception. The glass cylinder reminded many of an electrical insulator, a showy way of pointing out that the figure was perfectly isolated on the stage. But as the spectators stared at the glass cylinder, they never suspected that it was the actual air inside it that was responsible for the illusion. A conjurer could hope for nothing more invisible.

What prevented it from being a perfect deception was the provisional patent, which had been a big mistake. It was Maskelyne's first patent, a public document that had outlined the basis of the invention:

The object of his invention is to set in action by invisible agency clockwork mechanism, or trains of wheelwork actuated by weights or springs [and] as the controlling power we employ compressed air or gas . . . a small pedestal highly charged with compressed air or gas [combined with] bellows within the automaton figure.

Barely a year after Psycho's premiere, Dr. W. Pole, a writer on games and card table strategy, had noticed the patent and quickly explained in *McMillain's Magazine* how Psycho could be controlled by air pressure through the cylinder. Other exposures quickly followed in the newspapers and books on magic. Maskelyne, however clever a mechanic, was an even better showman. As a showman, he saw these exposures as fuel to the fire, a bucket of kerosene rather than a bucket of water. It was at this point that Maskelyne's ingenuity was most formidable.

Believe it or not, most magicians try not to lie. They resist not out of any particular morality or an effort to compensate for their deceptions. Audiences anticipate lies from magicians, and tend to challenge their statements. A lie often works against the deception, so the performer will avoid making statements that invite challenges or plant dangerous suggestions. If the magician starts his routine by holding up a glass and saying "an ordinary, everyday, unprepared drinking glass," it sounds preposterously dishonest. Isn't every glass ordinary? Why would he say that this glass is unprepared? How could it be prepared? Once the audience begins thinking along these lines, they might wander dangerously close to the truth.

Because of this, when magicians give accounts of their own tricks, there's usually a code to what they won't say as well as what they will say. If a listener is aware of the code, there's a lot that is revealed by a magician's statements. The performer will invariably dance around dishonesty rather than embrace it, indulging in a series of tiny untruths, not big lies.

Maskelyne was the exception to that rule. He told every story from a showman's point of view, using spectacular untruths to eke out a bit more credit for his wonders or scoff at a challenge. Even the fantastic story of his start in magic—the curtain that fell away at the precise moment to expose the Davenports' secret—was retold with wonderful embellishments: Once Maskelyne had made his pronouncement, he would claim he had reduced the séance to a shambles. Or perhaps, he hinted to his family, he had engineered the whole thing by signaling a friend to open the curtain at the precise moment. The whole story may be a myth. It's worth considering that, as a local boy attending an important show, he was awfully clever to stop the séance and promise to repeat it. It was a spectacular way to start a career and an irresistible way to guarantee an audience. He was expert at just these sorts of tricks.

In an 1895 magazine article, when asked about his use of mirror illusions, Maskelyne was blunt and defiant:

> *I have not employed any kind of mirror upon my stage for several years. It is true I have used them in every conceivable manner, and they are still used frequently in appearing and disappearing illusions at music halls, but the audiences here are much more critical, being largely composed of persons who take an interest in mysteries. Therefore, mirrors are practically useless to me, for the merest tyro in optics can detect by the 'fit-up' the presence of looking glasses the moment he glances at the stage.*

Of course, he used mirrors repeatedly and ingeniously throughout his entire fifty-year career. Maskelyne's various comments on Psycho seem equally disarming. He never shied away from the suggestion of air pressure, but paused only slightly to admire the ingenuity of the idea before relegating it somewhere between the dogs and the dwarves. In an 1877 program note, he boldly called attention to Pole's article, and credited him with an "ingenious" suggestion for Psycho's method.

> *We believe it is almost possible to construct an android upon Pole's principle, though not with the variety of movements Psycho is able to go through. Mr. Maskelyne . . . will*

shew that Dr. Pole's clever idea does not afford a satisfactory
solution to the Psycho mystery.

John Algernon Clarke, Maskelyne's partner in Psycho's invention,
offered a more astonishing smokescreen. Somehow he had been positioned to write the long essay on "Magic, White," for the 9th edition of
the *Encyclopedia Britannica*. As Clarke's only excursion into the world
of conjuring seemed to be Psycho, it's surprising that he was deemed to
be an expert in the field and capable of the authoritative article. Naturally, one senses the fine hand of the Chief in every sentence. Not surprisingly, the praise for Maskelyne is abundant and unchecked.

> *A new era in optical tricks began in 1863 when John Nevil*
> *Maskelyne, a Cheltenham artist in jewelry, invented a wood*
> *cabinet in which persons vanished and were made to re-*
> *appear. . . . The general principle undoubtedly was this: If a*
> *looking-glass be set upright in the corner of a room, bisecting*
> *the right angle formed by the walls, the side wall reflected*
> *will appear as if it were the back, and hence an object may*
> *be hidden behind the glass. . . . Two years later the same*
> *principle appeared in "The Cabinet of Proteus" patented by*
> *Tobin and Pepper of the Polytechnic Institution.*

Perhaps the Chief was still smarting over Sexton's suggestion that
the Gorilla Den was only a copy of Tobin and Pepper's Proteus. He
solved the problem by having Clarke insinuate a fictional timeline
into the *Encyclopedia Britannica*, which proclaimed that Maskelyne
had invented the mirror principle, and Tobin had probably copied him.
In private letters, Maskelyne quietly suggested that his mirror tricks
preceded Tobin's effects in London, which was obviously untrue.
Tobin and Pepper's illusion was patented in London a full month
before Maskelyne's first public performance in Cheltenham. The
magical Gorilla Den was first performed, according to playbills, over
a year and a half after Tobin and Pepper's effect.

Clarke then continued in the same vein, discussing the importance
of Psycho:

> In 1875 Maskelyne and Cooke produced at Egyptian Hall, in
> London, an automaton whist player, Psycho, which, from
> the manner in which it is placed upon the stage, appears to
> be perfectly isolated from any mechanical communication
> without. . . . What the mysterious means of connection are
> has not been discovered; or, at any rate, down to the time of
> writing this article there has appeared no correct imitation
> of this joint invention of John Nevil Maskelyne and John
> Algernon Clarke. . . . It may be mentioned that, in the same
> year in which Psycho appeared, the joint inventors patented
> a method of controlling the speed of clockwork mechanism
> by compressed air or gas. . . . But it is not known whether the
> principle obscurely described in the specification was appli-
> cable in any way to the invisible agency employed in
> Psycho.

The punch line was that the article was signed "John Algernon
Clarke." So the author claimed he was mystified by his own creation
and couldn't properly determine whether his own patent was a part of
the automaton he invented. It was a wry bit of showmanship that
should have never gotten past the encyclopedia's editors.

Maskelyne repaid Clarke by slowly draining away his credit. In an
1877 Egyptian Hall program, he praised Clarke's "cherished scheme
for the construction of a machine which should play cards, and yet be
perfectly isolated." Maskelyne had insisted that Clarke's name be cou-
pled with his as the joint inventor and chided other magicians who
"keep in the background the frequently needy inventor." Within several years, however, Maskelyne decided that the background was a
very good place for Clarke. Other programs or news articles failed to
mention him or awarded him merely grudging thanks. The Maskelyne
family came to refer to him simply as "a Lincolnshire farmer," suggesting a bumpkin stumbling into Piccadilly. Of course, Clarke technically was "a Lincolnshire farmer," but John Nevil Maskelyne was
similarly "a Gloucestershire horn player."

Maskelyne flatly denied that Psycho's secret had ever been discovered. One interviewer reported that, "to protect himself when he had

finished [Psycho], he took out a bogus patent, which threw all the curious off the scent." But Psycho survives in a London museum, so we now know the secret. Pole was right. It was air pressure. Still, Maskelyne boldly offered a reward of 2000 pounds sterling for "a Genuine Automaton capable of producing Psycho's movements with the same insulation and examination." It was an especially shrewd challenge, as Maskelyne himself could never have fulfilled the conditions. Psycho was never a "Genuine Automaton," because a hidden assistant operated it.

Maskelyne's challenges encouraged counterfeits, and once these copiers found that they had been finagled out of winning the prize money, the Psycho imitations naturally worked their way onto the stage in competition. One challenge brought Maskelyne to court. He had publicly offered 500 pounds for any trunk escape that could match his miraculous locked and sealed trunk that held the ape in "Will, the Witch and the Watchman." In 1898 two young inventors, Stollery and Evans, built their own trunk and applied for the money. Their imitation was a fascinating bit of machinery. A trapdoor was concealed in one end of the trunk. A metal ball bearing, hidden in an enclosed track in the side of the trunk, held the panel shut. It could be opened only if the trunk were turned in a certain sequence of moves—rolling the ball bearing down several concealed tracks—before it was upended and placed in the cabinet. Maskelyne examined their trunk but refused to award the prize money. The case dragged through the courts for months (in appeals). Maskelyne insisted that their mechanical trunk didn't match his own, but steadfastly refused to expose his own secret to the court. A jury logically decided that the imitation trunk provided just as good an effect as Maskelyne's. He was ordered to pay the award, then privately admitted that it had all been worth it in free publicity.

Magicians have long debated the actual secret of Maskelyne's trunk trick, which he would not have made as complicated or puzzle-like as the Stollery and Evans version. Several of Maskelyne's contemporaries insisted that, because the escape always took place in his magic cabinet, where an actor was already concealed, the trunk was completely ordinary. After the front doors of the cabinet were closed, the actor came out from behind the mirrors, opened the locks and ropes, and simply released the other person inside. It would have been the ultimate Maskelyne challenge to his audiences, and the ultimate Maskelyne deception: no trick at all. We now know, through reconstructions of the apparatus and research into his secrets, that Maskelyne's trunk was specially made so it could be opened by the man locked inside, but the Chief always remained silent on the issue, encouraging as much speculation as possible.

The exposures and imitations only excited controversy and kept Maskelyne's name before the public for many years. Even if Dr. Sexton could make the tricks sound unimpressive, Maskelyne knew that, once the audience was lured to the theatre, they were bound to be mystified. The carefully arranged transformations of "Will, the Witch and the Watchman," for example, would have surprised anyone who thought the secret was a simple matter of mirrors or a trick box. Nevil Maskelyne proudly pointed out that the magic play had been performed for over forty years—over 11,000 performances in London or touring shows. Psycho, the whist-playing automaton, was a particular favorite and appeared in over 4000 consecutive performances at Egyptian Hall. The Chief brought Psycho out of retirement in 1885 and again in 1910, after the machine had been completely refurbished and redesigned by its originator.

Every year Maskelyne and Cook took their London show on tour. In the fall they would return to the little theatre of "England's Home of Mystery." Their original three-month tenancy extended to more than thirty years at Egyptian Hall. On any given night, their audiences, anxious to see their latest wonders, climbed the stairs in the dark, creaky building, contemplated the weird Egyptian snakes and goddesses staring down at them, and found their seats in the showroom. As the musical director offered an overture on the grand piano, he was accompanied by ringing bells, gongs, drums, and a harp that, suspended on thin cords, dangled above the stage. This was Maskelyne's Mechanical and Automatic Orchestra, the instruments that seemed to play by themselves.

Maskelyne might open the show with his spinning plates and an exhibition of his magical automata. Psycho would play a game of cards. Zoë, a mechanical girl seated on a wooden pedestal, sketched pictures. Fanfare and Labial, two automatons dressed in evening clothes, played music on two horns.

There often was another magician on the program, someone who could offer sleight of hand. There might be an interlude with Mel B. Spurr at the piano: comic songs and verses, or a demonstration of mind reading. The evening usually ended with a short magic play designed around several of the latest Maskelyne inventions. For many years John Nevil and son experimented with levitation illusions, changing and combining methods in search of the ideal mystery. Many of the magic plays had plots about Spiritualism or witchcraft; most were comedies or farces, involving a mixture of actors and magicians to play the parts. Maskelyne often took the part of the burlesque spirit medium or wizard. His son Nevil seemed to specialize in gruff authority figures.

Egyptian Hall was a perfect showplace for magic, and it attracted important performers. In 1886 Joseph Buatier deKolta, from Lyon, France, joined the company. DeKolta was a pudgy little man with a thick black beard and wild, unkempt hair; he would appear on stage in a baggy tailcoat and knee britches. But for all his lack of elegance, his tricks were astonishing. Everything he performed was his own invention, with a neat, quirky simplicity that accentuated the magic. The French magician benefited from his seasons at Egyptian Hall, utilizing Maskelyne's mechanical expertise for several of his own effects. In turn, he brought crowds to the theatre, daily at three and eight, to see his artistic conjuring.

His most famous and most copied effect was unquestionably the Vanishing Birdcage. DeKolta entered with a small, rectangular brass cage held between his fingertips, containing a bright yellow canary. He made a gesture as if to toss the cage in the air, but as it left his fingertips, it seemed to dissolve in the air. The cage was gone.

Early in his career he was famous for his manipulations with billiard balls or silk handkerchiefs. A famous Buatier deKolta sequence involved the production of small, variously colored silk handkerchiefs at his fingertips. He then showed two porcelain soup bowls, placing them mouth-to-mouth on his table. Picking up the handkerchiefs and carrying them forward, he gradually rolled them into a bundle in his hand, then slowly opened his fingers to show that the handkerchiefs had disappeared. When the bowls were separated, the handkerchiefs were found inside.

The use of two porcelain bowls and several bits of colored silk was deliberate in its stark artistry; the generation of Robert-Houdin would have been horrified by the ordinariness of it all. Not surprisingly, deKolta disdained the elaborate boxes and cabinets used by other magicians. "I can do anything if I am allowed to put up a bedstead on the stage," he told one colleague. The remark must have referred to the large mirror cabinets that were then being used on Maskelyne's stage. Although famous for his own modern approach, deKolta seldom thought in terms of the latest fashion: optical conjuring. Instead, he typically solved his problems with sleight of hand or mechanics. In 1886 he was one of the first performers in Europe to experiment with a new optical principle, involving light and shadow to conceal an object. DeKolta used it for only a momentary effect. He was clearly not comfortable with optical illusions.

One of his greatest creations was the original Vanishing Lady illusion, which he performed at Egyptian Hall. He began by unfolding a sheet of newspaper on the stage—reminding the audience that this prevented him from using a trapdoor—then positioning a small dining chair on top of it. His wife was invited to sit on the chair, and he covered her with a long silk shawl. As he gestured, throwing his arms apart, the shawl and the lady instantly vanished. He picked up the chair, folded the paper, and took his bow. A magician who saw him perform this recalled, many years later, how deKolta had carelessly turned his prominent backside to the audience before bending down to unfold the paper. The audience quickly overlooked this sort of coarseness; the trick was a masterpiece.

The Vanishing Lady was quickly copied throughout Europe and in the United States, and deKolta did his best to keep up with the demand, organizing his own tours or deputizing others to present the illusion for him. Few bothered with his fussy little touches, like the newspaper on the floor or the simultaneous disappearance of the cloth. For deKolta's original version, he had worked out a clever arrangement of pulleys and cords under his coat, fixed around one foot and extending to a hand; by throwing open his arms, the enormous piece of silk was quickly pulled up one sleeve. DeKolta made it work perfectly, but other magicians were terrified of this particular touch—when it failed the cloth was dangling from the performer's cuff, which made the entire illusion seem laughable. They chose to simply whisk the cloth away and show that the lady had disappeared.

Buatier deKolta left Egyptian Hall in 1891 and toured through the United States, dying in New Orleans in 1903. Despite his important career, his ideas always seemed of more value to other performers than they were to him, and dozens of important magicians made their reputations by featuring one or two of the effects that had been incidental in his own act. Part of the problem might have been deKolta's awkward presentations. Part of the problem was certainly the impatience of a natural inventor, abandoning the last idea and determined to move on to the next idea that fascinated him.

Still, it's hard to overestimate deKolta's influence on his generation of magicians. He began a cult of creativity that certainly inspired two remarkable performers who followed him onto the Egyptian Hall stage. One, David Devant, is remembered today as Britain's greatest magician. The other, Charles Morritt, is largely forgotten today, a peripatetic old showman who may have fooled us all.

6
Two Wizards

*I am telling you in confidence that I have
got some new stuff . . . entirely different
and by far the best.*
—Charles Morritt

hen magicians are good at their jobs, it is because they anticipate the way an audience thinks. They are able to suggest a series of clues that guide the audience to the deception. Great magicians don't leave the audience's thought patterns to chance; they depend on the audience's bringing something to the table—preconceptions or assumptions that can be naturally exploited. That's why, despite what most people think, children are often bad audiences for magic. They have little experience and make few assumptions. They might not take for granted that holding your hand in a certain way indicates that it's empty, or that walking around a table in a specific manner implies that it's just an ordinary piece of furniture. A magic show is built on these tiny allowances; children may not grant them.

Alternatively, anyone with a firm system of beliefs, anyone who has been forced to categorize or analyze information, is ripe for a skillful deception. This is why there are famous and embarrassing examples of learned men of science being badly fooled by the simple tricks of fake psychics.

Our preconceptions include the things that catch our attention and the things we ignore. For example, there are brown paper bags. Most of us have seen a bag boy at a supermarket pick up a bag, snap it in the air with a "crack" so that it opens, and drop it flat on the tabletop, ready to receive groceries. I can depend on the sound and the gesture of opening that bag to suggest that the bag is empty. Every bag handled in that way is empty. Experts in handling bags open empty bags in precisely that manner.

Of course, the magician can use that gesture as part of a deception. The bag might have been prepared with a secret panel or hold a collapsible object, which can later open out to appear like a solid, three-dimensional object. But the performer would run a risk by saying, "Here I have an ordinary bag," calling undue attention to the bag. Casually snapping it open demonstrates the ordinariness of the bag.

Still, the same snapping gesture would be of no use if demonstrated to someone from another culture who had never seen a brown paper bag before. The odd noise and the flourish would naturally make them question the bag. "How did he make that noise? Why did he open it that way, rather than slowly unfolding it?" It would work against the suggestion that the bag was ordinary.

With every year that passes, the snapping paper bag becomes more and more suspicious. Today supermarkets use plastic bags, and when a paper bag is inserted, the bag boy slides the flat paper bag inside the plastic one, held open in a wire rack. He then presses down with his hand so that the paper bag opens out to fill the plastic bag. A magician would be foolish to snap open a bag for a group of children. They may have never seen anyone do this.

In Devant's day there were no paper bags. Grocers used large sheets of paper that were held between two hands and, with a smooth gesture, twisted into neat cones to hold flour or sugar. There are dozens of fascinating magic tricks from the start of the twentieth century, deceptions using specially prepared paper cones, which are virtually useless today because of the fashions in greengrocers' shops.

In 1889 Charles Morritt, known as the Yorkshire Conjurer, first stepped onto the small square stage at Egyptian Hall and arched an eyebrow at the audience. He looked the part. He was almost six feet tall, slender and imposing, with long, dark hair, an aquiline nose, and an elegant, waxed mustache. Dressed in a black swallowtail coat and a high starched collar, he was the perfect image of a Victorian conjurer. A formal portrait from those days, when Morritt was at the height of his career, shows an upturned head and a distant expression, slightly haughty perhaps, but not unbecoming in a great magician.

He was known for a characteristic energy on stage, and he performed, according to one critic, "in a spirited, dashing fashion, as though under the influence of strong but pleasurable excitement." His London audience would have noticed his flat Yorkshire vowels, mixed with sharp, exotic flashes of an American accent, a reminder of his recent successes overseas.

Before he appeared with Maskelyne, Morritt was famous for his mind-reading act, which was performed with his sister Lilian. She sat blindfolded on the stage as he paced the aisles of the theatre, selecting objects that were offered to him by the audience. As Morritt turned the objects over in his hands, Lilian took a breath, furrowed her brow, and slowly identified each one. "You're holding a gold watch . . . with Roman numerals. It was made on the Continent. . . . You're holding a cigarette case, of enamel and silver. . . . You're holding a purse, a small purse, made of silk. . . ."

In Paris the act had been a specialty of Robert-Houdin, who called it Second Sight and presented it over forty years earlier using his young son as the blindfolded medium. Robert-Houdin's original version depended upon a spoken code. His casual instructions to the audience—"Here's an interesting object. Yes, please hand it over. I'll ask you to concentrate on this. Pray tell us what we have"—contained the proper sequence of code words that indicated objects, materials, and characteristics. The act was something of a cliché by Morritt's time, but Charles and Lilian made a remarkable improvement. The normally talkative magician was pointedly quiet during the presentation, saying only the same simple words, "Yes, thank you . . . yes, thank you" at each phase of the routine. The simplicity and monotony of the presentation was calculated to madden anyone who suspected a code; when Charles and Lilian performed it, it felt like the real thing.

Charles Morritt jealously kept his secrets throughout his life, but during a lean time, early in his career, he was forced to offer his method of silent thought transmission to a British magician named Hercat for some much-needed cash. Visiting Hercat at his own theatre at the Crystal Palace, Charles and Lilian gave an impromptu demonstration. Hercat couldn't bring himself to pay the price being asked, but he was completely baffled by the effect. One day Hercat was discussing the mystery with a friend of his, a captain in the United States cavalry, who realized how Morritt must have done it. "Time, my boy!" the captain told Hercat. "We use that method of signaling on the field." Hercat described the secret in a small, obscure book, but politely declined to give the name of the magician, "then unknown, but who has since come to the front as an entertainer." According to the dates and theatres in Hercat's account, it was clearly Charles Morritt, who went on to sell the secret to the American magician Harry Kellar. Morritt's idea was ingenious. Knowing that audiences were listening for words, Morritt had created a code based on silence. Or, more properly, the code was based on the precise amount of silence between his sparse words.

We now know that Hercat was correct. The secret was synchronized counting. Charles and Lillian had learned to simultaneously count silently to themselves—very quickly and at exactly the same pace. Any sound—a spoken word, a click of his heel, a tap of a piece of chalk against a slate—cued the number. "One, two, three . . ." she would think to herself. "Yes?" Charles would say. "One, two, three, four, five, six, seven . . ." she mentally raced through the numbers. "Thank you," he said, taking the next object. She then repeated the thirty-seventh item on their memorized list, "A silk purse." By subtly shifting to other lists, Morritt could ask for additional characteristics, letters, names, or numbers.

It was a daunting routine, two performers working on a knife-edge while affecting a perfect nonchalance. Few performers would have attempted it. Over the years at Egyptian Hall, as John Nevil Maskelyne presented less and less magic, he depended on other conjurers to round out his programs. Morritt, who didn't specialize, was equally adept with deKolta's silk handkerchiefs, or billiard balls, coins, cards, and bouquets of flowers. He was also a glib hypnotist, hand-shadow artist, and mind reader. At the little theatre in Piccadilly, he was a valuable addition to the bill.

Charles Morritt was born in 1860 near Tadcaster, Yorkshire, to a gentleman farmer. His first inspiration had been the Davenport brothers, and one of his earliest experiments had been a crude wooden cabinet with a trapdoor in the back wall through which someone could appear or disappear. He sold the cabinet to the Hudson Surprise Company, a show then touring India, and the following year boldly started his career with a performance in the Public Hall in Selby. Morritt later admitted, "I had the courage, or audacity, to make my first [performance] with no other person on the bill." Fortunately, the show was a success in the opinion of the local paper. He was given a position at the music hall in Leeds, where he became something of a producer.

By the time he was twenty-one, he owned two music halls and managed some half-dozen others in the north of England.

Charles and Lilian first appeared in London in 1886 with producer Charles Duval at Prince's Hall, presenting their mind-reading act. After a brief tour of England, they were brought to America, where the popular magician Alexander Herrmann—who had performed for a thousand nights at Egyptian Hall—saw them and gave them a contract to appear with him at Niblo's Garden Theatre in New York. Shortly after their return in 1888, they began working for Maskelyne and Cooke.

Morritt would learn a lot from his years in London. He shared a rooming house with Buatier deKolta, and many additions to his program, like his flower production, billiard ball, or handkerchief manipulations, were based on deKolta's innovations. Collaborating with Nevil Maskelyne, J. N.'s clever son, Morritt developed a new illusion, which was titled Oh!!!, or The Mahatmas' Outdone. It was the instantaneous disappearance of a man seated in a chair and hidden in a curtained enclosure as a committee from the audience surrounded him. One of the spectators actually held the man's hand, which projected through a slit in the curtain, just a moment before the man disappeared. Suddenly, as the man's hand was released, the fabric was pulled away, showing that he had disappeared. It was a breathtaking, split-second deception.

Lilian Morritt, besides assisting in her brother's act, was also recruited for the Maskelyne repertory company, taking various parts in the magic plays. When "Will, the Witch and the Watchman" closed the show, her role was Dolly, the heroine. This gave Morritt an opportunity to stand in the wings and study the famous Maskelyne effects. He was disdainful of the play, which included too much dialogue and moved too slowly for his tastes. But the use of mirrors inside the cabinet fascinated Morritt, and the variations and possibilities of these principles became an obsession with him.

Morritt's greatest fault seems to have been a certain restlessness, which manifested in his magic on the stage and in his contracts off the stage. In later years he tended to work too quickly, substituting a fevered pace for the nicer touches of showmanship, which might have earned him more applause. One magician, commenting on a later

Morritt performance of various stage illusions, thought that Morritt was dependent on "too much noise . . . too much pistol shooting," presenting an act infused with cheap energy which left the audience cold. Even his famous mind-reading effects came to feel perfunctory and rushed.

Spoiled by his early music hall self-management, Morritt developed impatience under anyone else's employment, continually scheming to develop his own productions. In 1892 he suddenly left Maskelyne and Cooke, appearing at the Empire Theatre on a bill of music hall acts, where he introduced a new illusion titled the Convict's Escape.

Morritt had found a convenient workshop, which guaranteed privacy, in the basement of a silversmith near the London Pavilion. The illusion he built and rehearsed there was a large cage, about five feet wide, mounted on a raised platform above the stage. There were vertical bars on the sides and back of the cage, but the front was completely open. Centered within this large cage was a narrow cage of vertical bars, just large enough for a man to stand inside.

Dressed as a convict, Morritt's assistant was locked inside the narrow cage, and spring roller blinds were pulled down around it. Seconds later, Morritt pulled a cord releasing the blinds, which flew up to show that the inner cage was completely empty. The man had not only escaped—he had completely disappeared.

In many ways this first experiment was a slavish copy of Maskelyne's "Will,

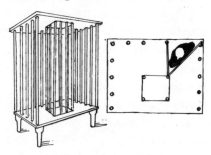

Morritt's Cage, and the view from the top

the Witch and the Watchman" cabinet. Morritt used the same arrangement of mirrors, the same sharp wedge formed by 90- and 45-degree angles, which was just large enough to contain a person. Even the jail theme was reminiscent of "Will, the Witch and the Watchman." But Morritt's apparatus wasn't made of solid wooden panels, just vertical bars. The audience could see between the jail bars to the curtain behind it, in the style of Tobin and Stodare's original Sphinx. The idea displayed a number of ingenious trademarks, which were later evident in all the Morritt mirror effects. It was beautifully proportioned, using the large outer cage to make the small cage seem even smaller. It was optically deceptive, emphasizing the transparency of the apparatus by arranging foreground objects (the bars of the cage) and background objects (the stage curtains, several feet away) to reflect perfectly. And it made the very most of its secret; by choreographing his own movements around the corner of the cage without the mirrors, Morritt could casually show off the deception. It seemed that the open cages could not possibly have provided a hiding place big enough to contain a rabbit. It seemed astonishing when a grown man disappeared so quickly.

Armed with the Convict's Escape and several other illusions, in 1893 Morritt assembled his own show, "Morritt's Afternoon Entertainment," which copied the Egyptian Hall formula for daily matinees. As an additional insult to his former employers, he was in competition just down the street from Maskelyne and Cooke, at Prince's Hall. The show included several of Morritt's specialties: sleight of hand, hand shadows, and mind reading, interspersed with Veveys' Musical Dog and James Dunn on the Banjo. Several months into the run, with the box office lagging, Morritt cleverly hired Arthur Orton, the famous Tichborne Claimant, as his co-star, so that he could make him disappear as he was seated in a chair.

The genius of Morritt's idea was wish fulfillment: All of London had been waiting for Orton to disappear, and many were happy to pay the price of a ticket to see it. In 1867, Orton, a fat, uneducated red-haired butcher from Wapping, first insisted that he was Roger Tichborne, the long-lost heir to the title of baron and the Tichborne family money. Roger Tichborne had been a slender, brown-haired, multilingual soldier, who had disappeared in a shipwreck some thirteen years before. The case fascinated the public with its mixture of tragedy, aristocracy, fortune, and fraud, but it dragged through the courts for years, until Orton's audacity was apparent to everyone. He served ten years in prison for perjury and was scorned by the British population. When he was released in 1884, he attempted to trade on his notoriety by taking a series of quick jobs—dime museum novelty, bartender, music hall lecturer. His most enduring contribution to entertainment might have been serving as the namesake for Little Tich, the famous diminutive comic who danced somersaults in long, pointed shoes. Little Tich took his name to distinguish himself from that other music hall attraction, Big Titch.

When Morritt contacted him, the Tichborne Claimant realized that being a magician's assistant was no worse than any of his recent jobs. Every afternoon the tall, suave Morritt introduced the dour, gray Orton. The Claimant was strapped in a chair, which was attached to ropes in a tall framework and lifted in the air. The stage lights flickered, the ropes were released, and the chair tumbled to the ground, empty. The audience cheered.

By the time Orton fulfilled his contract, the Prince's Hall audiences had tired of gaping at the famous ex-convict. Morritt secured another minor celebrity, a Mr. Edward Scott, who figured in a notorious Edinburgh court case, known as the Ardlamont murder. A. J. Monson had been accused of killing his ward, seventeen-year-old Cecil Hambrough, for insurance money. The mysterious Scott was a principal witness to the crime but avoided testifying by fleeing to London, and the case against Monson was officially "not proven." Described in the press as "the Missing Man," Scott was hired by Morritt four months later and paraded onto the stage by the magician at Prince's Hall. London audiences were eager to have a look at Scott, comparing him with the physical descriptions given in court. Morritt strapped his guest into the magic chair and made him disappear on cue.

Other than the novelty of these headline-making illusions, Morritt's afternoon show was only a moderate success. Yet his burst of independence must have angered Mr. Maskelyne. Charles and Lilian had been a valued part of the Maskelyne and Cooke company until Morritt's treacherous competition in Piccadilly. Maskelyne also must have noticed the resemblance between the popular Convict's Escape and his own magic cabinet, which only convinced him of Morritt's duplicity.

With Charles Morritt's irritating departure from his employ, Maskelyne suddenly found that he had an opening at Egyptian Hall for a conjurer. It was one of those astonishing confluences of the right time, right place, right person. The young magician who got the job was David Devant.

• • •

England's greatest magician—arguably the greatest magician of the twentieth century—was born David Wighton in London in 1868. His father, James Wighton, was an Edinburgh artist who supplied illustrations for the *Illustrated London News* and other periodicals. David had limited schooling and worked as a pageboy, a refreshment boy at Euston Station, and a telephone operator. When he was ten years old he saw a traveling showman named Dr. Holden and became interested in conjuring, obsessively seeking out any source for tricks and secrets.

He located the requisite mysteries at a London magic shop—the vanishing egg in a cup and dissolving penny, the same tricks that are sold today to beginners—and was delighted by the ability to amaze his younger sisters and brother. He also spent his pennies buying assorted secrets from a street busker named Kasper in Euston Road, who advertised himself as the "Great Court Conjurer." One Sunday Kasper announced that he was going away to Nottingham. He'd been impressed with David's young friend, a painter, and proposed a three-way trade for his moving sale. "Look 'ere," the Court Conjurer told David, "if you'll get your friend to do me a picture according to my orders, I'll give the 'ole game away to yer . . . all the blooming tricks there ever was, is, or could be." David found the offer irresistible. His friend, the artist, was flattered. But soon they both came to realize the ridiculous nature of the commission:

> The scene was to be the largest stateroom in Windsor Castle. The two principal figures in the picture were to be the "Great Court Conjurer" and his wife. The lady was to be sitting on the throne, her eyes were to be bandaged and the "Great Court Conjurer" was to be holding up a pocket handkerchief.

Kasper wanted himself portrayed amazing Queen Victoria with the old mindreading act. He imagined the title of the painting as a Cockney version of his mindreading patter.

*The picture, according to the man's own directions, was to
be called: "What 'ave we here! The State Performance." The
Queen and all the members of the Royal Family were to be
sitting or standing near the two performers.*

After Kasper supervised every detail of the painting—extra diamonds on the ladies, a different colored handkerchief, more of a curl
to his mustache—the artwork was delivered to him, and David, the
triumphant amateur magician, arrived in Euston Road for his lessons,
his pen poised, an empty notebook in hand.

"You needn't trouble to write nothin'," Kasper dismissed him with
a wave of the hand. "Get two books called *Modern Magic* by Professor
Hoffman and Houdin's *Masterpieces*. They're all explained there. Get
the books and read them."

Young David Wighton was crestfallen but came to realize that he'd
been given very good advice. *Modern Magic*, first published in 1876,
was filled with the latest Victorian magic, and Robert-Houdin's 1868
text offered the state of the art. He studied the books and regularly
analyzed the magicians he observed at Egyptian Hall, especially
deKolta. One day at an art gallery with his father, he saw a French
painting with a biblical theme. He leaned over to read the title,
"David devant Goliath," and thought it suggested a very good stage
name: David Devant. Not only was the alliteration sharp and distinctive, but he also hoped the meaning might be significant for his
career: David in front.

By all accounts he was a natural magician and a charismatic performer, equally adept at sleight of hand, children's magic, hand
shadows, or stage illusions. Portraits from early in his career show a
young man of average height with a bright smile, square shoulders, and
a barrel chest. His mop of dark, curly hair and a wide mustache gave
him a Bohemian look. He was engaged for two seasons to manage a
British tour with the American midgets, General and Mrs. Mite.
During this tour, he presented his magic show and a lecture about
the honored, miniature guests. In 1888, while performing in Margate,
he met a lady named Marion Melville. Quite fitting for a magician, he
saw her first by noticing her reflection in a large mirror. They married

three months later, and she joined his act. They circled London in various variety theatres, and his manager optimistically contacted John Nevil Maskelyne to try and secure an engagement at Egyptian Hall, but Maskelyne was satisfied with Morritt's success and had no reason to consider a new performer. When Devant heard that Morritt had suddenly left, he approached Maskelyne again. He invited Maskelyne to come down to the Crystal Palace and see his latest illusion, which was titled Vice Versa, after a popular novel of the time by F. Anstey. Maskelyne, whose theatre attracted every ambitious magician, demurred, suggesting that he could only attend if the engagement were a bit closer to him, in the West End of London. Devant contacted a friend at the West End's Trocadero and arranged for a morning audition.

Vice Versa was a wonderful idea. A tall, narrow skeleton cabinet was seen on the stage: simply a platform and roof supported with narrow upright posts. Devant introduced his assistant, a man. The magician dramatically unfurled a long, wide satin ribbon. The center of the ribbon was carefully knotted around the waist of Devant's assistant, and this man stepped up into the cabinet, facing the audience. Spectators in the front row of the theatre held the ends of the ribbon. Devant pointed out how the spectators could easily feel if the man was making any suspicious movements in the center of the ribbon. Devant lowered a set of roller curtains, quickly closing the four sides of the cabinet. He paused for a few seconds, then raised the curtains again. In place of the man was Devant's wife, Marion, and the ribbon was still tied tightly around her waist. The ribbon was cut away and the knots were examined. Devant and Marion took a bow.

Maskelyne applauded, but he wasn't fooled. The secret was something he had used at Egyptian Hall. Still, the Chief had been impressed with Devant: a talented, ambitious young conjurer who was comfortable with stage illusions and not afraid of experimenting with new ideas. Unfortunately, the tall framework cabinet used in Vice Versa was much too large for Maskelyne's stage. He asked Devant if he could suggest an alternative illusion for Egyptian Hall.

Devant called on Maskelyne just five days later with sketches and a rough model of something he called the Artist's Dream, a full-length portrait of a woman that came to life. Maskelyne liked it, and he suggested that it be arranged as a short play about an artist imagining a vision of his dead wife. Mel B. Spurr, the musical entertainer at the hall, was engaged to write "The Artist's Dream's" script and melodies. As always, Maskelyne kept a tight rein on his new artists: Devant did not actually appear in his own "Artist's Dream." J. B. Hansard, an actor with the company, took the part of the artist. Devant was added to the program to perform conjuring, and his wife Marion joined the cast as the lady in the painting.

David Devant was twenty-five years old. John Nevil Maskelyne was delighted that his new magician was creative and trustworthy. Still, it didn't take long before Devant began confounding the Chief. Their association was ideal for the programs at Egyptian Hall, but once Devant became a star on the stage, sparks between the two magicians—who represented the old and new styles of conjuring—were inevitable.

Although Devant always set his sights on the right engagements or the first-class theatres, taking definite steps to further his career, Charles Morritt's performances became erratic, as he bounced between theatres and unexpectedly changed the nature of his act. He acquired a fondness for alcohol. This was something of an occupational hazard in the music halls, where refreshments were available in the lobby or balcony during the shows, and performers, between their turns, were welcomed at the bars. It was tempting to step off the stage, change clothes and drift to the front of the house, where the theatre manager may want to swap show business stories over a cigar and a pint, or a patron was happy to compliment the Yorkshire Conjurer and treat him to a scotch. Morritt's caricature appeared in the 1894 comic journal, *Ally Sloper's Half Holiday,* with a description of his favorite drink, "For Bonnie Scotland and Scotch whisky has been, is, and always will be his battle cry."

After leaving Maskelyne and Cooke, Morritt presented a number of clever illusions around London, but he was summoned to the London courts in 1895 for selling alcohol without a license during an engagement at the Eden Theatre of Varieties. Morritt, who was then billing himself as Professor Morritt, a hypnotist, telegraphed that he was currently performing in Edinburgh and had placed several people under a trance. He insisted that he couldn't risk leaving for London before they had fully recovered. The London officials, unimpressed, fined Morritt twenty pounds.

It was during this Edinburgh appearance that Morritt staged another publicity stunt based on the Andlamont murder trial. He publicly "hypnotized" the main suspect, Monson, on a music hall stage and—not very convincingly—solicited Monson's testimony that he was completely innocent. At the Royal Aquarium and Crystal Palace, Professor Morritt exhibited A Man in a Trance, a local volunteer who, under his hypnotic spell, would remain motionless for days or weeks at a time. The Professor welcomed any controversy caused by these demonstrations. His playbill boasted that the feat stirred debate by local physicians and politicians, but that Home Secretary (later Prime Minister) Herbert Henry Asquith "kindly consented to a continuation of Mr. Morritt's Experiments," despite the minor authorities' ethical complaints.

Around this time, Morritt introduced into his program a wonderful bit of magic which was based on an old con game. He took the part of a racecourse swindler and presented the Purse Trick. He invited two men to the stage, asking them to sit at small tables. Morritt began by showing two silver coins, half crowns, which were placed in a small change purse and entrusted to one man. "I want you, Sir, to imagine that you have two half-crown seats in the stalls of a theatre. Here are the two half crowns to represent your preferment." On the opposite side of the stage, Morritt showed copper pennies, slipping them into another purse, which was held by the other spectator. These, he explained, represented two seats in the upper balcony. Morritt told the men that he would demonstrate how they could "change places" in the theatre. When they opened their purses they found that their coins had changed places.

Today any accomplished magician can tell you that the Purse Trick calls for the delicate touch of an artist. During the routine, Morritt concealed two of the coins in his fingers and deftly tossed the purse from hand to hand. But few performers can match the manipulation with the ability to "sell" this tiny trick—just four coins—to a theatre full of people. Morritt's presentation was a brassy bit of showmanship, a perfect example of how a small trick could be made important through its presentation, that the two men—the working man in the balcony and the swell in the stalls—could change places.

Harry Rickards, a popular music hall comic whom Morritt had employed in Leeds, took Morritt to Australia for eight months in 1897. For those performances, Morritt introduced a new variation on his cage illusion in which four ladies were magically produced as they burst through four large frames of paper. Instead of a wall of vertical bars, the surrounding framework was draped in fabric netting. Morritt called it Turkish Delight.

After the Australia tour, he introduced a new, striking effect at the London Pavilion. The curtains opened on a stage where four men were supporting a large board, four feet square, by the corners. They held it between them at waist height. Next, a female assistant dressed as a ballerina was lifted up so that she was standing in the center of the board, and then Morritt held up a small Oriental screen to hide the lady. She was covered for only several seconds. Morritt turned on his heel, grabbed the screen, and tossed it to the stage floor. As it fell flat on the stage, the audience was amazed to see that the lady was gone. The pointed simplicity of the props, just a wooden board held by four people, and a small Oriental screen, made the illusion especially magical.

It was amazing just how much Morritt had managed to accomplish with two pieces of looking glass. This time the wedge of mirrors was beneath the table, and the legs of the men concealed the edges of the mirror. For two of the men, the right leg was reflected as the left, or vice versa. Or one man's legs would be completely replaced by the reflection of another man. On stage, sur-

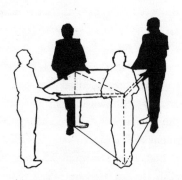

Morritt's illusion with four men and a board

rounded by curtains, it created a perfect optical illusion: no apparatus at all, just a plain board. Once concealed by the screen, the lady quickly ducked behind the mirrors, and she seemed to disappear.

He also presented a similar illusion with a stack of three four-legged tables, each slightly smaller than the one below it and all arranged like a tall ziggurat. The top table was covered with a long tablecloth, which completely obscured it. A ladder was put against the tables at one corner, and a lady climbed up and ducked under the tablecloth. The ladder was pulled away, Morritt tugged at the tablecloth, and the lady was gone.

The stack of tables was dramatic, but the actual secret was no different from Morritt's previous illusion. The center table was fitted with a wedge of mirrors, reflecting the back and side curtains. When the lady reached the top table and was hidden by the tablecloth, she climbed down through a trapdoor, hiding behind the mirrors in the center table. The cloth was pulled away seconds later, and she had disappeared.

Magicians avoid repeating the same effect for an audience because once they have an idea what to expect and there is no element of surprise, they can watch more critically. Similarly, magicians generally avoid using the same secret over and over in the same show. If every illusion depends upon the same arrangement of trapdoors or mirrors, the audience will begin to connect the dots and discern the secret. Reading an account of Morritt's shows, it's surprising how boldly he ignored this rule. Often he would include several versions of the same effect in the same show—his wedge of mirrors. He'd developed an unusual confidence in these optical illusions.

Morritt's wife recalled to a friend how Charlie always returned to mirror illusions, infatuated with their principles and eager to work out the next idea. She described how he used to retire for the evening with small pieces of looking glass under his pillow. In bed he would arrange them and rearrange them, "in an effort to discover something fresh." If he had known more about geometry, he would not have bothered. Morritt was frustrated to find that the 45- and 90-degree angles of the mirrors were a cold and hard mathematical formula. Forty years earlier, at the Polytechnic, that's what the architect Tobin had discovered in our world of perpendicular walls and floors. Morritt had been turning over these same principles, again and again, in his illusions.

To Morritt, these new ideas became lifelines to his next engagement. In 1903 he suddenly changed his program again, teaming up with another performer. Morritt worked as an impresario for a blind memory man who recited facts and figures in response to questions from the audience. His shows took him farther and farther from London, working in museums or halls, and Morritt became known for his bouts of drinking, which had severely jeopardized his work and his health. Morritt would disappear for long stretches of time, then turn up in a provincial theatre, scrambling to organize a show or scrape together an attraction. He could always fall back on the old sensation, his hypnotic sideshow exhibit, "A Man in a Trance." At Pickard's British Museum, Waxwork and Zoo in Glasgow, he shared the bill with a "Gipsy Palmist," "Solomon and his Wife, the World Famous Educated Chimpanzees," and a wax figure of the murderer Dr. Crippen:

> *Professor Morritt will place a Man in a Hypnotic Sleep at Pickard's British Museum, Trongate, Where he will remain ASLEEP IN A CASKET for THIRTEEN DAYS AND TWELVE NIGHTS . . . All Visitors will be allowed to touch the Man after he is placed in the Hypnotic Sleep.*

Morritt should have remained a top music hall performer. At his peak, he had been as innovative and professional as any magician in London. But his career became a series of unexpected, pendulum-like swings of fortune, as he performed in museums, provincial theatres, and store-front sideshows. It seemed as if he had slowly run out of inventions, schemes, or publicity stunts. The entertainers who used to cross paths with Morritt during their tours completely lost track of the old showman. By 1910 the news was gradually assembled from rumors and suspicions: Charlie Morritt, the once-dashing Yorkshire Conjurer of Egyptian Hall, the man who had worked so hard to improve his mirror illusions, was dead. His London associates, who knew him and fretted over his drinking and declining career, weren't surprised to hear that he was gone.

* * *

One night in 1896 David Devant saw a show at the Polytechnic on Regent Street, featuring a device called the Cinématographe that projected animated pictures on a large screen. It was a striking improvement on the old Magic Lantern shows, which consisted of still images of drawings or photos. Now the pictures actually moved, recreating action from life. The short films included a train arriving at a station, workers emerging from a factory, men playing cards. The Cinématographe was the invention of the Lumière brothers in France and had been unveiled just the year before.

For years the large painted slides of the Magic Lantern had been included in Maskelyne's shows. Devant thought these new moving pictures had magical potential and deserved to be featured at Egyptian Hall. The following night he cajoled John Nevil and Nevil Maskelyne into accompanying him to the Polytechnic to see the show. They both dismissed it. The Chief told Devant not to trouble with it, that the animated pictures would be a "nine days wonder."

Thinking that he might make a contract on his own, Devant returned to talk to Felician Trewey, a French magician who was a friend of the Lumières and was managing the show at the Polytechnic. Trewey had intended the Polytechnic shows as an audition for music hall managers and was anxious to secure bookings for the new device. Unfortunately, he had set a price that was impossible for Devant to pay. The machine was only available for rental, at 100 pounds (the equivalent of $500) per week. The Empire Theatre had already engaged the machine at this price and would shortly be featuring the pictures in London.

Just days later Devant happened to be reading a copy of a journal, *The English Mechanic*, and found a mention of the animated projected images of R. W. Paul. Feeling a particular urgency, Devant left his dinner, hailed a hansom cab and went to the office of the paper, where he discovered that Paul was a maker of scientific instruments who lived in London at Hatton Gardens. Dashing to Paul's address, he found him leaving his house with crates and boxes. Paul explained that he was just off for the Olympia to display his invention in a sideshow and invited Devant to join him.

Devant used the cab ride to press Paul for a price and was promised that he could buy the first projector for 100 pounds. The next day he proudly repeated the offer to Mr. Maskelyne, who still wasn't interested. But Maskelyne agreed reluctantly that if Devant insisted on buying the device, he could lease it to Egyptian Hall for five pounds a week for one month. Maskelyne was sure the interest wouldn't last longer than that.

Two days after the Lumière device premiered at the Empire, animated pictures provided by Paul's device were presented at Egyptian Hall, and created an immediate furor. Devant was sent scurrying for additional films. Working with Paul's camera, Devant shot footage of Queen Victoria and the royal family. The magician also appeared in several short scenes photographed by Paul on the rooftop of the Alhambra Theatre; in one, he gave a broad smile, reached into an opera hat, and produced a rabbit. Through Paul, Devant sold several of Paul's "Animatographe" projectors to a fellow magician, George Méliès, who was managing the Theatre Robert-Houdin in Paris and had developed a similar obsession with the idea of combining moving pictures with magic. Méliès studied Paul's projector and devised his own camera, producing a series of fantasy films that made him world famous. His unusual films combined magic illusions with his own innovative stop-motion effects. Devant acted as agent for Méliès in Great Britain, selling his films. Devant purchased additional projectors for his own private shows and tours, which were advertised as "David Devant's Animated Pictures, Direct from Maskelyne and Cooke's, Egyptian Hall, Piccadilly." Devant's original R. W. Paul projector was used, continuously, for more than twenty years.

Through the efforts of performers like Devant, Trewey, and Méliès, the earliest motion pictures were produced, sold, and exhibited by magicians, including Carl Hertz and Albert Smith. By the first decade of the twentieth century, the cinema had become big business and no longer relied on independent showmen. Film production moved to New York, then Chicago, and finally settled in Hollywood. Motion pictures were exhibited in the largest theatres of every major city.

Shortly after his initial success with the films, Devant made an ambitious business plan to consolidate Maskelyne and Cooke's touring shows into a Provincial Company from Egyptian Hall, with Devant as the managing partner. Again, Maskelyne was doubtful of the plan, but Devant, with his usual enthusiasm, made several attractive concessions. He included Nevil Maskelyne as a partner, and found an understudy for his own performances at Egyptian Hall, German sleight-of-hand artist Herr Paul Valadon. Valadon presented several illusions and performed mind reading with his wife, but his specialty, like Devant's, was the production of billiard balls at his fingertips. He finished with a handful of large white balls that dropped one at a time onto a porcelain plate, each one landing with a sharp ping, proving they were solid.

In 1902, while on tour with the Egyptian Hall company in Manchester, Devant introduced a new magic sketch called "The Honeysuckle and the Bee." It was a brief play set on a plantation in the southern United States. Devant played Dick Harwood, a young planter who was being threatened by a detective. At the suggestion of an old witch, he hid inside a tall woven wicker beehive, pulling it down around him. The detective arrived and dramatically lifted the hive. But Devant had disappeared. Now there was a young lady standing in the wicker hive. When the witch pulled a disguise off the detective, the audience was surprised to find Devant, who had appeared in his place.

Devant produced the play without telling John Nevil Maskelyne, secretly constructing props, purchasing costumes and scenery, and commissioning a script. He had located a magician and mechanic named Henry Bate, who could construct special apparatus according to Devant's instructions. Now he was no longer dependent on Nevil Maskelyne's workshop at Egyptian Hall. With "The Honeysuckle and the Bee," Devant may have been trying to impress the Chief as one would try to impress a stern parent, while simultaneously flaunting his independence.

With enormous pride and not a little arrogance, Devant sent a glowing review of the performance from the next day's *Manchester Guardian*. When it tumbled onto Maskelyne's desk in London, it was the first time the Chief had heard of "The Honeysuckle and the Bee."

Maskelyne responded with threats and reprimands, but both of them knew that David Devant now had the upper hand. "I protested that I had the right as managing partner to make what I considered a perfectly legitimate hit off my own bat for the good of the firm," Devant wrote. His various schemes and plans—the animated pictures, the touring company, and the new effects—had been lucrative for Maskelyne and Cooke. No one could argue with his success. And yet, Devant's increasing fame and autonomy threatened Maskelyne's pride. The Chief's ideal partner had always been Cooke, a man who remained in the shadows, took the role of assistant, and never sought any credit. Maskelyne's solution was to keep Devant out of town and busy on tour—sending the profits back to London—and to retain the German magician Paul Valadon for Egyptian Hall. Valadon pleased the audiences in an old-fashioned way, with solid, charming sleight of hand, and he was happy to take roles in Maskelyne's latest magic sketches. Maskelyne felt that Valadon could be trusted; he was the perfect man to replace Devant at Egyptian Hall.

Soon, the personalities and intrigues of the little theatre would prove more memorable than any character or play that passed across its stage. Nearly three decades after they premiered in London, Maskelyne and Cooke unveiled their latest farce titled "The Entranced Fakir," which featured an amazing illusion. By all accounts, it was a nearly perfect deception, a levitation of a human being. It left other magicians stunned, which only served to raise the stakes among competitors.

One night the curtain rose on "The Entranced Fakir" and Mr. Maskelyne stepped out onto the stage in the part of Dan'l Daw, a stubborn old showman in a flashy vest and a pearl grey top hat. He glanced over the footlights and saw the American magician Harry Kellar—a real-life flashy, stubborn showman—grinning back from the audience. At that moment, the redoubtable Mr. Maskelyne realized that Kellar was there for a specific reason. He wanted the secret. But the Chief didn't know what Kellar had in store for him.

7
Father and Son

*The conjurer is not a juggler; he is an actor
playing the part of a magician.*
—Robert-Houdin

In 1845, at the premiere of his elegant little theatre in the Palais Royal in Paris, the French magician Robert-Houdin borrowed a lady's handkerchief.

He rolled it into a small bundle and placed it on his table alongside an egg, a lemon, and an orange. Picking up the handkerchief, he rubbed it between his hands—smaller and smaller—until it disappeared completely. It had been passed into the interior of the egg, he explained to the audience.

Delicately holding the egg at his fingertips, he may have been expected by the audience to break it open, prove his point, and conclude the illusion. Instead, the egg was rolled between his hands until it, too, had vanished. The egg—he told them with a sly smile—had been passed into the lemon. He repeated the process with the lemon, pointing out that it now resided within the orange.

The orange was lifted from his table and rolled, smaller and smaller, between his palms. He paused several times to open his fingers and show the orange reduced in size. Finally he crushed his hands together, then opened them to reveal just a powder. This was delicately sprinkled into a silver vial, covered with spirits, and ignited.

A small orange tree, about eighteen inches across and sprouting from a decorative wooden box, was brought on the stage and placed on the table. The blue flame of the burning vial was placed beneath it, and as the vapors reached the foliage, the audience was surprised to see the leaves spreading, twisting, and falling to reveal bright white blossoms. Robert-Houdin waved his wand. The flowers disappeared and flashes of orange fruit were revealed on the tree . . . now slowly growing larger and larger until the green leaves were spotted with full-sized oranges.

The magician picked several of the oranges and offered them to his spectators, who were surprised to find that they were real. One orange remained at the top of the tree. Gesturing with his wand one final time, he commanded this orange to open. It split into sections, revealing the borrowed handkerchief tucked inside. Two clockwork butterflies, flapping their tiny wings, appeared from behind the tree, lifted the corners of the handkerchief and spread it open in the air as the magician took his bow and the curtains closed.

• • •

Over a hundred years before Robert-Houdin appeared on a stage, magicians had exhibited automaton trees that, through a combination of clockworks, compressed air, or pull-strings, gave the impression of blooming flowers or growing fruit. For hundreds of years magicians had offered sleight of hand with eggs or lemons, or destroyed a borrowed handkerchief only to find it tucked away in some safe, surprising location. Mechanical apparatus or sleight of hand: these were the two basic categories of secrets for Victorian magicians.

Robert-Houdin improved the mechanism of the tree, added the butterflies, and devised a beautiful routine with the handkerchief, egg, and lemon, but the real "invention" of his Marvelous Orange Tree was combining sleight of hand and secret machinery into one seamless fantasy, deliberately blurring his techniques so that one started as the other left off. Some conjurers had specialized in displays of mechanical wonders—trick vases, boxes, or wind-up figures with magical abilities. The fashion was to open the curtain on shelves and shelves of brightly nickel-plated apparatus, interspersed with candelabra to dazzle the eye and boast of the conjurer's expensive taste. The magician took the part of a scientific lecturer, showing off his inventions. More than likely, only a fraction of the apparatus would actually be used during the performance.

Then, in the mid-1800s, a new trend was to eliminate the elaborate apparatus and austerely emphasize pure manipulation, using only objects borrowed from audience members, cards, coins, simple tables, or hats. All too often, these magicians filled their performances with pointless manipulations that called attention to their own skill, like a pianist who performs finger exercises up and down the keyboard.

The dichotomy continues today. As beginners, magicians love the colorful boxes they first saw on magic shop shelves—the trick props that seem able to do anything. As sophisticates, they learn that these mechanical props are no substitutes for pure ability—a stark, aesthetic approach to sleight of hand. But to an audience, the answer lies somewhere in between—as in Robert-Houdin's tasteful example. Accomplished by an invisible mix of deceptions, his illusion pleased his spectators as a visual jewel and surprised them with a reassuring fairy tale.

Every magician at the turn of the twentieth century was haunted by Robert-Houdin, who cast an enormous shadow over their generation. It's easy to see his influence over John Nevil Maskelyne. For example, Maskelyne claimed that his early training in Cheltenham, like that of the French magician, was as a "watchmaker." Maskelyne opened his own theatre of magic in a capital city, later aspiring to be more than a magician—producing the shows of other performers, working on commercial inventions, researching the unexplained and the tricks of gamblers, following Robert-Houdin's lead by portraying himself as a scientist.

The model magician was Robert-Houdin because, more than anything else, magicians had been captivated by his astounding memoirs, an inspiring piece of literature that painted the portrait of a magician as an artist. It might be the most influential book in the world of magic. Thanks to Houdini, it has also become one of the most debated.

Robert-Houdin's book was first published as *Confidences d'un Prestiditateur* in France in 1858. The first English translation was published the following year under the title *Memoirs of Robert-Houdin*, which was reviewed by Charles Dickens in the April 9, 1859 issue of *Household Words*. Dickens was himself an amateur magician.

According to the memoirs, he was born Jean Eugene Robert in 1805 in Blois, France, and originally trained as a watchmaker, getting his introduction to conjuring from a series of odd coincidences. During his time as an apprentice, he had intended to pick up a set of volumes on clockmaking at a bookseller's. The shopkeeper was distracted and accidentally wrapped up two volumes that explained physical amusements, scientific tricks, and sleight of hand. Rather than return the books, young Jean Robert was fascinated by the discovery and secretly studied the books late into the night:

> I was eagerly devouring every line of the magic book which
> described the astounding tricks; my head was a-glow,

and I at times gave way to thought which plunged me in
ecstasy. . . . How often since have I blessed this providential
error, without which I should have probably vegetated as a
country watchmaker!

Not much later, when he was twenty-two years old and had just finished his apprenticeship, he suffered a bout of food poisoning. Attempting to return home, he took a stagecoach destined for Blois, but, in agony, felt unable to endure the ride. He threw himself from the vehicle and collapsed on the roadside, delirious. Days later he regained consciousness to discover that he was riding across the countryside in a large wagon, carefully being nursed back to health by a mysterious stranger:

[H]e was a man of about fifty, above the average height, and
his face, though sad and serious, displayed a degree of kind-
ness which prepossessed me. His long black hair fell on his
shoulders in natural curls, and he was dressed in a blouse
and trousers of unbleached cloth, with a yellow silk pocket-
handkerchief as a cravat. My surprise was increased by
finding him constantly at my side and nursing me like the
fondest of mothers.

Jean Robert was surprised to find that his savior was Torrini, an itinerant magician, who traveled in an expandable wagon that doubled as a theatre. Torrini was a romantic, gypsy-like conjurer who shared his secrets with Jean Robert and confessed his tragic story. His real name was deGrisy, and he was a renowned performer who had appeared before Pope Pius VII and worked in competition with a famous Italian magician, Pinetti. Years later, while in Germany, he presented his version of the famous Gun Trick. Inspired by the tale of William Tell, Torrini would fire a marked bullet at his son; the bullet would be found lodged in an apple on his son's head. But one evening, through a tragic mistake, the trick failed and Torrini fatally shot his son on stage.

He was imprisoned for the killing and nearly driven mad with grief, but after serving his sentence, Torrini resumed his tours, upon which he encountered Jean Robert on the side of the road. Robert was nursed back to health in Torrini's wagon, where he was taught the fine points of magic presentation and craftsmanship.

It's now clear that one of Robert-Houdin's most ingenious deceptions was Torrini himself. Almost certainly, there was no Torrini, but his sad tragedy had been constructed from bits of other performer's lives and several object lessons that the author attributed to his mysterious mentor. Most of all, the tale was a way to avoid explaining why this middle-class watchmaker's son, who had been given a good education and apprenticeship in his father's trade, was drawn to the less reputable world of conjuring. In recent years, researchers have discovered a more likely story. A wealthy amateur magician named Mr. David was a friend of Jean Robert's uncle. He probably provided the youth with the rudiments of the art, and Robert perfected his own skills in small town shows or at fairgrounds.

This would also explain another puzzle of his memoirs, for after meeting Torrini the author seems to have had a successful career as a watchmaker, then suddenly burst forth as a proficient, ingratiating performer. He was an experienced showman with an expressive face and a graceful sense of movement; these attributes are clear even from engravings of his show. But this was a remarkable transformation, from quiet craftsman to star magician and polished performer. According to his book, after finishing his season with the mysterious Torrini, Robert moved to Paris to work with Jacques Houdin, a well-known clockmaker, and the following year married his daughter, Cécile, adding her name to his own to become Robert-Houdin. For the following fifteen years he lived and worked in Paris as a clockmaker and automaton maker in the capital before beginning his own magic shows, titled the "Soirées Fantastiques." These shows were first produced in 1845, when Robert-Houdin was almost forty years old, installed in his own small theatre at the Palais Royal in Paris:

> *Remembering Torrini's principles, I intended to have an*
> *elegant and simple stage, unencumbered by all the*

> *paraphernalia of the ordinary conjurer. Real sleight of hand*
> *must not be the tinman's work, but the artist's, and people*
> *do not visit the latter to see instruments perform. Of course,*
> *I abstained from any eccentric costume, and I never thought*
> *of making any change in the attire civilized society has*
> *agreed to accept for evening dress. My only fear was whether*
> *the public would accept these important reforms and such*
> *elegant simplicity.*

There's no question that his performances quickly attracted French society. His magic was original, thoughtful, and adorned with an elegant setting of gilded Louis Quatorze furniture. Robert-Houdin had announced to Paris that magic was not an amusement for children or fairground ruffians; it belonged in a theatre, and it attracted a respectable audience. But almost certainly, these ingenious performances represented the climax of a clever career, not the beginning. Although not mentioned in his elegant memoirs, during his years in Paris he had been producing magical apparatus for other leading magicians and must have honed his skills in numerous amateur performances.

Although Robert-Houdin has the reputation of simplifying magic, by today's standards his performances were reliant upon paraphernalia and elaborate mechanical automatons, which were integrated into the performances. His revolution in magic was one of taste, degree, and selection; Robert-Houdin seemed to crystallize a number of experimental trends, including some, like performing in evening clothes or emphasizing sleight of hand, which had already been introduced by other magicians. The importance of his decisions and creations are clear, for his contemporaries and imitators quickly adopted them, copying such illusions as his levitation trick, mind-reading routine, or the beautiful Orange Tree. He became the important transitional figure in the art.

Robert-Houdin's career before the public was surprisingly short. He toured very little—he worked on the Continent briefly and appeared in Great Britain, being honored by a command performance for Queen

Victoria in 1848—and after only seven years retired from his own theatre in Paris, turning it over to his brother-in-law.

But his career as a magician had a spectacular encore. After he returned to his home near Blois, he was called out of retirement in 1856. He received an unusual request and was put in a peculiar situation: the government of Louis-Napoleon suggested that Robert-Houdin participate in a "pacification" of the tribes in French Algeria. Specifically, a tribe of religious mystics, the Marabout, who claimed magical abilities in the name of Allah, were reluctant to accept French rule. Perhaps, his government suggested, Robert-Houdin could demonstrate that French magic was superior.

The mission involved a formal show at a city theatre as well as several special galas before the country's tribal chiefs. An example of his approach to this curious diplomatic mission was his performance of the Light and Heavy Chest. This had been a novelty in his Paris shows, a small wooden box about a foot wide, that he introduced and deposited on the stage. A spectator was invited to lift it, but found it deceptively heavy—actually impossible to move. A moment later, the chest could be lifted and moved with ease. In his "Soirée Fantastique," Robert-Houdin's effect was presented as a magical box that could become heavy or light at will and thus protect itself from thieves. It was accomplished with a metal-lined box and an electromagnet beneath the stage—in the 1840s such magnets were little understood by the general public and not likely to be suspected. In Algeria, the Light and Heavy Chest was given a dramatic new presentation. Robert-Houdin cleverly shifted the focus to the lifting man instead of the box. He claimed the ability to drain the strength from a man. A particularly strong, skeptical tribal member was invited onto the stage by the magician. He lifted the box effortlessly, then replaced it on the stage. Robert-Houdin gestured gravely with his wand, explaining that the man was now weaker than a child. As the Algerian bent over to lift the chest with a quick snap, he found himself thrown off balance. He couldn't budge it. He planted his feet, grasped the handle and applied his full force. The audience laughed nervously to see that he was powerless. The magician added a purposeful climax, designed to remove all doubt: On a signal, he had a brief electric shock sent through the handle of the chest:

But, wonder of wonders! This Hercules, a moment since so strong and proud, now bows his head; his arms, riveted to the box, undergo a violent muscular contraction; his legs give way and he falls on his knees with a yell of agony!

"Allah! Allah!" he exclaimed, full of terror, then wrapping himself up quickly in the folds of his burnoose, as if to hide his disgrace, he rushed through the ranks of the spectators and gained the front entrance. . . . My audience had become grave and silent.

The magician was rewarded for his service to the French government; they were convinced that his magical demonstration had intimidated the Marabout and quelled any potential uprising. Robert-Houdin returned to Blois and wrote his *Confidences d'un Prestiditateur*, including his remarkable Algerian adventure. In retirement he continued his experiments with ophthalmology and electricity—and may have produced one of the first experimental electric light bulbs.

He also wrote several books on the techniques of magic, including inspired sleight-of-hand routines and accounts of his own stage inventions as well as the innovations of the Davenports, Pepper, Dircks, Tobin, and Stodare. His account of the Davenports' performances, for example, was remarkably even-handed and informative, even though he made some bad guesses about their secrets. Pepper's Ghost especially fascinated him. He analyzed it like a scientist and displayed a remarkable understanding of its intricacies. In his chapter on the Ghost, he explained why it worked, the most important parts of the formula, and a simple, intuitive system for calculating the size and position of the glass. In fact, his description was far more accurate than Pepper and Dircks's original patent.

The French magician died at Blois in 1871, but his books went on to become standard texts, and his famous theatre in Paris survived into the next century, managed by a number of clever magicians including George Méliès, the artist and early filmmaker. Méliès' programs regularly featured some of the automata, which had been handmade and performed by Robert-Houdin.

• • •

The Memoirs of Robert-Houdin, Ambassador, Author and Conjurer,
as the American edition of his book was titled, provided a special
inspiration for the young boy named Erich Weiss:

> *To my unsophisticated mind, his* Memoirs *gave to the pro-*
> *fession a dignity worth attaining at the cost of earnest, life-*
> *long effort. When it became necessary for me to take a*
> *stage-name . . . a fellow player, possessing a veneer of cul-*
> *ture, told me that if I would add the letter "i" to Houdin's*
> *name it would mean, in the French language, "like Houdin."*
> *I asked nothing more of life than to become in my profession*
> *"like Robert-Houdin."*

It seems more logical that "Houdini" was an amalgam of the names
of the teacher and his pupil, Torrini and Robert-Houdin. Young Erich
Weiss, misunderstanding the hyphenated name, didn't realize that
Houdin was the maiden name of his wife. Years later Houdini
explained that the name had been intended as a sincere homage, while
show business at the time was filled with imitators, not disciples. In
his prime, Houdini faced his own imitators with names like Oudini,
Szeny, and Undina; he clearly felt no honor by their names and
attacked them mercilessly. But part of the mystery of Houdini was his
childish, arbitrary mix of devotion and hatred, which bubbled to the
surface in unexpected ways.

Erich Weiss had been born in Budapest, Hungary in 1874, the son of
a rabbi. The family immigrated to the United States several years
later, first settling in the farming community of Appleton, Wisconsin,
where his father had a small congregation. Several years later the
family moved to Milwaukee and then New York City. Erich had long
been interested in magic, but it was in 1891, when he was seventeen,
that he read the memoirs of Robert-Houdin, and decided to quit his
job as a lining cutter in the garment district, determined to become a
professional magician under the name Harry Houdini.

Working in New York City with a friend, Jack Haymen, and later with his younger brother Theo, Houdini presented a series of such standard tricks as producing a flower in his buttonhole, materializing a silk handkerchief from the flame of a candle, and performing a series of card manipulations. The finale of the act was an escape he called Metamorphosis. Harry would have his hands tied behind his back, then be tied inside a cloth sack and locked inside a large steamer trunk. Theo stood next to the trunk, and then pulled a curtain closed, concealing himself and the trunk from the audience. He clapped hs hands three times.

It was Harry that dramatically pulled the curtains open and took his bow while the audience noticed that the trunk was still tightly sealed and Theo had disappeared. Harry quickly opened the trunk and the cloth sack, showing Theo inside.

The Brothers Houdini performed on the Midway at Chicago's Columbian Exposition in 1893, and the following year the act was improved with the addition of a tiny brunette, Wilhelmina Beatrice Rahner, of the song and dance act called The Floral Sisters. Wilhelmina, nicknamed Bess, quickly became Harry's wife and replaced Theo as the other person inside the trunk. Mr. and Mrs. Houdini performed at Tony Pastor's famous vaudeville theatre in New York, but they earned only a lukewarm letter of endorsement from Pastor: "satisfactory and interesting." Houdini performed as the "King of Cards," presenting a series of flashy manipulations. Harry and Bess also found work in dime museums, sharing the platforms with freaks; or in traveling circuses or medicine shows. Gradually, he added additional escape routines into his act, derived from the rope ties used by mediums, and also escapes from handcuffs.

Returning to New York, frustrated by his lack of success, Houdini even advertised a School of Magic, offering to sell his secrets, through the mail, for several dollars each. In 1898 he wrote to John Nevil Maskelyne, asking for work at Egyptian Hall. If Houdini had sent press clippings, which he probably did, Maskelyne must have been bemused. Here was an American magician who had arrogantly named himself after France's greatest wizard, Robert-Houdin, the "Father of Modern Magic."

Even stranger, this American had taken Robert-Houdin's name but exhibited no trace of his fine example. Houdini's press clippings would have indicated that he performed a standard magic act and several escape effects, including a trunk escape. Wasn't this simply the Davenport brothers' act with an additional veneer of honesty and Yankee nerve? More to the point, wasn't this a simplification of the trunk escape from "Will, the Witch and the Watchman"? It would be hard to imagine an act less suited to Egyptian Hall. The Chief penned a quick response of the sort he must have written hundreds of times:

> Dear Sir,
> I have no room for any addition to my company. I seldom change my artists.
> > Yours very truly,
> > J. N. Maskelyne

It was fortunate for Houdini that Maskelyne didn't hire him, because the American was on the verge of an important breakthrough. The following year, while fulfilling a typical engagement at a beer hall in St. Paul, he was visited backstage by Martin Beck, the head of the Orpheum vaudeville circuit. Beck told him that the various escapes—the handcuff and trunk tricks—were interesting, but wondered why Houdini bothered with the handkerchief and card tricks, which seemed so ordinary. He joked with Houdini about whether he could escape from Beck's own handcuffs, and Houdini, eager to please, treated this as a serious challenge and quickly agreed. The following day, Beck returned to the vaudeville show with several pairs of handcuffs he'd purchased, sending them up to the stage during Houdini's act.

Houdini had the cuffs locked in place, retired to his curtained cabinet and quickly emerged, free, to the cheers of the audience. Beck tried him out for a week in one of his theatres, and Houdini dropped the magic tricks, concentrating instead on escapes. Houdini worked hard for Beck, performing publicity stunts, devising challenges, and displaying a knack for making headlines in any city. Martin Beck managed his interests carefully, increasing his salary at regular intervals. By

1899 Houdini was one of the stars of the Orpheum circuit, playing week after week in first-class vaudeville theatres across America.

In 1900 he began his first European tour, opening at the Alhambra Theatre in London as part of the music hall bill and creating a sensation with his brash and unusual act. In Europe he became famous as an archetype of the new world, arrogantly challenging anyone to restrain him. Europeans called him "the Syllable Accenting American." He later explained his sharp techniques for addressing an audience and vitalizing his act:

> *I never spoke to the first row. I would walk down to the footlights, actually put one foot over the electric globes as if I were going to spring among the people, and then hurl my voice, saying, "Ladies and Gentlemen."*

He toured Great Britain, then appeared in France and throughout Germany and Russia. His sensational act inspired imitators, but Houdini stayed one step ahead of them. His challenges at Scotland Yard, the dare of the *Mirror* handcuffs, or escaping from a Russian transport cell made headlines and brought crowds to the theatre. He returned to the United States in 1905 with a sure-fire repertoire for the vaudeville stage, and became one of its highest-paid performers. Three years later, as the handcuff act started to lose its edge, he introduced the Milk Can escape, which allowed him to demonstrate his spectacular underwater escapes on a stage. An oversized metal milk can was filled to the brim with water. Houdini would squeeze inside; the can was barely large enough to hold him. As he slid into the water, he urged the audience to hold their breaths along with him. He ducked his head beneath the surface as the can was topped off with gallons of water. The lid was slammed on top and locked in place with six padlocks. A curtained cabinet surrounded the can, and assistants stood nearby watching, waiting with fire axes ready to smash the locks. The band played ominously. "Awful suspense," one account recorded. The audience, one by one, exploded in gasps as they ran out of air. As the tension became unbearable, Houdini pulled the curtain aside, drenched with water and stumbling forward to take his bow. The can was still sealed, still locked with six padlocks from the outside, still filled with water.

Compared with other magicians, Houdini was not especially artistic or versatile. He could not succeed as a typical conjurer. But he had perfectly mastered his greatest creation, "Harry Houdini," and had an unerring knack for appealing to an audience. In this sense, he was a genius. Houdini once boasted, "I get more advertising space without paying for it than anyone." His career was enhanced by a string of irresistible publicity stunts. In later years he would be locked in a trunk and thrown into the local river, only to escape; or wriggle out of a straitjacket while dangling upside down from the cornice of a building before a gaping lunch-hour crowd.

There are many accounts of his enthralling performances, which seem remarkable even by today's standards. Often a great deal of the act consisted of staring at a curtained cabinet, listening to the band, and waiting expectantly for a flutter of drapery to see when Houdini had made his escape. In presenting his various challenges, he was a charismatic, magnetic performer. Publicity photos artfully displayed the muscular Houdini posed in chains and cuffs, nearly naked; on stage he was quick to rip away his jacket and vest or perform in a bathing suit. An early Martin Beck ad emphasized the difference between Houdini and other acts:

> The Weird, Mystifying and Inexplicable
> Harry Houdini
> The Famous Handcuff King!
> Positively the Only Conjurer in the World Who Strips Stark
> Naked

Of course, it wasn't really conjuring at all, even if his novel act had been derived from the world of magicians. Houdini created his own product. The drama of his performances was the sight of the little man challenged, playing David to society's endless Goliaths, the archetypal victim who, within the strict confines of the vaudeville turn, rose to be the victor. His rough-and-ready energy, which had seemed so out of place when he performed card tricks, was perfectly suited to his escape act.

The end result sometimes felt as oddly surreal as the Davenport brothers' phenomena a generation before. Houdini's most heralded escapes—being nailed in a crate and dropped into a river; freeing himself from the jail cell that had held Charles Guiteau, who assassinated President Garfield in 1881; emerging from the deadly upside-down Water Torture Cell—never seemed to be mere tricks. They couldn't be explained by a simple lock-pick or a practical knowledge of knots. They were demonstrations of a particular power, a weird force possessed by Houdini. The illusion was so strong that some psychics and spiritualists suspected that Houdini was concealing the ability to actually dematerialize and free himself; when he denied this, they refused to believe him.

Houdini never wrote a full autobiography, but he filled his publicity with tall tales from his life. He lied about the place of his birth—he claimed to have been born in America—invented academic honors for his father, and manufactured tales about escaping beneath an ice-covered river, his early career as an aerial act, his experience as a locksmith, and his innovations as a card manipulator. Even his loud claim that he originated the challenge escape act has been debated. One of Houdini's enduring myths is that he took his secrets to the grave. Actually, many of his effects were willed to his brother, and almost all of his secrets are known today. Houdini's act called for physical stamina and daring, but the actual secrets were ingeniously simple and dependable. Often Houdini depended on his crew of devoted assistants, who surreptitiously supervised the on-stage escapes or oversaw the publicity stunts. Many of the challenges were instigated and orchestrated by Houdini: "challengers" were solicited, publicity was arranged, and the "extemporaneous" performances were carefully planned. Houdini was trained as a magician, not a daredevil; he took fewer chances than audiences ever suspected.

As Houdini's fame as an escape artist increased, he took deliberate steps to tie himself to the world of magicians. He became a collector of magic memorabilia and planned to write an authoritative book on the history of the art. He associated with magic organizations and,

in 1906, he even became the editor and publisher of a monthly journal
for magicians, called *The Conjurer's Magazine*. His role as editor
seemed to be about Houdini settling scores. *The Conjurer's Magazine* was, from its first issue, filled with gossip about magicians
he didn't like, encouragement for his friends, criticisms of his imitators, and numerous assurances about his importance to the world
of magic.

The magazine's most unusual feature, which ran for a full year, was
a series of articles he first titled "Unknown Facts concerning Robert-
Houdin," and later titled "Robert-Houdin's Place in the History of
Magic":

> *No doubt all this material regarding Robert-Houdin will
> cause a great deal of controversy, but let it be known that at
> one time, years ago, on first reading his* Memoirs, *I firmly
> believed everything in them, even as if I had been an actual
> witness of each deed and action. I resolved that should Fate
> ever grant me the means of looking up his life, I would do so
> in order to find material he had not published.*

But Houdini's motivation was clear from the first page of his article.
He wrote that in France he had called upon the widow and family of
Robert-Houdin, lavishly announcing his presence by sending letters
of introduction, asking to be allowed to place a wreath on the French
magician's grave, or inquiring about the purchase of mementos of his
career. No doubt they were surprised to find a magician working
under the name Houdini. Robert-Houdin's daughter-in-law quietly
passed the word that they did not care to see anyone. Houdini wrote
in his magazine,

> *I was treated most discourteously by Madame W. Emile
> Robert-Houdin, who is the widow of Emile Houdin. . . . Per-
> sonally, I think she should have shown a little common
> courtesy to the memory of Robert Houdin, especially as she
> is now living in her old age on the proceeds of his
> endeavors.*

When he spoke to older magicians, many of whom had seen Robert-Houdin perform, Houdini heard mixed reviews. He was told that the famous French magician, his idol, was "only a little above the average entertainer." Robert-Houdin's contemporaries insisted that he was being credited with inventions that he did not invent, or lavished with praise he did not deserve. Houdini seemed to be shocked by the revelations that Robert-Houdin was a careful, calculating businessman, that he was a skillful publicist, and may have exaggerated some stories to appeal to his public.

Houdini was himself a master of publicity and self-aggrandizement, yet he also championed the little guy and had a fondness for old retired showmen. It's easy to imagine the conversations he had with Robert-Houdin's contemporaries, who would have been eager to tell their own stories. Robert-Houdin had been a brilliant light, which unfortunately cast all of his contemporaries into shadow; the continuing sparkle of his book had made Robert-Houdin the focus of the mid-1800s. Unfairly, if accidentally, a number of interesting magicians had been neglected while all the attention turned toward the "Father of Modern Magic."

Houdini had been guilty of just this sort of bias. He'd begun his research believing "everything in [the *Memoirs*], as if I had been an actual witness of each deed and action." In attempting to enshrine his hero, he discovered that additional information on Robert-Houdin was difficult to obtain—perhaps because of Houdini's own clumsy attempts with Robert-Houdin's family—and the stories of other magicians were waiting to be told. He then displayed his typical difficulty with moderation or balance. Houdini worked in shocking headlines. He decided to portray Robert-Houdin as a liar and thief who was completely incompetent as a magician.

Houdini had developed a hatred for his spiritual father.

In 1908 his collection of articles was gathered together, expanded, and sold to a London publisher. By comparing the original articles with the finished book, it's clear that Houdini employed a ghostwriter to polish the language and clarify his points. Other surviving manuscripts from

Houdini demonstrate that most of Houdini's writing depended on ghostwriters. The theme of his book on Robert-Houdin was sharpened to a razor's edge, and was now titled *The Unmasking of Robert-Houdin*. Houdini took aim at the French wizard:

> *In the course of his* Memoirs, Robert-Houdin, *over his own signature, claimed credit for the invention of many tricks and automata which may be said to have marked the golden age of magic. My investigations disproved each claim in order. [His] explanation of tricks performed by other magicians proved so incorrect and inaccurate as to brand him an ignoramus in certain lines of conjuring.*

The Unmasking is a mess of a book. Houdini's original intention was to write a history of magic. In fact, there was a great deal of genuine research in Houdini's manuscript, including brief biographies of a number of interesting performers, but it became polluted with his unusual premise and his tiresome, impudent attack.

The most embarrassing aspect of *The Unmasking* was that Robert-Houdin had fooled Houdini so completely. Houdini never realized that the Torrini story was a fabrication. He continually referred to Torrini's lessons and experience, pointing out that they should have been examples to Robert-Houdin. The Torrini chapters, wildly coincidental and unsubstantiated in any other source, should never have gotten past Houdini, who boasted about holding every element of the story to his expert magnifying glass.

Instead, Houdini passed along the gossip that Robert-Houdin might have used a ghostwriter for his memoirs. We now have the master's handwritten manuscript copies and know he did not. Houdini pointed out that many of Robert-Houdin's effects were derived from earlier illusions, but ignored the enormous mechanical and artistic improvements that made Robert-Houdin's effects the envy of his contemporaries. Houdini pilloried Robert-Houdin for claims he never made, like being the first to perform in evening clothes. He ridiculed him for being fooled by the Davenport brothers' basic rope techniques. Houdini, after speaking with Ira Davenport, boasted that he knew exactly how they were done. He also scorned Robert-Houdin for writing about the delicate touch needed to palm several coins. Houdini had personally found no such delicacy necessary:

> *So ends the true history of Robert-Houdin. The master magician, unmasked, stands forth in all the hideous nakedness of historical proof, the prince of pilferers. . . . The day of reckoning is come. Upon the history of magic as promulgated by Robert-Houdin the searchlight of modern investigation has been turned. . . . My task is finished.*

Despite Houdini's self-congratulations, in the years since *The Unmasking of Robert-Houdin* was written, a number of researchers and authors have dismissed his claims and defended Robert-Houdin's reputation. Many of Houdini's basic criticisms—that Robert-Houdin used a ghostwriter, that he exaggerated his successes, minimized his failures, romanticized his life, overstepped his claims for credit, overstated his creativity and knowledge of magic, and underplayed his own vanity—have left most authors slack-jawed. These were exactly the traits for which Houdini was infamous. Most analyses of *The Unmasking* easily confront the arguments of dates, names, or inventions but are helpless in attempting to explain the blindness and double standards of its author.

The simple explanation is that Houdini wasn't hypocritical at all, just jealous. Houdini had idolized Robert-Houdin as his ideal in magic, a pure artist. Robert-Houdin represented an archetype in magic that had been denied to Houdini, who wanted to be recognized as a magician but was successful only as an escape artist. Even more revealing, Houdini's research must have demonstrated that the French magician exhibited not only the refined traits of a nineteenth-century artist, but the cagy self-awareness of a twentieth-century performer. As Houdini recognized some of his own skills and shortcomings, he came to hate his idol, who outclassed him. It was a kind of Oedipal complex; Robert-Houdin was the spiritual father in the art and Houdini was his literal namesake. Houdini wasn't unmasking Robert-Houdin, he was unmasking himself.

• • •

With typical bravado, Houdini advertised his book with a banner headline. "$250.00 Reward!! . . . To anyone who can bring a book which has taken so much time, energy, travel and money, with such authentic data regarding real magical inventions, a reward of $250.00 will be paid." Magicians were disappointed by Houdini's book. Many who knew Houdini had been amused by his personality; now they were shocked to see the ruthless, unexpected level of his attack. Houdini never really expressed any regrets. To several friends he made the enigmatic statement that he was completely correct but that the book should have been published as "a History of Magic." Since then it's been debated whether this was an admission of his mistaken emphasis or a boast of the importance of his research.

He was confident that he had taken on the old traditions and conquered the Victorian golden age. He had deposed the king and contemplated the empty throne. Houdini set his sights on one more challenge. He wanted to be not only an escape artist, but also, in the eyes of his audiences, America's greatest magician. For Houdini it wasn't simply a matter of artistry, or originality, or appealing to the tastes of the public. Like all of his challenges, which started with an impossibility that he would flamboyantly struggle to overcome, this would be a fight to the bitter end.

8
Stealing Secrets

Feed with mystery the human mind,
which dearly loves mystery.
—Harry Kellar

ertain tricks are perfectly suited to certain personalities or techniques. Harry Kellar observed, "every magician I have met performs some trick much better than anyone else." Maybe it's just like some songs being well suited to certain voices or accents. A particular illusion, in the hands of one performer, may be flat and obvious. Another, investing the same trick with indefinable touches of presentation, can turn it into a miracle.

Devant once wrote about how he had interviewed a young magician backstage at Egyptian Hall. He casually asked the young man how many tricks he knew. His visitor responded by making a rapid calculation. "About three hundred," he said. Devant furrowed his brow, explaining, "Actually, I know about eight, myself."

He seemed to be very puzzled, but he is puzzled no longer by [my] reply, for he is now a very popular performer; he now appreciates the difference between knowing how a trick is done and knowing how to do it.

Not every magician of his time understood Devant's insight or valued the intellectual property of others. Often, magicians instinctively feel a greedy desire for secrets and end up collecting them and treating them with sacred reverence, then boasting of knowing secrets as a measure of success. If they chanced upon a great idea, they might have taken extraordinary steps to guard it from other professionals. But stage doors could always be opened, and assistants could always be bribed.

In the late 1870s, during one of Buatier deKolta's early successes in Paris, he was performing his flower trick. He deftly twisted a large sheet of stiff paper into a cone and shook it gently, revealing that it was filled to overflowing with pastel tissue flowers, which cascaded out of the cone and into an upturned parasol. DeKolta had every intention of keeping his secrets, but one night at the Eden Theatre a slight draft from the wings wafted several of the flowers beyond the footlights, and they tumbled off the stage. A magician in the audience

reached down to pick one up and rushed from the theatre with his discovery: an important key to the trick was the ingenious construction
of each paper flower. For the next hundred years, the famous deKolta
flowers could be purchased for a few dollars at magic shops.

Servais LeRoy, an artistic Belgian illusionist, appeared in early
vaudeville at the start of the twentieth century. One of his most memorable creations was an illusion he first called The Garden of Sleep, in
which his wife, Talma, was covered with a silk sheet and floated high
above the stage. As LeRoy plucked the cloth away, Talma instantly
disappeared in mid-air. In combining the succinct imagery of two distinct effects, LeRoy had hinted at much more than illusion—death,
afterlife, and the soul. By touching these symbols, he provided a jewel-
like setting for his ingenious invention. There were many small
secrets to The Garden of Sleep: the lighting, the backdrop, and a clever
arrangement of wires above the stage. But the most important element was a specially shaped piece of metal, the key to it all. After
every show, LeRoy personally locked it away in a little wooden
packing crate. In 1910, after an engagement at the Alhambra Theatre
in Paris, the company loaded their equipment and set off for another
city. Backstage in the next theatre, as LeRoy opened his crate, he felt
the blood drain from his face. The lock had been picked and a single
piece of metal stolen. Within weeks The Garden of Sleep was in the
programs of his rivals.

In 1897, during a Maskelyne sketch called "Trapped by Magic," David
Devant made his first appearance in a magic play. It was the usual
Egyptian Hall farce, with Devant and J.N. Maskelyne playing
Japanese jugglers. Devant included a sequence in which he manipu-
lated transparent crystal spheres, making them multiply or change
color and size at his fingertips, but the highlight of "Trapped by
Magic" was the levitation illusion.

John Nevil Maskelyne had been working on levitations since the
start of his career, and he produced some half dozen versions over
the years, always incorporating his latest experiments or improvements. His 1894 play was called "Modern Witchery," a parody of

theosophy written by his son Nevil. In it, a character named Koot
Hoomi, a mystical mahatma, was strapped to a wooden plank that was
laid across the backs of two chairs. Carefully, the chairs were removed,
but the mahatma floated in the air, rising slowly, then descending
again. Maskelyne used several fine steel wires, which were secretly
attached to the plank during the preparations for the illusion. The
scenery and lighting were carefully arranged to conceal the wires, and
the illusion he created was quite eerie.

The wire idea fascinated Maskelyne, and in several of his early illusions he developed a technique for using a fan of wires—a multitude
of fine, thin wires rather than just one or two thicker wires. It's a little
trickier than you'd think, as each wire must be meticulously adjusted
to carry the correct proportion of the load. Otherwise one or two fine
wires might snap, and the others, unable to carry the weight, would
break in a domino effect. The advantage, of course, was that thin wires
were another form of invisibility. They could be used on stage under
bright lights.

Three years later, for "Trapped by Magic," the Maskelynes had
changed techniques. Now a steel rod was pushed up vertically through
the stage. It was hidden behind the leg of the magician, who stood on
a precise mark facing the audience. At the top of the rod, a horizontal
bar curved around the magician's body and connected to a metal
cradle or back support, which held the horizontal lady. She could rise
or fall with the mechanism. Unlike the previous illusion, the magician could wave his hands over the floating lady, indicating that there
were no wires connecting from above.

The Maskelynes compulsively fixed and adjusted their illusions.
Just one week into the run of "Trapped by Magic," Nevil Maskelyne
added an improvement to the mechanism, which allowed him to
pass a seamless hoop over the floating lady. Instead of the metal cradle
attaching directly to the rod, he had the metal wrought in several tight
gooseneck twists, a sort of wide, thin "S" shape hidden against the
lady's side. These gooseneck turns extended toward her feet, then doubled back toward her head.

Nevil Maskelyne stood behind the floating lady as she rose into the
air, one of his legs concealing the upright support. He held the hoop

in his hand and passed it over her head. The curve of the gooseneck allowed the hoop to pass nearly to her feet. At that point he swung the front portion of the hoop off her feet and held it behind her body. As far as the audience was concerned, the hoop had been passed from one end of the lady to the other; they weren't aware that the back edge of the hoop was still trapped within the gooseneck track. Following a dif-

ferent curve of the gooseneck, he swung the hoop over her head again and then repeated his moves, slowly moving the hoop along the length of her body. On the second pass, the hoop had been unhooked from the gooseneck track and came completely off her feet. To the audience, it appeared as if the solid metal hoop had been passed over the lady head to toe, then moved to her head again and passed over her a second time.

*Nevil Maskelyne's gooseneck
for the Levitation*

Although it was a great idea, John Nevil and his son Nevil were now faced with an embarrassment of riches. They had made two discoveries—the use of many fine wires that supported the person from above, and the use of a metal gooseneck that supported the person from behind. Both were interesting and each was mutually exclusive of the other.

"Modern Witchery" and "Trapped by Magic" turned out to be promising experiments leading up to a masterpiece. After almost thirty years of levitations, John Nevil Maskelyne captured the best of both worlds on April 6, 1901, with the premiere of his play entitled "The Entranced Fakir."

George Cooke played Dryanard Boo Sing, a fakir with a long white beard. Maskelyne played Dan'l Daw, the old showman. Also in the cast was Herr Valadon, the German sleight-of-hand artist, who portrayed a Chinese magician. David Devant was busy with the Maskelyne touring company at the time and wasn't a part of the play.

During the plot, Cooke was laid in a horizontal sarcophagus that was supported on two trestles. Maskelyne gestured over the top of the sarcophagus, and Cooke's rigid form slowly floated up into the air. When Cooke was high above the coffin, Maskelyne took a hoop and passed it over Cooke twice, giving every impression that he was really floating. Cooke slowly descended into the coffin again.

The levitation took place in bright light, and Cooke floated many feet from the backdrop and any other scenery. Unlike his previous effects, Maskelyne was not trapped by the mechanism, forced to stand in one spot to conceal a lifting apparatus. He walked around the floating figure, waved his hands above and below and passed an examined, solid metal hoop over Cooke, according to his son's wonderful formula.

Magicians had always regarded Egyptian Hall as a laboratory of new ideas. Many considered it a badge of honor to keep up with Maskelyne's latest developments, which were analyzed and discussed over a late night drink and scribbles on a scrap of paper. Although Mr. Maskelyne was careful with his secrets, most of his best effects had been discerned by clever magicians and copied for their own acts. But "The Entranced Fakir" found magicians stumbling onto the pavement of Piccadilly and blinking at each other in stunned silence. A man had been floating in the air, and there was simply nothing else to dissect.

David Tobias Bamberg, a proud old magician who was a favorite of King William III of Holland, accompanied his son Theo to see Maskelyne's latest play. They were the third and fourth generations of a family of innovative Dutch magicians. Theo later described the experience:

> *Both my father and I were utterly baffled by the illusion. After the performance my father was still completely carried away by the spectacle. "Theo, my boy," he said, "this really hurts my pride. I always was under the impression that no illusion could mystify me. Of all the illusions I have seen in my time, I could make out a little theory of my own regarding the technique—even those of Robert-Houdin, in Paris, although I came away highly impressed. But, my boy, what I saw today is beyond any comprehension. I haven't one percent of an idea how that could be done!*

• • •

Harry Kellar was also badly fooled when he saw it in the summer of 1901. He was America's greatest magician, a rough-and-tumble showman. He'd been born Heinrich Keller in 1848 in Erie, Pennsylvania. As a boy, Harry worked as a drugstore clerk, a newsboy, and custodian for the Erie Railroad before he ended up in Buffalo, New York and responded to a newspaper advertisement for a magician's assistant. He toured with the Fakir of Ava for six years, learned the business of magic, and struck out in 1867 with his own modest show through small towns in the Midwest. His tour ended with his equipment in the hands of creditors and Harry talking his way onto a freight train. In LaCrosse, Wisconsin, he met up with the famous Davenport brothers and Fay, and his career made a sudden change.

The Davenports were looking for a new road manager, and Kellar desperately needed a job, any job. He ended up working for two seasons as the Davenports' general manager, and also as understudy to William Davenport. Already well-versed in magic, he didn't take long to discover the secret of their act and master it himself, which he did in secret sessions backstage with their cabinet. He organized their tours through the eastern states and Canada, but he didn't get along with the brothers. William Davenport traveled with a dog and a monkey, disagreeable pets barely endured by everyone on the tour. One day in Philadelphia, William told Kellar to take his pets into the Pullman car. Kellar told him that he couldn't, that the conductor would insist they travel in baggage. They began to argue, and William cut him off by declaring "You do as I tell you, Harry. You might as well know it now. You're my servant." Kellar quit, and persuaded their longtime partner William Fay to leave with him.

Kellar was just twenty-four years old, tall and handsome with thin, sandy hair and an enormous mustache. Within a few seasons he'd learned the toughest lessons in show business and the secrets of one of the most successful acts. Kellar and Fay set out on their own, presenting a skillful imitation of the famous séance act, touring through southern states, into Mexico and throughout South America. They made a fortune in gold and uncut Brazilian diamonds, lost it all when their ship was wrecked in the Bay of Biscay, and decided to start again from scratch. Fay left to rejoin the Davenports, and Kellar moved on to London.

It was there in 1875 that he visited Egyptian Hall for the first time and was fascinated by Buatier deKolta's mechanical effects. He met him backstage and paid deKolta a handsome fee for his spare Vanishing Birdcage. This became a feature for Kellar, who used it to slowly rebuild his act. He also borrowed Maskelyne and Cooke's billing of "Royal Illusionists," forming his own troupe of contortionists, fire eaters, and magicians, and making two full world tours, performing before Queen Victoria and touring through the Orient, India, and Australia.

Kellar had an excellent taste for material, but he was always an imitator, borrowing secrets, presentations, and advertising techniques from Maskelyne, Stodare, or the Davenports. Much like John Nevil Maskelyne, he had little interest in conjuring, filling his program with mechanical wonders and "honest" simulations of the spirit world. Under different circumstances, Maskelyne and Kellar might have become good friends. They shared a sort of hard-boiled pragmatism and showmanship; they both were inspired by the Davenports and felt it a mission to expose Spiritualist frauds.

After years of touring, Kellar returned to the United States to find that the leading magician was Alexander Herrmann, the Satanic, goateed sleight-of-hand artist who had made his name by performing at Egyptian Hall in 1870. Herrmann was famous for his leisurely, Parisian-accented puns as he borrowed a hat from the audience, caught coins in the air, or hurled playing cards into the theatre. For years, Kellar and Herrmann played in opposition, jumping each others' routes or pasting over each other's posters, until Herrmann suddenly died in 1896, leaving the field to the homegrown American wizard.

Kellar was the complete opposite of Herrmann, a big man with the twinkling blue eyes and crooked smile of the most charming con artists. Audiences loved him. By that time he was forty-seven years old, completely bald and clean-shaven. His presentations were charming and earnest, never silly or frivolous. Kellar was almost certainly the inspiration for the wizened Wizard of Oz described by author L. Frank Baum; he was America's leading magician when Baum's book was written.

Kellar had thick, stubby fingers, not the hands of a magician. For the obligatory coin or handkerchief manipulations, he depended upon small, flesh-colored metal gimmicks, which could be pinched between his fingers. Such subterfuges got the job done, but magicians respected him most as an "operator of mechanical illusions." At the end of his career, a writer who had worked with him offered back-handed praise for his

> *masterly simulation of sleight of hand and his admirable acting. On stage he is the magician par excellence, he is today the Admirable Crichton of conjurers. In view of these qualities, it is almost unbelievable that this man cannot manipulate a pack of cards, that he cannot execute the sim-plest pass with coins, and that he is "out of the running," so to speak, when . . . no apparatus is used.*

His show was never about such delicate conjuring. Kellar worked hard to bring his audiences the finest magic from around the world. He had paid Charles Morritt handsomely for the secret of silent thought reading and developed the principle into an impressive act with his wife, Eva Medley Kellar. He performed his own version of the Davenport rope tie, presented an improved séance, and was famous for his wonderful, methodical handling of Stodare's flower trick. The Fakir of Ava had taught it to him, suggesting that it would suit him well. In this effect, Kellar grew two real rose plants from two tiny sprouts by covering them with an empty cardboard tube. One bush was red and pink with blooms, the other white and cream. Mrs. Kellar helped him snip off the roses and distribute them to the audience.

He billed his show lavishly with beautiful stone lithographs that often portrayed him with little red devils cavorting on the stage or sit-ting on his shoulder, whispering secrets into his ear. Most of all, Kellar was a perfectionist with every piece of apparatus, every hinge, back-drop, and costume. A friend of his recalled one season when Kellar was using a beautifully made, expensive trick box in his program. At one performance, a spectator from the audience happened to indicate that he knew how the box worked. After the show, Kellar took the box out to the alley behind the theatre and smashed it to pieces with an axe. "Now we'll build a new one that no one will figure out," he told his mechanics.

Kellar was always anxious for new material. Playing the part of the hard-nosed businessman, Kellar made offers to buy illusions from Egyptian Hall. Maskelyne, playing the high-handed artist, rebuffed him. In response, Kellar sought out copies of many of Maskelyne's finest creations. These included two different levitations, the whist-playing automaton and the two musical automata, a small spirit cabinet, and several popular deKolta effects. In 1884, Kellar went so far as to start his own permanent theatre of magic in Philadelphia, for which he borrowed the title "Egyptian Hall." The enterprise lasted less than a year.

Maskelyne was exasperated when Kellar returned to London every summer for his vacation, to study the latest illusions. It was inevitable that when "The Entranced Fakir" appeared in 1901, Kellar would be there. Kellar was also fascinated with levitation illusions, following Maskelyne's improvements by always revising the levitation effects in his own show. Kellar arrogantly told Maskelyne that he would figure out his latest floating man marvel. Maskelyne invited him to buy as many tickets as he liked; anyone was free to come to his theatre. Kellar brought his chief mechanic, Phillip Claudi, returning for several shows, sitting at different spots in the small theatre, alternately scowling through the performance and whispering to each other. On some evenings he arrived with opera glasses, which amused the cast.

Finally, one night Kellar chose a seat in front and waited patiently until Cooke began to rise from the sarcophagus. The American magician stood up, walked to the edge of the stage, and mounted the steps. The actors froze. Maskelyne glared at him. Kellar took a good look at the apparatus, turned around, and left the theatre.

We now have a pretty good idea what was visible to Kellar beyond the footlights—a mass of wires, an iron platform, and a tangle of overhead leaf springs. It would have been just enough to drive him mad. The physics of Maskelyne's levitation was much more intricate than what Kellar saw. Maskelyne realized that Kellar would be looking for an informer to bribe, and he recruited a member of his cast, a comic actor named Teague, as a double agent. Teague played Stumpy, "a Factotum," the character that stood on stage during the levitation, handed over the hoop and assisted Maskelyne. Kellar would realize that Teague had a privileged view of the apparatus. Maskelyne coached Teague in the role of spy and armed him with sketches that would throw Kellar off the scent should the American ask for the secret.

Kellar never fell for it. He had already been bribing his own spy. Incredibly, he had chosen Paul Valadon, the current star at Egyptian Hall. Valadon, handpicked by David Devant to fill in during his tours, had been working four seasons for Maskelyne. He had also been given a role in "The Entranced Fakir," which meant he'd had a chance to see the secret. Kellar told Valadon that his talents were being wasted in London. He wanted the German magician for his American tour, asking him to join the company and present his own act. Valadon was in a bind. He must have been loyal to Maskelyne for his success, but realized that, in the shadow of the famous David Devant, he would never be more than one of the many magicians at Egyptian Hall.

As a final inducement, Kellar hinted that he would be retiring soon and would introduce another magician as his successor. Valadon's sense of fair play must have quickly curdled with the promise of his own American career. Kellar asked if Valadon could possibly describe the apparatus that was being used at Egyptian Hall, just a simple diagram and description. Where do the wires connect? What are they made of? What's above the stage and what's below it? Kellar helpfully suggested that he would be happy to take it from there.

The secret of Maskelyne's levitation, which in America became known as the Kellar Levitation, is the closest thing magicians have ever had to the Holy Grail. It was treated like stolen plunder, then bestowed like the crown jewels, proudly polished and displayed by the greatest magicians of the century. It was technology turned into poetry.

Valadon accepted the assignment, delivered his rough sketches and clandestinely met with Kellar to discuss what he knew about the illusion. He revealed that the levitation was a sophisticated lever. Cooke

A version of Pepper's famous Ghost was exhibited at Henri Robin's Paris theatre. (*Author's Collection, hereafter* AC)

The climax of the Davenports' séance act featured an audience member tied inside the cabinet with the two brothers. (*Mike Caveney, Egyptian Hall; hereafter* MCEH)

Ira Davenport and Harry Houdini, at their meeting in Mayville, New York, 1910. (MCEH)

Egyptian Hall in London was built as a museum and later housed Maskelyne's famous theatre of magic. (MCEH)

John Nevil Maskelyne, standing, with his mechanical automatons on stage. Psycho, the card-playing mechanical man, is on the left. (AC)

Buatier deKolta and his assistant Lizzie Allen, producing hundreds of flowers from an empty paper cone. (MCEH)

left • Charles Morritt ties the "Missing Man," Ted Scott, into the chair before making him disappear. (AC)

below left • Robert-Houdin and his son, with his automaton Orange Tree at his theatre in Paris. (AC)

below right • Harry Houdini with his book that attacked his idol, *The Unmasking of Robert-Houdin.* (AC)

above • A Harry Kellar advertising lithograph, featuring his improved version of the Spirit Cabinet act. (MCEH) *below left* • Theo Bamberg witnessed the Maskelyne Levitation in London, then later toured with Thurston's show. (MCEH)
below right • Paul Valadon, featured in a Kellar poster during the seasons they toured together, brought the secret of the Levitation from London. (MCEH)

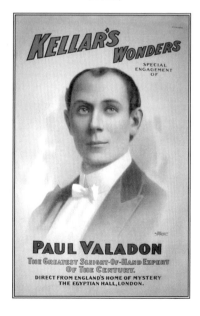

above left • David Devant, the popular St. George's Hall magician, with a publicity photograph to dramatize the Mascot Moth illusion. (MCEH)

above right • "All Done by Kindness:" Devant with the simple mystery, Boy, Girl and Eggs. (MCEH)

right • Guy Jarrett, backstage during his season with the Thurston show, standing next to his famous Bangkok Bungalow illusion. (AC)

above • Howard Thurston, standing, and the famous Levitation of Princess Karnac, the illusion Kellar had stolen from London. (MCEH)
below • Harry Houdini with Charles Morritt; Morritt had his own secret for making an elephant disappear. (AC)

above • The New York Hippodrome theatre, on Sixth Avenue, was the largest stage in America and the site of Houdini's Vanishing Elephant illusion. (MCEH)

left • Servais LeRoy, who perfected his own levitation illusion, always considered his friend Houdini an incompetent magician. (AC)

below • P. T. Selbit, standing at right, with Betty Barker in the wooden box, presenting his original illusion of Sawing Through a Woman. (MCEH)

above • Howard Thurston presented Goldin's version of Sawing a Lady in Half in his touring show. (MCEH) *below left* • Horace Goldin, the American vaudeville star, set a new pace for magic and developed his own Sawing illusion. (MCEH) *below right* • Thurston, left, producing a rabbit from a hat for a children's benefit, backstage at his show. (MCEH)

was lying on a metal cradle, which supported his back and legs. This extended backwards like a shelf, away from his audience, for several inches. Just next to him was the Maskelyne gooseneck, so the hoop could be passed over him. Beyond the gooseneck were two short metal bars. Attached to these were the sets of fine wires that spread up toward the ceiling. By lifting the wires, Cooke and the cradle would be lifted straight up, over the stage.

Except, of course, for leverage. The cradle would naturally tip forward when pulled up by the wires, spilling Cooke onto the stage. Maskelyne compensated for this by adding another point several inches further behind the cradle. This attached to a fan of fine wires

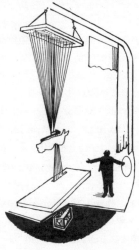

The improved version of Maskelyne's Levitation

that passed down, through a narrow slot in the stage, where they were attached to a heavy box of weights. If you imagine the cradle as a short little lever, Cooke was at one end of the lever, the wires pulling up formed the fulcrum, and the wires pulling down formed the counterweight. When the system was perfectly balanced—weights could be added beneath the stage—Cooke appeared to be floating.

But the lever was even more complicated than that. First, the fulcrum was spread between two points so that the balance was far more stable; remember that the cradle could not be permitted to suddenly swing up as Cooke was lifted off of it at the end of the trick. In physics, this is called a "sliding moment"; the fulcrum had to function in both situations. Maskelyne had also designed a second lever, arranged from head to toe on the floating assistant. The fulcrum was roughly at Cooke's thigh as he was lying on the cradle, and the counterweight, pulling down, was at his ankle. This meant that there were no wires near Cooke's head, allowing the magician to pass his hands around this space.

Previously, when magicians used wires, they had tried to use as few as possible so they were not seen. What Maskelyne had realized was that once the system of fine wires had been worked out, it mattered very little whether one was lifting ten pounds or one hundred pounds. The only thing that changed was the number of wires, and each individual wire would be invisible to the audience. This allowed him to lift a very heavy arrangement: the weight of Cooke, plus the weight of the metal cradle, plus the considerable counterweight on the other side. The whole thing was nearly 400 pounds. Above the curtains, the wires were fixed to a metal grid, which was then raised or lowered with a heavy winch.

If the wires were chemically treated to darken them, the illusion looked nearly perfect, but there was always a slight haze or cloudy effect just above the floating man. Kellar must have seen this through his opera glasses. Careful lighting and a patterned backdrop could minimize this, but it was always there, caused by the multiplicity of wires, which converged just before they attached to the cradle.

Ironically, Maskelyne might have discouraged Kellar if he had only put his arm around his shoulder, invited him backstage, and shown him the whole apparatus, for Kellar could never have used the illusion the way it had been built. The high-carbon spring wire was a source of endless difficulty; if the wires were not under tension, they would twist and coil. If the wires were nicked or creased, they could easily snap. In London, Maskelyne had delicately looped the wires around grooves on the apparatus so they were always held in tension, but it took weeks of adjustments to ready it for the stage, and wires were often breaking. After carefully being set on the stage, the effect could not be moved.

Once he'd resolved to steal the illusion, nothing could stop Kellar from making it work. A rumor among American magicians was that he had paid the Otis Elevator Company $10,000 to work out his levitation apparatus. We can't be sure. Otis' records from this period have been lost, and it seems like a preposterous amount of money to spend on a magic trick. Still, it sounds like a typically hard-headed way for Kellar to attack the problem, and Kellar benefited from someone's sophisticated understanding of the winch, wire strength, and balance. His real improvement for the illusion was a small device that you could hold in your hand; it would twist a perfect eyelet in the end of the fine spring wire. He also used large, felt-covered rollers in wooden crates, which allowed him to carefully coil the wires for storage backstage. These devices made it possible to handle the delicate spring wires, move them from city to city or install them in new theatres.

In Kellar's final apparatus, the floating lady was held aloft with fifty-four wires, each about the thickness of sewing thread. Another thirty-two wires, passing down through the stage, provided the balance. One technician who worked with the illusion provided an account of the apparatus:

> I can say that all the drawings purporting to explain [the Levitation] are very little like the mechanism that does the trick. With the drapes, it packs in nine big trunks, easily a ton and a half. The first time in a new house, it takes three men four hours to set it. Of course, that includes stalling and going out for beer. For each performance, it takes three men thirty minutes to set, and it strikes and packs away immediately after it acts.

Each wire was connected to a leaf spring, in the grid above the curtains, which helped to keep the proper tension. After they were installed, the wires were plucked and tightened, the way one would tune a musical instrument. Once the twangs were identical, the wires were sure to carry the same amount of weight. Finally, each wire would be chemically treated to remove the shine and give it a dark, dull finish so that it wouldn't reflect in the stage lights. After the trick was performed, the fans of wires were carefully retracted on the felt-covered rollers, which left the stage clear for Kellar's other illusions.

Valadon and Kellar concealed their plan for almost a year. As Kellar had the illusion quietly constructed in America, Valadon continued to work for Maskelyne, presenting his act and starring in the magic plays at Egyptian Hall. During this time, Devant came to the United States. Unaware of the plot to steal the Chief's treasured secret, he actually met with Kellar in Philadelphia and New York. Devant seemed to share a genuine friendship with Kellar. He used Kellar's distinctive graphic elements in his own posters and, several years later, hired Kellar's chief assistant for his own touring company. Kellar, in turn, was grateful when Devant improved a new trick for him, a wooden ball that mysteriously rolled up and down a plank. Early in 1904, Devant first heard rumors from America that Valadon might be leaving Egyptian Hall and planning to join Kellar. He hesitated telling Maskelyne, but did begin auditioning performers who could take over in an emergency.

Valadon stayed as long as he could and finally quit Egyptian Hall around the time Kellar introduced his new levitation in America. He joined Kellar's show about eight months later. When Maskelyne finally realized what had happened he felt double-crossed by Paul Valadon, who he had always considered a valuable member of his company. But he was also mystified by Kellar's success with the temperamental illusion. Although he publicly insisted that Kellar's illusion was only a poor copy of his own, the Chief did pay to have someone in America sneak backstage and take a flash photo of Kellar's apparatus, sending it off to London so he could study any improvements. That photo, like Kellar's bold visit to the Egyptian Hall stage, wouldn't have shown him very much. It was actually the little tool that made the eyelets, and the felt-covered rollers—two simple additions that never looked very impressive backstage—that had made all the difference.

On January 17, 1904, in Baltimore, Kellar took the stage and introduced his latest and greatest illusion. The presentation was a mix of exotic, oriental elements. He performed it with an assistant dressed as an Indian maiden, and used a name based on the name of a city in Egypt, The Levitation of Princess Karnac:

> *Some six years ago, my company and I made a trip to India, the land of magic, where magic is not written in books, but is handed down from father to son by word*

of mouth. While on this tour, it was our good fortune to wit-
ness a performance of the Great Ali Ben Bey. We saw him
lay a native Hindu lad, seven or eight years of age, upon
the sand at his feet. After Hindu incantations, of which nei-
ther I nor my company understood a single word, the boy
rose into the air to a height of possibly five or six feet, defying
all law of gravitation, there being no visible means of
support.

It was vintage Kellar, earnest and sincere, a modern fairy tale about
his faraway travels. Of course, it was also pure fiction, filled with suggestions to mislead the audience: that it had been performed outdoors,
that the secret was ancient and primitive.

He then passed for inspection a hoop made from the bark of
some native tree of India. The hoop was wrapped with
leather thongs, which resembled our own American pigskin,
but most likely was the skin of some wild animal. After we
were satisfied it was without break or split, it was passed
completely over the floating body, not once but twice,
proving the absence of all means of support known to
mechanical science.

Here was another clever bit of storytelling, emphasizing how the
Indian magician passed the hoop twice, which had supposedly convinced Kellar of the miracle. Passing the hoop twice was actually a
flaw in the trick, a necessary step to make the gooseneck work. The
presentation told the audience that this was intended, a deliberate re-
creation of what was seen in India. Rather than questioning it, the
audience would anticipate it.

After this most satisfying demonstration of a magic new to
both my company and me, I went to the Hindu magician
with an offer which, if he had accepted at the time, I would
have been unable to pay.
*   He, being a Hindu and reared within the circle of magic*

and mystery, refused to part with his wonderful secret. I,
being an American and determined as all Americans are,
followed our Hindu friend. Three weeks later I found him on
the banks of the Ganges River and discovered the secret of
this grandest of all mysteries. I now present it to you as wit-
nessed in India six years ago.

This was the twinkle in Kellar's eye; his fantasy ended with an echo
of the truth. As a determined American, he proudly pursued it and
stole it for his audience.

Ladies and gentlemen, the Levitation of Princess Karnac.

Kellar's program boasted that he had recreated "the miraculous
tales of levitation that come out of India," and that this single illusion
was the "sensational marvel of the twentieth century and the
crowning achievement of Mr. Kellar's career." There's no question
that he considered the Levitation as his greatest accomplishment; for
Kellar the thrill of the chase—backstage intrigue, secret meetings, and
mechanical challenges—had just added to the excitement and convinced him of its value.

When it reached the stage, the illusion lived up to every promise.
The Levitation of Princess Karnac was beautiful and astonishing,
something that many in the audience would remember for the rest of
their lives. For his fellow magicians, Kellar had demonstrated that this
single illusion—like a real Holy Grail—was worth any amount of
deceit, espionage, and thievery. Now it was Kellar's turn to try and
protect it.

9
Special Effects

*In conjuring, we work under the eye of
the public. In filmmaking, we are far
from the public sight.*
—George Méliès

oday George Méliès is renowned as the originator of special effects for films, the creator of a new kind of magic for a new medium, but we've forgotten that he did it through his own vocabulary of a Victorian magic show. His new techniques for special effects were natural extensions of his magic and the same optical principles that had been used on stages since 1862.

Pepper's Ghost had combined two images through a careful mix of illuminated objects and black areas. In the oven everything else was swathed in black velvet so it didn't cause any stray reflections in the glass. The ghost would look transparent if its reflection appeared in front of another person or scenery. It could be made to look more opaque if it were reflected on top of a black area on stage.

These formulas were applied to photographic plates sometime in the 1870s. If the plate was secretly exposed twice, transparent "spirits" could be seen hovering near portraits of the living. Like Pepper's Ghost, these photographic ghosts were surrounded by black, and their transparency could be controlled by carefully aligning the images around darker areas.

Méliès photographed images by reexposing the same strip of film, so that he could put two images on it. For example, in one of his famous films, Méliès's dismembered head appeared on a table. He accomplished it by first filming the scene with the empty table, keeping an area of dense blackness, an alcove, directly behind the table. The same strip of film was exposed a second time. Covering his body with black velvet and working against a black background, Méliès's head appeared to be decapitated. By aligning the image so that the head appeared to rest on the tabletop and was in front of the dark alcove, this head appeared perfectly opaque, not ghostly and transparent.

The same techniques had been described in print by Henry Dircks and Robert-Houdin: pale colors and black, with bright light and shadows, one image placed on top of the other. Instead of using the large sheet of glass to combine the images, Méliès had now done it on a strip of film.

Méliès's early special-effect films were designed to appeal as illusions, surprising the audience with their tricks. Today special effects have become integral elements on the stage and in film. These special effects are often still compared to magicians' effects, but the end results are very different things; a chef and a chemist can use similar skills to produce a velvety sauce and a dangerous poison, respectively.

The ultimate goal of any special effect is that the audience ignores it and feels that it has been completely integrated into the story and subsumed within the action. If an audience stops the action of the play to applaud for a special effect, it's as much of an insult as a compliment. When watching a film, people should believe that Superman can fly or aliens can dematerialize. These effects shouldn't jar them into thinking outside of the story or start them questioning just how it's all been accomplished.

A magician doesn't share this goal. He can't risk having the illusions ignored or accepted as part of a larger context. The effects must be held apart from anything else happening on stage and treated as unique.

This evening, if a painting were to fall off your wall, you might think nothing of it—a frayed wire or a loose nail. You might repair it tomorrow and forget that it ever happened. But if a medium were holding a séance in that room at the precise moment that the picture fell, that single incident could change your life. The only difference is the medium, who directs your attention and provides the interpretations. When the painting falls, it is a special effect. It is the presentation of the séance that makes it magic.

Ultimately, like any really successful storytelling, a magic show is an example of dictatorial control by the performer. The magician takes charge of every aspect of the story, pointing your head in certain directions at certain moments, emphasizing the importance of certain occurrences and minimizing others, hinting at every surprise, and imparting specific meanings. If the performance is successful, it is because the storytelling has been successful. If it stops being simply a puzzle and becomes magical, it is because the audience has succumbed to the magician's direction and interpretations.

•   •   •

The famous Egyptian Hall had never been more than a small exhibit room, just twenty-three feet by sixty feet, that had been fitted with a stage and curtains at one end of the room. It seated barely two hundred people. A serious problem was the lack of space beneath the stage, just forty inches, which made it difficult to use effects with elaborate trapdoors and mechanisms. In 1905 Maskelyne lost the lease when the building was scheduled to be demolished. He transferred his business to St. George's Hall, an austere auditorium in Langham Place, in the shadow of All Soul's Church off Regent Street. It had been the site of the Davenport brothers' last appearance in London. With St. George's Hall, Maskelyne had a real theatre. It seated over four hundred people and had an impressive, deep stage and a full basement beneath it to accommodate the Maskelyne inventions.

John Nevil Maskelyne had a dramatically different business plan for the new theatre. He would produce full plays, opening with a sensational drama adapted from Lord Lytton's science fiction novel, *The Coming Race*. He would produce the show, supply the special effects, and hire leading actors for the roles. The usual magic show mixture would be used only for matinee programs.

Part of this change of focus was that the Maskelyne family never really considered themselves conjurers and weren't particularly adept at presenting magic. This was especially obvious when David Devant joined the company. Devant was proud to be a magician and treated his profession with sincerity and seriousness, writing about the fine touches of performance, inventing new illusions for the stage, experimenting with presentations that would be appealing to his audiences. His style of performing was especially modern in its honesty and lack of pretension. For example, he eliminated the traditional address to the audience, the welcome to the "ladies and gentlemen." Instead, he stepped out on stage, walked directly to his first illusion, and began to "magish"—as his patter would have it—for the audience. Devant also deliberately never used a wand in any of his tricks, feeling it was an old-fashioned conceit, a symbol of mysticism that was beneath his audiences. Unlike the Chief, he was not mechanically inclined and had to depend on stage mechanics to develop and build his apparatus.

But Devant was blunt about what he felt belonged in a good magic show. He doubted the value of magic plays, which had been staples of the Maskelyne program, feeling they were expensive and inefficient. The magic could easily be lost within the action of the play. With typical pragmatism, he later wrote that plays could be sometimes useful as an artifice:

> *Magical sketches are an excellent means of making one or two illusions go a long way. They are also very important, or can be made to seem important by atmosphere and setting, thereby greatly enhancing the total effect of the illusion.*

Nevil Maskelyne's Victorian romps and farces had shuffled a number of illusions in comic situations. Devant's approach required scripts that were more restrained, more self-conscious. The illusions were placed intricately within the play to show them off. Most Devant sketches escalated toward one single effect, a sentimental situation that was resolved with an illusion or a spell. Some scripts, quite inelegantly, concerned a magician presenting a magic show. One can feel Devant continually holding the action in check to provide the perfect buildup, climax, and bow for his illusions.

John Nevil Maskelyne was always quick to portray himself as an important inventor and producer. His son Nevil considered himself a scientist, experimenting with wireless telegraphy, and was also an amateur astronomer. He worked on his own model for a film projector, which was a failure. Nevil regularly took part in the family business at Egyptian Hall, appearing in the plays or touring shows, but like his father, he was prone to rather dry, expository presentations, without the twinkle and flourishes of Devant. The Chief's younger son, Archie, was also recruited to perform in the shows.

Reading through the programs at Egyptian Hall, people would see an advertisement announcing that David Devant was available for private engagements and lessons, or that the other conjurers could be engaged through the Maskelyne Entertainment Agency. But the Maskelynes were above this sort of entertaining. On the back cover of the program, elaborate engravings boasted of J. N. Maskelyne's inventions: his typewriter was "The Most Perfect Writing Machine

Yet Produced," and his mechanical cashier "A Boon to Shopkeepers."
The typewriter offered variable spacing in each line, far more complicated than other commercial typewriters. But it was not a success.
The Maskelyne mechanical cash box was no more popular. Probably
his most popular commercial invention was a coin-operated lock that
was especially simple and durable; it was used for decades on pay toi-
lets in London.

To an inventor and producer like Maskelyne, the idea of presenting
a full play filled with special effects must have seemed like a logical
step; for the last few decades, popular melodramas and pantomimes
had been filled with spectacle and sensation. Actor–producers Henry
Irving and Herbert Beerbohm Tree used crowd-pleasing effects to
ensure that Goethe and Shakespeare were box office successes.
Maskelyne realized that these effects, which filled West End theatres,
were simply large, coarse stage illusions.

For example, in 1902 London had been thrilled by a revival of
Irving's sensational production of "Faust" at the Lyceum. It was an
evening of supernatural thrills. Irving himself took the role of
Mephistopheles. The famous Brocken scene, pure spectacle that he
had added to Goethe's script, was a supernatural summoning of
spirits, including hundreds of witches and goblins cavorting on a
blasted mountaintop, then flying overhead. Irving included peals of
thunder, flashes of lightning, mist, and moonlight. For the sword duel,
Maskelyne had been specially consulted and supplied Irving with electrical rapiers, which sparked and hummed with a surreal blue flame.

The following year Tree's "Richard II" opened in London, delighting his
audiences with a procession of horses and a mob of people onstage. For
"The Tempest," Tree began with a dramatic shipwreck, then filled the
stage with a number of romantic tableau views of the enchanted island.

Meanwhile, other London theatres, like the Adelphi, Hippodrome,
and Drury Lane, offered a regular diet of spectacular effects. Often
enough the shows were written around the scenic effects. On the
Drury Lane stage, submarines sailed, horses raced, locomotives col-
lided, giants marched, and hot-air balloons ascended—these were the
"sensation scenes" that formed the core of the melodramas. In 1902
Drury Lane imported the American melodrama "Ben Hur," featuring

a Roman galley sinking within canvas waves and the famous chariot race, in which real horses galloped atop treadmills in the stage as rolling scenery completed the illusion.

John Nevil Maskelyne must have felt that he could do better. At sixty-five, having long been associated with the tourist attraction and the quaint little shows at Egyptian Hall, he felt he deserved a reputation in the theatre and the press reported that that "one of the dreams of his life" was to produce a drama with magic effects.

Maskelyne spent lavishly on the first show in his new theatre, "The Coming Race," which included extensive changes to the stage at St. George's Hall, including new trapdoors and a modern electrical lighting system. Devant was kept busy touring during this time; his receipts were essential to the work being done at the new theatre. Nevil Maskelyne and David Christie Murray, a British journalist, collaborated on the script, which was an early science fiction fantasy about an advanced race of people, the Vril-ya, who lived beneath the surface of the Earth; they were accidentally discovered during a mining accident. The Vril-ya have mastery of a supernatural power called Vril. The plot allowed for a number of amazing effects— exploding mines, tumbling boulders, and a gigantic prehistoric lizard. The supernatural power of Vril was used to include several levitation illusions, and the sophisticated culture of the Vril-ya allowed the Maskelynes to include scenes with airships and hovering robots.

Nevil Maskelyne was the stage manager. His brother Archie was the business manager. John Nevil and Nevil worked out the many special effects and illusions, including much of their secret technology developed at Egyptian Hall. Several of the Vril-ya levitation effects seem to have used the wire arrangement from "The Entranced Fakir." But as the production grew more complicated, the Chief was faced with delays; the coordination of illusions, props, cast, and scenery was far beyond anything he'd done in the past. Maskelyne postponed the opening, missing most of the holiday theatre season, and gave the first performance on January 2, 1905.

Devant was in Edinburgh with the Maskelyne touring company, generating the cash that was now being poured into the London company. He wrote many years later of the "The Coming Race":

> It was lavishly staged and beautifully produced. Unfortunately, however, it failed to draw the public and was withdrawn, after eight weeks' run. Opinions differed as to the reason for the failure of the play, and as I never saw it, I cannot express one. Many thought the play was "over the heads" of the public; others thought the alteration in the form of the entertainment was of too drastic a nature. . . . The public expected more magic from Mr. Maskelyne than he gave them.

Devant politely suggested that the new theatre itself might have been to blame, being cold and uninviting, or that the advertising was at fault. We know that the first performances were plagued with uncomfortable pauses as the stage was set and long, awkward scenes. The show ended up as a strange mix of somber situations, music, and weird effects. But most concluded that "The Coming Race" was a miscalculation.

Ten days before "The Coming Race" opened, another show premiered at the Duke of York's Theatre in the West End, J. M. Barrie's strange new fairy tale titled "Peter Pan." It's ironic that these two shows opened in competition, for the less technologically advanced "Peter Pan" proved, from the first night, to be a memorably magical fantasy— including scenes with pirate ships, mermaids, and red Indian campfires. Throughout the play Peter and the children took to the air through the magic of "fairy dust," flying high over the stage. The Kirby family, long known for lifting dancers in aerial ballet effects and pantomime spectacles, supplied the flying effects, which were traditional and basic, nothing like the Maskelyne family's sophisticated system of fine wires. The Kirbys used leather harnesses hidden beneath the actors' costumes. Attached to the harnesses were thick, black wires, which lifted the children into the air, swung them from side to side in dramatic, pendulum-like swoops, or tracked them across the stage. In "Peter Pan" the wires were plainly visible against the painted scenery. The pirate ship was painted flats of wood. The mermaid's rock was a papier-mache mound in the middle of a stage of canvas waves.

"Peter Pan" was exactly the collection of crude, obvious effects that Maskelyne thought he could improve upon. The levitation in "The Coming Race" was far more astonishing than "Peter Pan"'s, but the Maskelynes had made a mistake by confusing special effects with illusion, and deception with magic. "Peter Pan"'s "fairy dust" was far more magical for the audience than "Vril."

Maskelyne's advantage had always been the magicians in his theatres—who took the part of the storyteller in a fantasy or the medium at a séance—efficiently establishing the reality for the audience and then transforming theatrical artifice into magic. Without this advantage, his product was no better than the collection of fantasy found in any London theatre. Audiences were willing to ignore the wire that held up Peter Pan, because of the inherent magic of the story. On that level John Nevil Maskelyne simply couldn't compete.

For several years Maskelyne had kept Devant out of the London spotlight, where his ambitions could work to the advantage of the Provincial Company. But in the dire circumstances of "The Coming Race," Maskelyne realized that his younger associate and his magic shows could be the salvation of St. George's Hall. He took the train to Edinburgh to see Devant and plead for his help, explaining his options for keeping the play open. Devant respectfully listened to the Chief and analyzed his business problems. Devant urged him to close the play immediately. He would lend Maskelyne the reserve fund of his touring Provincial Company and then return to London at his first opportunity to organize a first-rate magic show. "I felt a keen sense of responsibility to save the sinking ship," Devant wrote. Maskelyne agreed to the plan but pressed Devant to use many of the costly elements from the play for his new magic show. Devant declined, insisting that he be given an opportunity to arrange the best program and feeling comfortable with the material he had been perfecting during his seasons on tour. Maskelyne soberly agreed; he had little choice but to fully trust Devant.

On April 24, 1905, David Devant stepped through the curtain for the first time at St. George's Hall, taking the principal role in "A Feast of Magic." Reading a list of his effects, it's surprising how traditional and safe it all was—especially since audiences had been lured to the theatre just weeks before with explosions and prehistoric monsters. This was typical of Devant, who emphasized the magic and the magician rather than reaching out for the flashy touches typical of most showmen. That night in London, Devant opened with the trick he had invented for Kellar, the large wooden ball that rolled up and down the plank by itself. He presented tricks with flags, a mindreading routine with his sister, and a levitation illusion.

Later he presented his Obliging Kettle, stepping to the edge of the stage and standing in the spotlight:

> This kettle has a story attached, as well as a handle and a spout. When in Edinburgh I was taken to a shebeen. A shebeen is a place where one buys drinks during prohibited hours, but I don't suppose there is such a place in London.

Devant held a deliberately ordinary, large tin kettle.

> The reason I went to the shebeen was not to get a drink. I went there to interview the old gentleman, now passed away, who kept the place. He had the reputation of being a magician. He showed me one or two of his tricks and I showed him one or two of mine, and as a souvenir of my visit the old man gave me this tin kettle. The trick he did with the kettle was this: Suppose a person came in to buy a glass of whisky. The old man would pour it out of the kettle as I'm doing now.

Picking up a glass, Devant tilted the kettle and poured a small, neat serving of amber-colored liquid.

*Is there any gentleman here who happens to know the taste
of whisky?*

An assistant appeared with a tray and took the whisky to a man in
the audience.

*Is that good whisky, sir? Good! Now, supposing a policeman,
or any other total abstainer, came in and asked the proprietor what he kept in that kettle, he would pour out a glass
of cold, white, wet water.*

Tipping the kettle, Devant filled the next glass with clear liquid.

*Now is there a gentleman who knows the taste of water? I
have improved this kettle. It will oblige with any recognized
drink you would like to name, ales, wines or spirits.
Liqueurs or cordials. Now, don't shout! Just whisper your
orders to the attendants.*

Moving to a tray of glasses, Devant poured out dozens of glasses in
quick succession: sweet gin, claret, Benedictine, port, and Chartreuse.
As the assistants dashed up and down the aisles serving the mysterious drinks, Devant continued with Crême de Menthe and Kummell,
finishing with a large glass of milk.

The idea of pouring different liquors from a single bottle was an old
one by the time of Robert-Houdin. Devant realized that for his audience the trick was so old that it would be new again. Besides, it gave
him a wonderful opportunity to establish a rapport with the audience,
by filling his presentation with light jokes as he served them
free drinks. Devant concluded his "Feast of Magic" with a quick
sequence of illusions, including Morritt's Cage and deKolta's Vanishing Lady.

By all accounts, it was an exquisite program of magic, presented
with charm and style. By this time Devant had the look of a pros-
perous, friendly banker in evening clothes. He was solidly built with
a square jaw and a wide, bright smile, and moved with surprising grace

from illusion to illusion, without a touch of the exotic or mysterious—no affectations. The motto for his performance, "All Done by
Kindness," was in evidence. His trademark was to perform with deliberately ordinary apparatus: a simple table and chair, several hats and
handkerchiefs, a vase of water.

Old George Cooke, Maskelyne's original partner, had died just
months before, which only added to the gloom over "The Coming
Race." The Chief was surprised to see the receipts steadily climb under
Devant's steady hand and thrilled to see that his luck had turned.
Maskelyne offered the magician managing-partner status in the whole
business and property "on very flattering terms," according to Devant,
"that is to say, the purchase price was to be paid only out of profits."
Not only did the business become Maskelyne and Devant, but St.
George's Hall, Maskelyne's dream of theatrical magic, quickly
became David Devant's stage.

Over the next decade Devant's inventive powers produced a continual
string of marvels at St. George's Hall. The formula at Egyptian Hall
had been to change the program only once or twice in a year; old
favorites were economically used to fill out the shows. Devant, seeing
his part in the business as the creative one, felt that the public would
be drawn to his theatre by a regular change of program; it seems astonishing how many ideas Devant was able to introduce in quick succession. Part of the formula must have been Henry Bate, his friend, an
amateur magician, craftsman, and photographer. With Bate building
his new illusions—he constructed the Mystic Kettle, for example—
Devant was no longer subject to the Maskelyne family's fussy adjustments or their second-guessing. We also have to assume that in St.
George's Hall, Devant had a well-equipped, full-sized theatre that now
allowed him to experiment with ideas that he might have been planning for many years.

Just months after his first appearance at the theatre, he introduced
a new illusion, the disappearance of a lady at the climax of a short play
titled "The Mascot Moth." He later wrote that the idea came to him
in a dream, which he had virtually forgotten the following morning:

One night my wife saw me get up, light a candle at the bed-
side and sit watching the flame intently for some time. I
then blew the candle out and got back to bed. In the
morning [when she reminded me of this,] I told her that I
had a wonderful dream. I had dreamt I was chasing a moth
about the stage, a moth who was a human being with wings,
and was trying to tempt it towards me with the candle flame
when it suddenly shriveled up and disappeared.

Devant's illusion was a paradigm of his understanding as a magician, a transcendent mixture of perception and mechanics. The
Mascot Moth was a miracle.

Following his own formula, Devant created a simple play that
would enhance the illusion. The first script, written by H.L. Adams,
was an especially dark story about an entomologist in the jungle who
is searching for the elusive moth. At the finish of the play, the disappearance of the moth served as a lucky omen, bringing news of the
death of a romantic rival. The story must have seemed especially
oppressive and sinister to the St. George's Hall audiences. Devant,
eager to showcase his new illusion, rewrote the play himself,
including an additional sequence of conjuring and a lighter, more
innocent plot.

The new play was set in an army officer's bungalow just outside of
Rajpoor, India, on a sultry evening. A group of British colonists passed
the time with various amusements. Several of the men were engaged
in a high-stakes poker game. Max, a mysterious stranger to the group,
is winning big. Bob Wentworth, the role taken by Devant, was a young
lieutenant losing precariously—gambling away the money needed to
marry his fiancée, Maude.

The poker game moved offstage as two Indian fakirs entered. Munga
and Patna had been engaged by the Colonel to entertain the ladies,
Maude and her mother. The jugglers presented a series of amazing
effects, materializing flowers and fruit.

As the conjuring performance came to a climax, so did the offstage
card game. Bob entered, ruined, losing not only his bankroll but any
hopes of marriage. Munga, the conjurer, overheard his dilemma and

promised to show him his very best trick, the Mascot Moth. The fakir enthusiastically promised that the Moth "comes only once in twenty years. When it comes, it is luck!"

Munga pulled away a curtain at the window, revealing the Moth, a lady in a voluminous winged costume, hovering several feet above the stage. Slowly, she descended, stepped forward, paused center stage, and folded her wings around her face.

Bob circled, curious about the apparition. "But where does the luck come in?" he asked. "You touch it, sahib!" Munga urged. Bob approached tentatively, stepping to the shrouded figure as if to envelop her in his arms. Just as he reached out to the Moth, there was a momentary flash of movement. In a split second the Moth seemed to wither and disappear, the same way a flame can suddenly burst and then be extinguished in an updraft. Bob whirled around, opening his arms and realizing that the mysterious moth had eluded his grasp. His surprise was broken as another poker player entered to announce that Bob's fortune had been saved. Max was discovered to be a swindler, he explained; all of the money was recovered. Bob and Maude embraced as the curtain closed.

The script was a crisp example of Devant's approach to a magic play: using a number of tricks to establish the skills of the Indian magician but building the action around the single disappearance of the Moth. That split-second illusion, the climax of the poker game, and the resolution of the conflict all coincided perfectly.

But the real achievement was the illusion. The necessary secrets overlapped and complemented each other, just as the various elements of the story had been knotted tightly at the conclusion of the play. "She vanished as quickly as an electric light goes out when the switch is turned," Devant later wrote, "shriveled up in full view." The amazing effect is apparent from Devant's careful account of just how it was accomplished:

> *I had the happy thought of bringing a tube up through the stage behind the person to be vanished, who would be wearing a special dress. This dress was made in such a way that it could be supported by the tube and looked the same*

*whether she was in it or not. In the first place it all hung
from the neck, and the collar, or yoke, was formed by a steel
spring shape.*

A vertical black tube, about four inches in diameter, was slid up
through the stage just against the lady's back. Naturally, the audience
didn't see this tube. A plug at the top of the dress, in the small of the
back of the lady, slipped into the end of the tube. This plug supported
the costume, which hung from wire shapes in the shoulders.

*Attached to [the costume] was a rubber-covered reel . . . the
reel had some strong cord wound on it. In one of my various
journeys to the lady I picked out this reel and dropped it
down the tube which was behind her. [Beneath the stage, one
of my stagehands] had looped the cord from the reel over two
pulley blocks, one in the floor and one in the ceiling above his
head, so that he could get a strong, quick pull on it.*

Not only was the dress being held upright by the tube, but a strong
cord, dropped down the tube, was now held by a stagehand, ready for
his cue.

The second part of the secret was the disappearance of the lady. She
had stopped on a precise mark, standing on a narrow, rectangular trapdoor that could descend like an elevator. She

*folded her wings across her face and locked them together by
a steel wire which ran through the top of each wing and
hooked them together. Now the weight of the dress was
entirely on the tube, the lady gave three taps with her toe
and [the trap door] would glide gently downward.*

Once the lady had covered her face and been lowered through the
costume, the upright dress gave the appearance that she was still
standing in place in the center of the stage. The dress was now an
empty shell supported by the narrow black tube. The man under the
stage held the cord, ready to pull it quickly.

Meanwhile, standing on the stage just above his assistants, Devant was engaged in a delicate bit of choreography:

> *My part of it was to get my left foot in front of the tube, so*
> *that I could get into the right position when I wanted to*
> *work the "vanish."*

Standing at the right side of the "lady," with his right side toward the audience, Devant slid his left foot behind the figure. He threw his arms open, as if to embrace her, then gave a cue:

> *The cord was pulled on my giving a shout.*

From beneath the stage the cord was rapidly pulled in one quick motion—the spring wire shapes collapsing so the entire dress was pulled through the end of the upright tube. As this happened, Devant lunged forward, pressing his body against the black tube:

> *Immediately afterwards the tube was drawn down and the*
> *process covered by my right foot being brought up sharply*
> *with the left, the heel of the left foot going into the side of*
> *the right foot. In this position the tube was entirely covered*
> *in its passage downwards.*

By sweeping both feet together, he concealed the tube for the split second that it dropped through the stage floor. Devant could then step away from the spot, clearly showing that the lady had disappeared.

More than anything, the illusion demonstrated Devant's under-standing of stage illusions and an audience's perceptions. There was seemingly no apparatus involved; the lady stood at the center of the stage and disappeared instantly, without the obligatory sheet of fabric or wooden cabinet or even an obscuring puff of smoke. More than likely, he had been inspired by several other illusions, including deKolta's Vanishing Lady. When deKolta performed the illusion—

pulling the large silk sheet up his sleeve—he had depended upon the quickness of his motions to disguise the action. Devant realized the fault in this:

> *It is a common mistake to suppose that the quickness of the hand deceives the eye. You cannot move your hand so quickly that its passage cannot be followed by anyone who is watching you.*

Similarly, Devant knew that the audience would perceive the movement of the costume as it disappeared in the Mascot Moth. The strength of the illusion was in this subtle, subliminal motion: The lady seemed to be rapidly drawn upward, to some indeterminate spot in space, where she quickly disappeared. The flash of movement, the quick compression of the fabric as the performer reaches for it, created a striking image. The tube supported the dress during a few critical moments in the illusion and then provided the means by which it could rapidly disappear.

Devant admitted, "It was a difficult thing to get right in rehearsal," which must have been something of an understatement. If the dress were pulled too slowly or without enough cover from Devant's body, it would give the appearance that it was being tugged into his costume, destroying the effect. If he provided too much cover, crowding the lady just before she disappeared, it would seem as if she simply dropped through a trapdoor.

When John Nevil Maskelyne saw the finished product, he shook his head and admitted that it was "the trickiest trick" he had ever seen. Devant must have been flattered by this indirect compliment from the Chief. It was high praise from a master of machinery. David Devant thought that the sudden disappearance of the Mascot Moth was "the best that I have ever done."

Devant followed his Moth with a number of striking effects. Often these were given the attractive titles of recent shows or novels: The Chocolate Soldier was an illusion in which a live marching soldier was surrounded by bright electric lights. A triangle of flags concealed the soldier for several seconds; when the flags were pulled away, he was seen to have shrunk to a tiny, mechanical marching soldier made of chocolate. Beau Brocade was the title of Devant's mysterious disappearance of a lady who was wrapped in a large, seamless sheet of fabric and held in his arms; as he carried the lady forward over the footlights, the cloth suddenly collapsed, and she was gone. She was discovered inside a large trunk, which had just minutes before been shown to be empty.

A Trick without a Title was an ingenious deception that was advertised with a contest; Maskelyne and Devant offered 50 pounds for the best name. An assistant was strapped against a framework of iron, which rested against his back. This in turn was lifted and bolted inside an extremely narrow, upright, coffin-sized cabinet. The cabinet was suspended on cables above the stage, and the front doors were closed on the man. Explaining the theory of voodoo, Devant showed a small doll dressed like the man inside. Holding the doll in his hand, he slowly turned it upside-down, then threw open the doors of the tiny cabinet to show that the man was still strapped inside, but now seen to be standing on his head. The winning title was the New Page—not only was the assistant dressed as a pageboy, but like a new page, he was "turning over."

As a sign of Devant's rapid success at St. George's Hall, shortly after his premiere at the theatre, he was busy forming three touring companies of the show. John Nevil Maskelyne, the Chief himself, took out the provincial tour in the autumn of 1905. Devant later wrote that Maskelyne "did me the honor of presenting my tricks" in part of the program, including Devant's popular Obliging Kettle.

Maskelyne's appearance in the tour represented the complete and sudden shift in the business. Just months earlier it was Devant who had been shuttled out of London, in charge of the provincial tours, presenting versions of the long-favorite Maskelyne effects. Now Devant was the London star, and as managing director of the new company, Maskelyne and Devant, he was much too valuable to the enterprise to leave St. George's Hall.

A year earlier Maskelyne had been the doyen of British magic, about to become London's latest theatre producer. But now, standing on a Bristol stage and holding a tin teakettle in his hand, he felt no particular honor in presenting the latest ideas from his younger partner. The Chief felt more like the proverbial old dog forced to learn some new tricks.

10
Magic Words

My object is to mystify and entertain.
I wouldn't deceive you for the world.
—Howard Thurston

ow I'll perform a piece of magic for you.

This strikes me as a convenient place to offer a demonstration that would naturally appeal to your intellect as a reader. Some piece of mind reading would be appropriate, a version of Charles Morritt's act, where you think of something and I tell you what you're thinking. Of course, my disadvantage is in attempting this through written words, which I had to type long ago so they could be printed and bound into this book. It doesn't leave me with many opportunities for improvisation.

At the same time it occurs to me that at this point you've been following all my words and the rhythm of the prose. I've taken advantage of a few sly opportunities to prepare you, dropping hints that you might not have noticed. And right now, if I asked you to carefully follow my instructions and make a completely free choice, I think I can count on influencing that choice.

I'm not going to read your mind. I'm going to see if you can accidentally read mine.

First, take a look at the following clock dial. You'll notice that there are no hands on the clock. That's because you're going to apparently

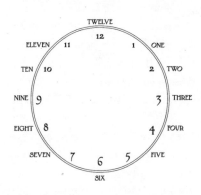

pick the time, and I don't want to give the impression that I'm influencing you.

Start by placing your fingertip at the top of the dial, on the twelve. Do that now. Now think of any number on the dial. You can think of the twelve if you'd like, or the one, two, three. . . . Go ahead and think of any of the twelve numbers. That is completely your choice, and you'll have to admit that it seems like a free one.

I'm now going to have you make three moves to arrive at a random number. Follow these instructions. First, I'm going to have you spell your number, the number you're thinking of, making one move clock-wise around the circle for each letter. In other words, if you thought of "twelve," you'd spell "t-w-e-l-v-e," moving your finger each time. Do that now.

Keep your finger right where it is, because you're now on a new number. I want you to spell the number that's under your finger, con-tinuing around the circle to a different number. Do that now.

Your finger is now on a new number. For the third time, please spell that number, moving your finger farther around the circle. Remember where your finger ends up. That's the random number you've selected.

Of course, you've made a free choice, and arrived at a final number based on that choice. It would be impossible for me to have antici-pated each and every move, unless you were particularly susceptible to my words.

You ended up with your finger at one o'clock, right?

It's a good thing that we're on friendly terms and I'm not concerned with deceiving you. I assume that right about now you'll want to go back and try that again to determine exactly how it's done—whether it was math, or luck, or psychology. Of course, the answer is right in front of you. It is all about words. In this case I'm relying on my ability to confuse words and numbers in your mind, causing you to overlook, for a moment, the fact that you're spelling numbers rather than counting them. I'm also taking advantage of your familiarity with a clock face, and the fact that you've developed a trust that I'd be telling you the truth about these secrets.

Hundreds of years ago, magic words were some vaguely Latin gib-berish that supposedly triggered spells: "hocus-pocus." For a magician the specific words in a script may be equally magical. They might sound like nonsense. They might sound vitally important and mean nothing at all. But often they are chosen with surgical precision. Film historian David Thompson called it "the dainty torture of a magic show, the small talk that traps."

• • •

Despite what he had been promised, Paul Valadon never got the job as Kellar's successor. He toured for three seasons with Kellar in America, presenting his own segment of the show. He supplied technical details on the levitation illusion and also copied "Will, the Witch, and the Watchman" for Kellar's show, providing the script and arranging for a duplicate of the Maskelyne cabinet from London. Contacting his old associates from England, he even hired one of Maskelyne's actors and David Devant's brother, Ernie Wighton, to play parts in Kellar's version. Kellar presented it for two seasons as "The Witch, the Sailor, and the Enchanted Monkey," taking the part of the Witch, with Valadon reprising his favorite role of Joe the Butcher.

The politics backstage were extremely delicate. Harry Kellar was unpredictable and temperamental; his staff was used to seeing him stomping and raving about inconsequential matters, then appearing the next day to offer a broad grin, a slap on the back, and an elaborate gift—his clumsy manner of apologizing. There was something silly and innocent about Kellar's explosions, but Mrs. Kellar, an Australian who was fifteen years younger than her husband, tended to drink and instigate smoldering arguments. Mrs. Kellar didn't get along with Mrs. Valadon. The Valadons had learned to excuse themselves quietly from potentially contentious situations, but one evening they were trapped by a fusillade of Mrs. Kellar's grumbling criticisms. Drawing on his long experience with Cockney stagehands, Valadon returned a string of colorful English phrases. Harry Kellar dutifully fired Valadon, who had become exhausted tiptoeing through the Kellars' nightly minefields.

The following season, in 1907, Kellar appeared with Howard Thurston, the handsome, ambitious American magician who had made his name in Europe as a card manipulator and then toured the world with his own large illusion show. Kellar's advertisements explained that the audience was witnessing

Kellar's Triumphant Farewell—After forty-seven years of phenomenal and unparalleled success the greatest of all magicians is introducing Howard Thurston as his successor, and will retire permanently from the stage at the close of the current season.

Thurston's official investiture had been given the glow of a royal appointment; he even advertised his new position with a large poster displaying Kellar, the old wizard, placing the "Mantle of Magic" upon the shoulders of the proud young magician. Like everything Kellar did, his arrangement with Thurston was much more business transaction than ceremony, but it put Kellar in the remarkable position of selecting, proclaiming, and appointing America's next greatest magician. After years of touring Kellar was looking forward to a long, relaxing retirement. On May 9, 1908, after a season together on stage, Kellar officially named Howard Thurston his successor and took his last, tearful bow from the stage of Ford's Opera House in Baltimore.

Howard Thurston became one of the great men of the American stage, a performer whose magic show became a national institution and an important franchise in the first decades of the twentieth century. He was born in Columbus, Ohio, in 1869, and as a boy he became a street tough. He had little formal education and worked as a newsboy and hopped freight cars from city to city. He gravitated toward racetracks—because he was small, he tried to become a jockey—and made his first real money selling racing programs. There's no question that he was also something of a con man. Thurston peddling cheap jewelry, switching the real article in and out so it would pass the occasional jeweler's loupe. He became well known on circuses throughout the Midwest as a "run 'em in and run 'em out man," the spieler in front of a carnival who eloquently promised what would be seen inside. He worked with the Sells Brothers Circus and the African Village at the World's Columbian Exposition in Chicago. His brother Harry, who started in the carnival business and financed several of Howard's enterprises, ended up running a peep show in the Levee, part of Chicago's notorious First Ward, negotiating patronage and politics from his back room.

But for all his ties to the shady side of show business, Howard Thurston also spent several years at the Mount Hermon School training for the ministry; he might also have been enrolled for a short period at Moody Bible Institute. He always dressed impeccably (even as the front man for a group of hootchy-kootch dancers) and had elegant, placid features. Most people remember his voice, a clear, resonant baritone, which was perfectly suited to the pulpit and hypnotically elegant on a sideshow platform.

Thurston had picked up card tricks both from books and other carnival workers and dreamed of becoming a magician. While traveling to the University of Pennsylvania to take an entrance exam and continue his schooling, he stopped to see Alexander Herrmann's show in Albany, New York. The next day at the train station, he saw Herrmann and his entourage. Thurston followed instinctively, standing behind the magician in the ticket line. At the window Thurston asked for a ticket to Philadelphia, but found that he'd accidentally been given a ticket for Syracuse—Herrmann's destination. Thurston accepted the ticket as an omen. He shadowed Herrmann, sitting near him in the train car and watching carefully, then following to the theatre to see Herrmann's show. He decided to abandon his plans for the ministry and turned his attention full-time to show business.

Thurston was the product of an interesting time in magic. Music halls and vaudeville theatres had created a market for short magic acts that could be sustained for seven, twelve, or twenty minutes. The old style of Robert-Houdin, Herrmann, Kellar, and Maskelyne was a full show dependent on establishing the performer's personality and introducing a wide variety of deceptions over the course of a couple of hours. The new acts were faster and flashier, emphasizing specific novelties.

For example, magicians had always talked to their audiences. They depended on their monologues to establish their effects and considered the quality of their patter, their funny remarks and puns, to be essential elements of the act. The idea of a silent magician, performing without speaking, seemed as ridiculous as a magician performing with a hand tied behind his back. Theo Bamberg, of the family of Dutch magicians, decided to start his own act in the 1890s, but a swimming accident had seriously affected his hearing, which in turn impaired his voice.

> *One day I said to my father, "What would you think if I could do magic without speaking?"*
>
> *My father thought me absolutely insane to entertain such a notion. "But what device would you use as an excuse for not speaking?" he said. "How could you get away with it?"*
>
> *"Well, I could pretend that I was a foreigner who couldn't speak the language, such as a Japanese or Chinese. . . ." That decided it.*

The conceit was successful for Bamberg. Silence was much more startling when Horace Goldin, a plump American magician at the turn of the twentieth century, deliberately began performing without speaking. Wearing a white tie and tails, Goldin, the "Whirlwind Illusionist," dashed onstage to present magic at breakneck speed—no time for talking—filling his vaudeville turn with dozens of tricks.

American magicians of Goldin's time became known as specialists, creating entire acts around artistically simple concepts. This was the period when Houdini became famous by performing an act that was exclusively escapes. T. Nelson Downs, who learned to manipulate coins while sitting in a telegraph office in Marshalltown, Iowa, billed himself as the "King of Koins," producing hundreds of half-dollars from the air and manipulating tall stacks of coins in his hands to the accompaniment of droll patter. George Stilwell performed an act just with handkerchiefs.

It was card tricks that made Howard Thurston famous. He performed his act at Tony Pastor's theatre in New York, and in 1900 he opened at the Palace Theatre in London, billed as "The King of Cards" or "The World's Premier Card Manipulator."

First, Thurston performed a series of amazing manipulations with a pack of cards, producing cards at his fingertips or making them disappear one by one. As the orchestra played "The Zenda Waltz," Thurston gracefully flexed each hand, slowly twisting his wrists to show his empty palms, then reaching out and plucking the cards from the air once again.

His second trick was a version of the famous Rising Card illusion. For over a century the trick had several playing cards selected by people in the audience, then shuffled back inside the deck. The deck was then placed upright in a glass, and the performer would call for the chosen cards. Each card rose several inches out of the pack, as if being pulled up by an invisible fingertip. Thurston improved the illusion by making it a full-stage effect. As he shuffled the deck, he asked for several spectators to call out the names of cards. Gripping the cards in his hand, he held his other hand high over the deck and gestured gracefully. One of the named cards slowly rose up, completely out of the deck, soaring up and into his outstretched hand. He tossed this card out to the spectators and then repeated the trick with every other named card. For the finale he left a card suspended in the air as he stepped away. The card responded to his commands, dramatically rising and falling in the air before floating up to his waiting fingertips.

Thurston's next flourish, the ability to throw individual playing cards far into the audience, was borrowed from Herrmann. Thurston could grip a card at his fingertips and, by cocking his arm like a baseball pitcher and snapping his wrist, send the card spinning horizontally, slicing through the air to the back row of a theatre or even into the balcony. He had a knack for delivering cards to individual spectators in their seats.

The card throwing was the crowd's favorite; invariably the act would end with spectators loudly calling for him to throw cards in their direction. The Rising Cards was a masterpiece of stagecraft, bestowing personalities and magical powers on the small rectangles of pasteboard. But it was another part of his act—his delicate sleight of hand with just a pack of cards while standing in a bare limelight— that established Thurston as an exceptional magician. He was one of the first to use a maneuver called the Back Palm. The title was a perfect misnomer. *Palming* is a term for concealing something in the hand, holding it with subtle, slight contractions of the muscles of the palm. The Back Palm doesn't involve the palm at all, though; the cards are pinched against the backs of the fingers.

The Back Palm has a mysterious history. One day in the mid-1890s, according to the legend, a Mexican magician appeared at Otto Maurer's magic shop in New York City. He demonstrated how he could make cards disappear, one by one, at his fingertips and then showed Maurer his technique. The Mexican left—Maurer never caught his name—but his innovative sleight of hand was taught to a few select magicians who passed through the magic shop. It now seems that Mark Schantz, a touring East Coast magician, was probably the originator of the Back Palm. Maurer might have thought Schantz was Mexican because he had a habit of speaking Spanish and manipulating Mexican coins; he liked their size and weight in his hands.

Although Thurston didn't originate the Back Palm, he was probably one of the first to perform it. The maneuver perfectly suited his long, muscular hands and his elegant style. A single playing card is held between thumb and fingers. The fingers curl against the back of the card, and the corners of the card are pinched between the fingers. When the hand is quickly opened flat, the card is carried to the back of the hand, gripped by its corners. The open hand is empty and the card is invisible as long as the magician's palm is facing the audience.

It's a notoriously easy move to bungle and a very difficult move to master. You've probably seen an uncle "perform" it at a holiday party. Few uncles have acquired the years of fine touches that make it really magical, transferring the cards to the back of the hand with an effort-less wave. Once the technique is flawless, the move can be covered with a slight upward toss, giving the impression that the card dis-solves as it leaves the fingers. In this way the flat hand is not the focus of the audience's attention; it just seems to be left behind once the card disappears.

Thurston improved the trick by showing both sides of his hands, rotating his hand and, at the same time, transferring the card from the back of his fingers to the front. The card was always kept away from the audience. Thurston made the move by momentarily swinging his hand behind his leg. He also included a sequence in which he picked up five cards one by one, making each disappear at his fingertips. He was Back-Palming all the cards at once, delicately adding single cards to the group already clipped behind his fingers. He would re-produce them, one by one, by peeling off single cards and returning the others to their concealment behind his hand.

Shortly after the turn of the twentieth century, when specialists were performing in American vaudeville or British music hall, a number of magicians wondered whether the fashion for Back-Palming was ruining magic. There was a craze for manipulation acts, and imitations of Thurston became a fashion. Most magicians reduced the moves to a series of silly hand-waving exercises and flourishes as cards tumbled from their fingertips—many seemed to stare intently at their hands through their acts, barely acknowledging the audience. It could easily seem like juggling, not magic.

There's no question that many of the new acts seemed dangerously stark, eliminating any mysterious feeling of magic. Maskelyne and Devant, for example, were disdainful of silent conjuring. (Thurston did not perform a silent act, though the manipulations he presented at the beginning of the act were performed only with music.) P.T. Selbit, an inventive British music hall magician and journalist, was aghast at Goldin's rapid pace onstage, which reminded many of watching a washerwoman at her board. Even worse, once the increased pace was established in the industry, others couldn't keep up. Selbit wrote in 1908,

> The public was quite satisfied with magic as it existed ten years ago . . . until Goldin came. In his first fifteen minutes on the English stage Goldin did more magic and more mischief than many others have done in a lifetime.

Even Devant's modern style—eliminating tricky-looking apparatus —could be taken to an extreme. One magician and writer glorified the good old days when stages looked colorful and apparatus were built specifically to look exotic and intriguing:

> Here in England we have many advocating the disuse of anything that looks magical. They advocate using ordinary, everyday articles, with the result that the stage would be littered with things from the kitchen, bedroom and sitting room. It all looks cheap and nasty.

•   •   •

Thurston could have performed his card act lucratively for many years in vaudeville, but he set his sights on a much more ambitious goal. He invested his money in an elaborate act, featuring a levitation illusion and a weird effect in which gallons of water gushed from an empty half-shell of a coconut. Thurston had no delusions about making marvels with "ordinary, everyday articles." He was creating an elaborate fantasy of an act, with impressive electrical, pyrotechnic, and fountain effects. He expensively included state-of-the-art lighting and exotic Oriental costumes; Thurston wore an Indian turban and a military jacket, suggesting an explorer returned from the distant empire.

Thurston was touring in Australia in 1906 when Mrs. Kellar, who had been traveling by herself in her homeland, saw the lavish show and recommended the magician to her husband. When Thurston heard of Kellar's plan to retire, he quickly wired him, suggesting that Kellar might consider him as a successor.

Thurston purchased Kellar's props and trunks, his route, and posters. Mostly, he purchased the right to be named America's leading magician. But after their one and only season together in the United States, Thurston surprised everyone by stripping the Kellar show of all its illusions except two, the Spirit Cabinet—an elaboration on the old Davenport act—and Kellar's remarkable Levitation. He admired Kellar but felt he was "the last of the old school magicians," later writing that in Kellar's show, "mystery came first with him; entertainment was not considered." Now Thurston was determined to rebuild the show according to his own galloping, entrepreneurial plan. The illusions became larger, the show faster and flashier, slowly taking on elements of a revue show, with novelty acts, musical numbers, and a growing cast.

Kellar received annual payments from Thurston, according to their contract for the show. He moved to Los Angeles, building a beautiful home, learning to drive a car, and sportfishing off the coast of Catalina Island. He became the revered dean of American magic, but in retirement he still habitually kept in touch with magicians, nervously following Thurston's show receipts and reviews, and was quick to offer his advice for new features. Kellar fretted over Thurston's rapid changes, feeling that he had unraveled many of the strongest parts of the show.

In particular, Kellar was horrified at the Levitation. The Levitation of Princess Karnac, "Mr. Kellar's Masterpiece," according to Thurston's earliest programs, was ideally suited to Thurston's beautiful voice and dramatic stage presence. But he never stopped tinkering with the routine, surrounding it with longer and longer presentations and tying it to other illusions. A number of years after obtaining the Kellar show, Thurston boldly changed the routine by describing the "Temples of Love" in India:

> On the seventh day of every seventh month in Alahabad, in Agra and Delhi, a high priest in the Temples of Love places a young lady in the air as I shall place this young lady in the air. Then lovers, lovers from all over the country who are not satisfied with their love affairs, who would like some mystic spell cast over the one they love or the one who loves them, gather into these temples for the blessings of the high priests. . . . Rest, Fernanda; dream, Fernanda; sleep, Fernanda.

With Fernanda, the Indian princess, suspended in the air, Thurston stepped to the footlights and broke the hypnotic silence by whispering a fascinating invitation to the audience:

> I am so anxious to convince you that she actually floats in space without any support, that this evening I shall ask on the stage a number of ladies and gentlemen. Anyone may come. Lawyers, doctors, scientists, students, those interested in the occult or mysterious: Come right down the aisle and on the stage; come as quietly as you can, please.

Once onstage, each spectator was taken to the floating princess and allowed to touch her ring as Thurston intoned a magical blessing:

> Hear me, hear me, each of you. I bring to you now the love blessing from India. Now is the chance to cause the one you love to love you. . . . Surakabaja, Surakabaja, Surakabaja.

It was an enchanting idea, and the presentation says a great deal about Thurston's stage presence, but Kellar exploded when he saw the new routine. He cursed the "crummy-looking people" who shambled up onto the stage and surrounded the floating princess, ruining the fairy-tale image of the illusion. Even worse, Kellar was reminded of his visit to Egyptian Hall: Anyone who stood beyond the spotlights could see the maze of wires responsible for the trick. Thurston was exposing the illusion to a handful of spectators each night.

Thurston depended on the spectators' being confused by what they saw, and, once on a stage, too awed to say anything; he also had a particular skill for "cueing," whispering cues or instructions under his breath, being able to direct the volunteers quietly. His novel presentation focused on the thousand people in the audience who did not step up onstage, calculating that by quietly exposing the trick to a few, he was creating a miracle for everyone else. Kellar, the famous perfectionist who once smashed a prop to pieces when one spectator whispered that he knew the secret, simply didn't understand this kind of math.

In later years, as Thurston continued to experiment with the Levitation, he eliminated the group of spectators, instead inviting one man and one little boy from the audience to come up on the stage. He led the man around the floating lady and then lifted the boy to touch the ring of the floating princess. For the finale he combined the illusion with Servais LeRoy's Garden of Sleep: The lady was covered with a cloth, floated high in the air near the footlights, and then disappeared suddenly as the cloth was pulled away. "She floats all over the stage and into the audience, then vanishes like a fading cloud," Thurston's posters proclaimed, with the requisite exaggeration.

A magician friend of mine was sitting at a diner one afternoon in the 1980s, when he started a conversation with the man next to him. It turns out that the man had, many years before as a little boy, been invited onto the stage during Thurston's famous Levitation. "What did you see?" my friend asked him. The man replied:

> *I saw more damn wires than I'd ever seen in my life! As Thurston lifted me up, he whispered, 'If you touch any of*

those blankety-blank wires. . . .' Well, I'd never heard lan-
guage like that in my life. At that moment, I opened my eyes
and my mouth wide, which made everyone in the audience
think that I was amazed at what I was seeing. They all
laughed and applauded. I was actually reacting to what
I'd just heard. You know, I couldn't have told my parents
what he'd said. They would have washed my mouth out
with soap.

Several magicians I've met remembered, with a certain horror, the occasional string of four-letter epithets from Thurston; with his particular eloquence, he could use them to good effect.

Kellar soon discovered another problem with his beloved Levitation. Two of his backstage assistants, Fritz and Carl Bucha, worked for one season with Thurston, then left to join another American illusionist, Charles Carter. Shortly after that, Carter suspiciously began performing his own Levitation, a perfect copy of Kellar's apparatus. It was obvious to everyone that the Bucha brothers had provided drawings of the apparatus for Carter—so obvious that Kellar, remembering how he had acquired the Levitation with Valadon's help, must have realized that this was his comeuppance. He kept his complaints private, which must have been difficult for the old master. In a letter to Thurston, he wrote,

Carter had the nerve to telegraph me for the stuff to blacken
wires, saying he was on a trip around the world. I didn't
even answer him as I might have said something I should
have been sorry for.

●　　●　　●

Kellar continually recommended specific ideas or personnel for the Thurston show; he was hoping that Thurston would improve the quality of the magic, which he always felt was carelessly presented. The retired magician persuaded Theo Bamberg to leave vaudeville for several years, giving up his Chinese magic to travel with Thurston. Bamberg presented his Hand Shadow act and developed new material, working as Thurston's "technical supervisor." More than likely, Kellar also suggested Guy Jarrett, an illusion builder and assistant, for Thurston's 1912 season.

Guy Jarrett wrote, "Kellar was so disappointed with the way Thurston botched up the show, he would take me out to eat somewhere and sit and cuss." Jarrett was one of the most colorful figures in magic, a "back-room boy" responsible for inventing and building illusions for leading performers. He was born in 1881 in Ohio and worked as a part-time telegraph operator and carnival pitchman in San Francisco just after the turn of the century. Jarrett had real talent for invention and—considering that he learned the fine points of the art on a sideshow platform—a surprisingly sophisticated approach to magic. Jarrett knew that people recognized hokum when they saw it, but they appreciated top-quality hokum, and he felt strongly that most magicians underestimated the intelligence and taste of their audiences.

Jarrett worked out each invention according to this formula and saw each illusion as a daring battle of wits with the audience. He built his apparatus meticulously, fitting and refitting the props to each assistant; he learned to work with wood, metal, resin, fabric, and glass, then painted the props like scenery so that they utilized the principles of highlight and camouflage to "cheat the eye."

After touring for one year with T. Nelson Downs, who attempted to enlarge his coin manipulation act with several stage illusions, Jarrett joined Thurston's company. Before the season started, Jarrett built several of his own illusions for the show at Thurston's Connecticut warehouse, including something he called the Siamese Cabinet, a small wooden closet that could be shown empty and then opened again to discharge nine people. As usual, Jarrett had worked it out down to the quarter inch, not only building in a secret compartment, but also squeezing the assistants inside a space that seemed impossibly small.

Thurston was never much of an originator, and although he was always desperate for new ideas, he had a tough time evaluating them. He went behind Jarrett's back, instructing the carpenters to add an additional eight inches to the dimensions of the cabinet, just to be sure that it was big enough. Thurston might have reasoned that if a cabinet looked empty, a big cabinet looked even emptier—magic is filled with these subjective sorts of guesses.

To Guy Jarrett, though, there was no guesswork, and fractions of inches were worthy of full-blown battles. He arrived the next day and, shaking his head, quietly sawed apart all the nicely doweled and glued panels, then reassembled the prop according to his original plans. "I can't remember a single time that Thurston was ever right about anything. He just didn't know," Jarrett often fumed.

Jarrett was a small, slender man, prematurely bald, with a serious expression and an intimidating squint. In Thurston's show he was a good, reliable performer who took part in the illusions he built; he was one of the nine assistants who emerged from the Siamese Cabinet.

In another illusion titled the Bangkok Bungalow, Jarrett performed a quick series of "here and there" appearances and disappearances. The presentation involved a narrow dollhouse in the shape of a tiny brownstone, which seemed big enough to just contain a medium-sized dog. During one disappearance Thurston insisted to the audience that Jarrett had been spirited inside the house. It was a ridiculous idea, of course, and the audience didn't believe it. They naturally suspected that Jarrett was hiding in the thick curtains of a magic cabinet. At the end of the routine, as the curtained cabinet was pulled apart to show that Jarrett had disappeared for one last time, the little house was effortlessly lifted by an assistant and tossed offstage into the wings. Seconds later Guy Jarrett reappeared in the aisle of the theatre.

The Bangkok Bungalow had an astonishing secret. During a crucial thirty seconds of the routine, Jarrett actually squeezed himself into the tiny house, like a contortionist. By then the audience had rejected the notion as a silly joke. The illusion was clinched when the house was picked up and tossed backstage. A fine, invisible steel wire, like the wires used to fly actors, was secretly clipped to the top of the house. As the onstage assistant lifted the little house, the wire was pulled as well, providing additional lift. This meant that the house could be picked up, carried, and tossed as if it weighed only a few pounds. Once safely in the wings, Jarrett ran around the side of the theatre and dashed down the aisle for his reappearance.

The routine was indicative of his thinking. Most magicians depend upon the audience's coming up short in their own explanations of illusions. They expect that people will never reach the point of understanding that cards can be held behind the hand, or that a mirror could be arranged inside a prop to deceive you, trusting such notions will be beyond them. Jarrett, who viewed magic as a great intellectual exercise, chose to present the secret to the audience, then forced them to rule it out in their own minds. This was how he guaranteed they would be fooled. As in the Bangkok Bungalow, a number of Jarrett's effects involved pointedly telling the audience how the trick was performed.

These sorts of routines, daring challenges, and delicate balances of lies and the truth can give performers weak knees. Thurston appreciated Jarrett's creativity, but Jarrett's hard-nosed, idealistic approach to illusion was something Thurston never understood. They worked together for only one season.

Shortly after Jarrett's year with Thurston, David Devant was on vacation in America and arranged a dinner with Jarrett. He had been impressed with his illusions in the Thurston show and wondered if Jarrett would be interested in working at St. George's Hall in London, creating magic for Maskelyne and Devant. Jarrett quickly proposed a salary of $30 per week, which was high enough to turn Devant red in the face and end the dinner with a long, uncomfortable silence. Jarrett shrugged, excused himself, and left the restaurant.

Jarrett moved to New York, creating illusions for vaudeville magicians and building props and special effects for Broadway shows and revues like "The Ziegfeld Follies" and "The Greenwich Village Follies." A 1914 newspaper article called him "the man with the know . . . whose brain builds the show for the big magician." Insiders knew Jarrett for his brilliant inventions and sought him out, but Jarrett was always cynical about what was happening to magic. He later wrote:

> *I have spoken personally to every magician . . . and there is not a single one with the desire or ambition to become great, or famous, or to earn real money. . . . Not a single one has guts or ideas or imagination. They just got hold of a bunch of*

*tricks and walked out on stage. So, they are only a bunch
of "drug store magicians."*

•   •   •

Jarrett was an uneasy collaborator, but Thurston and Devant forged a
successful relationship. The magicians were just over a year apart in
age and both had, within a short period of time, been proclaimed the
greatest magicians of their respective countries. The feud between
Kellar and Maskelyne seemed to have also created a good-natured truce
between Thurston and Devant, the second-generation wizards who
were now proud to make a point of their cooperation and camaraderie.

Thurston and Devant swapped ideas and professional advice.
Because he was always hungry for new material and unable to invent
his own magic, Thurston naturally depended on Devant for new
effects, and early in his career he presented a number of Devant's specialties, including the New Page, the man who turned upside down
inside the tiny box; the Problem of Diogenes, the production of an
assistant from an empty barrel; and the Window of a Haunted House,
Devant's masterful illusion in which hazy scenes of people came to
life inside an isolated window frame.

Thurston reciprocated by advising Devant where he could purchase
illusions. He also sent an account of one specific trick from his own
show. Thurston invited two children, a little girl and a little boy,
onstage to help him. He showed a bowler hat empty, then reached
inside and produced eggs. The eggs were handed to the little girl, who
in turn was instructed to place each egg in the arms of the little boy.
Thurston quickly produced more and more eggs from the hat, pretending to ignore the struggles of the children to hold them all. As
eggs fell and broke on the stage, the audience roared with laughter.

Pulling eggs from a hat: It wasn't much of a trick. But the situation
complemented Thurston's onstage rapport with children and his sense
of humor. In his show he didn't tell jokes; he presided over ridiculous,
magical situations with a kind of magisterial grace—which made the
tricks even funnier.

When Quentin Roosevelt, the son of President Theodore Roosevelt, was about ten years old he volunteered for Thurston's egg trick at a show in Washington, D.C. Quentin was a fan of Thurston's and had seen the trick before. As Thurston began producing eggs, Quentin reached under his coat and pulled out a large cloth sack, to ensure that he wouldn't drop any of the eggs. This in turn received even more laughs.

Thurston enthusiastically detailed the routine for Devant, urging him to use it:

> *This trick, if properly presented, will create as much talk as anything I have ever seen performed on the magic stage. It will also bring the children and increase your matinee business. If there is anything not perfectly clear in your mind, or if you cannot get seven minutes of good solid laughter from the trick, let me hear from you . . . and I will do what I can for you.*

The trick suited Devant even better than it had Thurston, and Boy, Girl, and Eggs, as Devant called it, became one of his most famous effects.

The slight differences in their routines gave evidence of their different approaches. Thurston's trick depended upon his silently cueing the children, guaranteeing certain responses during the routine:

> *[Calling to the boy in the aisle:] "Take the little girl by the arm and lead her down the aisle. You may as well start now, as you will have to do it later in life.*
>
> *"Now I have something to tell you. Hear me and pay attention, Jack, Alice. Listen. You are now standing on the magic carpet." (Here say to the boy and girl, so the audience does not hear, "Step back off the carpet.") [When they do so, the audience will] laugh. Place boy and girl on carpet again.*
>
> *"Now Jack, Alice, the only difference: You cannot see the same as I can see. For example, the air is full of eggs. Everywhere you look here are eggs, but you cannot see them."*

(Here quietly tell boy and girl to look around as if looking for eggs. Another laugh.)

At Devant's smaller theatre, it was more difficult to whisper cues without being heard, so the humor of the routine became gentler and more direct. For example, he started by softening the joke about leading the girl down the aisle. "Make her your best bow, give her your arm, and escort her down the aisle." As the children walked toward the stage, the band struck up Mendelssohn's "Wedding March"; the audience laughed because the children were oblivious to the joke.

Typically, Devant showed an expert's touch by deemphasizing the hat. He wanted to make the hat seem incidental to the routine, knowing that the audience would later remember that eggs had been produced in his hand.

> I made a great point of the development of the eggs by using the hat as a cover; there was no suggestion that I produced the eggs from the hat. "Can you see those little white atoms floating about in the air? I don't suppose you can. They are quite invisible except to a magician. All a magician has to do is to catch one of them, develop it, and it becomes an egg. Supposing I had caught an atom like this. . . . I use this old hat as a developing chamber; all I have to do is cover my hand for a moment with this hat and the atom becomes an egg, you see."

In 1912 the variety artists of Great Britain—jugglers, ventriloquists, acrobats, and singers—were honored by a request for their first Royal Command Performance; Devant was paid a considerable compliment of being the only magician who appeared on the bill. He could have included a number of large illusions or his most spectacular effects. Instead, he performed only two tricks, one in which an image materialized in a cheval mirror, and the Boy, Girl, and Eggs, knowing that this tiny bit of magic would quickly emphasize his strengths as a performer.

• • •

Both Thurston and Devant realized that routines like the egg trick might be audience favorites and deliver "seven minutes of good solid laughter," but it was the floating ladies, the tricks with pianos, horses, motorcycles, and marching soldiers that brought people to the theatre. Like his American counterpart, Devant was always in search of a new idea that would sell tickets—ultimately, this was his greatest value to his partners, the Maskelyne family. In 1912, shortly after his command performance, he happened to find one of these illusions. Devant was stunned to discover that it was the latest invention of a ghost.

11
Solomon

A conjuring performance cannot be properly appreciated by anyone who does not know something about the art.
—David Devant

I n 1981 the magician Doug Henning hired me as his magic designer, responsible for creating new effects for an upcoming television special and his second Broadway show, "Merlin." During the eight months that it played at the Mark Hellenger Theatre, "Merlin" became famous as an over-budget, overstuffed, and confused Broadway spectacle. Mixing a musical score with illusions was certainly a complication, but that was also the most interesting part of the experiment.

From its earliest drafts, "Merlin" was brimming with wonderful illusions. Doug Henning, a creator and the star of the show, worked to ensure that the magic would be breathtaking. A gigantic suit of armor, assembled of different pieces, came to life and walked off the stage. A horse and rider were raised high in the air in a wooden cart, then disappeared as the cart broke open. Seconds later the horse and rider reappeared on the opposite side of the stage. A black panther paced the perimeter inside a small gold cage. The cage was covered for several seconds and then uncovered to show that the panther had been transformed into a lady.

Each of these illusions posed enormous challenges—bigger, faster, and more amazing. As the illusions were integrated into the story, we were constantly working to deemphasize the apparatus so it would become part of the scenery.

Doug had decided that he wanted to perform David Devant's Mascot Moth as a part of a dream sequence in "Merlin." At that time the illusion hadn't been seen onstage for about forty years; it had been over sixty years since Devant himself last performed it. Our only information regarding the technical details came from a brief description in Devant's book, *Secrets of My Magic*. Together with John Gaughan, an expert in creating apparatus for professional magicians, we tried to transcribe Devant's few words into the necessary catches, traps, and footwork.

It was slow going. We cursed Devant for giving us perilously little information—nothing of any real substance. He offered no drawings, just a brief description of the sliding tube, an elevator trap, and some wire supporting the costume. The art to the illusion would be that in some indefinable way these coarse bits of metal and fabric would not only fit together but be integrated into a smooth, dreamlike vision. Standing in a workshop, surrounded by real props that were made of welded metal and painted wood, the Mascot Moth seemed to be mostly nothing at all.

Starting with the metal for the tube, we could determine the size and shape of the costume. Building a small rectangle of the stage floor in the shop, we could discover the size of the trapdoor and where the technicians could stand beneath it. Catches were tested and installed. Handles were moved. Springs were tightened. Metal surfaces were padded so that they wouldn't snap or clink in the silent seconds before the illusion.

At John's Los Angeles workshop, the result was an ungainly tower of steel tubing, eight feet tall, which contained the necessary traps and tracks. Overhead a sheet of four-by-eight-foot plywood was the staging area. By climbing a ladder and dodging the overhead beams, we could "perform" the illusion and test the apparatus, shouting at the technicians who were pulling on ropes underneath, dancing Devant's choreography around the tiny, wobbly stage.

With every step, we returned to Devant's description and were amazed to find more and more information. It was magical how the illusion became clearer and clearer as we re-read his text; Devant had implied subtle motions on the stage and the step-by-step work of the men operating it beneath the stage. We realized that Devant had fooled us badly, not by concealing information but by mysteriously hinting at it all:

> In one of my various journeys to the lady, I picked out the reel and dropped it down the tube which was behind her, then I fitted the plug into the tube, she having folded her wings across her face and locked them together. . . . My part of it was to get my left foot in front of the tube, which was facilitated by two stops let into the boards.

When the apparatus was finished, we were amazed at how much had been spelled out in his elegant, mysterious little paragraph. The efficiency of his description became apparent only when we were actually standing next to the equipment.

The Moth was the last illusion completed for "Merlin," a product of nervous experiments and constant second-guessing. The apparatus was taken apart and shipped to New York. The wire head-and-shoulder framework for the lady was sent off to be dressed inside a white silk costume. The metal tower was carefully lowered through a new show deck, an elaborate construction that replaced the current stage at the Mark Hellenger Theatre.

Other illusions could be approximated in the rehearsal hall, but when we came to the scene with the Moth, we could only stumble through the motions. These awkward rehearsals made the illusion seem even more mysterious and unmanageable. One afternoon I arranged with the stage managers for a secret rehearsal on the theatre stage, a quiet opportunity to test the apparatus and turn it over to our two magic technicians, Steve Kirsner and Willie Kennedy, so they could feel their way through it. No stars, no producers or directors. We swore our small team to secrecy, packed the rehearsal costume in a bag, and brought one of the dancers as we took the subway uptown from our rehearsal space on 19th Street. We met at the stage door, where the set was still being installed.

That evening in the Mark Hellenger, faced with an expanse of smooth, black floor, our job once again seemed frightening and intimidating. The apparatus had been swallowed up and completely disappeared beneath the stage—no tower of machinery, no staging area, no visual cause and effect. The stage floor separated the illusion into two separate worlds. Once again it seemed as if we had nothing at all.

During our secret rehearsal we worked through the cues mechanically, again and again, anticipating how we could combine the apparatus with the people. We learned that the Mascot Moth balanced fractional inches and split seconds. It could be accomplished only by four people working in perfect unison. Two people, the magician and the lady, worked above the stage, sliding into each mark, ensuring that the catches and connections were secure. Most important, they placed their bodies in the precise positions—second by second—to achieve the illusion. Beneath the stage two other people, Steve and

Willie, "performed" the apparatus. Many of the overlapping cues could be accomplished only by a sense of touch, feeling the weight of the lady on the trap, easing the tube into place, pulling the wire framework and costume through the tube in one smooth motion.

After a dozen rehearsals, after watching the illusion from various spots in the theatre, we bundled up the costume and left. We were all quiet, our stomachs in knots. We scattered at the stage door, anticipating the work ahead of us.

In "Merlin," with Doug Henning and his wife, Debby, performing the Mascot Moth onstage, it always seemed to me that this delicate illusion belied the notion of a mechanical trick. It was the manipulation of human beings, the equal of Valadon's sleight of hand with ivory billiard balls or Thurston's fancy palms and flourishes with playing cards, an art of synchronized intangibles.

In 1911 Devant and Nevil Maskelyne, the Chief's son, joined to write a book on magic. By that time Maskelyne and Devant's Magic had become a popular brand name in England. Playing off their trademark, the book was simply titled *Our Magic*, by Maskelyne and Devant.

Our Magic was a remarkable book with an astonishing premise. The authors intended to change the perception of the art, and invited readers to know everything about magic. Everything. As they explained in the introduction,

> *So far from feeling any reluctance toward letting the general public into the secrets of our procedure, we are most anxious to educate the public on such matters, in order that a proper understanding of our art may be disseminated among its votaries and patrons. The point is this. Tricks and dodges are of comparatively small importance in the art of magic. At the utmost, they display inventive ability, but nothing more. We hope that even the man in the street will have learned the fact that so-called "secrets" are to the magician little more than are, to the actor, the wigs, grease-paints and other make-up with which he prepares himself for appearance*

before the public. . . . Those devices are merely his work-
ing tools.

•   •   •

But beyond their introduction, *Our Magic* was significant in what it told the readers about Nevil Maskelyne and David Devant. There had been no collaboration in their writing. The thick book was divided almost perfectly in half. Nevil Maskelyne had written the first two sections, titled "The Art in Magic" and "The Theory of Magic." Always a reluctant performer, he had none of his father's taste for old-fashioned showmanship. Instead, he took an analytical approach to illusions. Nevil always fancied himself a scientist, inventor, and entrepreneur; in the book he defined terms, offered authoritative rules, suggested categories, and gave examples of principles. Promoting magic as a performing art, he quoted Aristotle. Explaining the steps of rehearsal, he quoted Tolstoy. His sections were often dry and occasionally pretentious or artistically vague. Maskelyne suggested that the climax should generally be at the end of the effect, the performer should work quickly but not too quickly, and say just enough but not too much:

> [Rule 12] *Although the antagonistic elements of surprise and repetition can scarcely be combined to produce a single effect, we may readily combine them in a presentation which comprises a dual effect. And, beyond doubt, that may be done, not only without confusion, but also with a marked amplification of the impression created.*

The remainder of the book, "The Practice of Magic," was written completely by Devant. In these chapters Devant decided to instruct by example, perfectly explaining twelve of his popular routines—every detail that was involved in performing these effects for an audience:

> *In the same way that the Japanese art collector does not confuse the senses of his visitors by exhibiting several specimens of one class of object, but submits one, and only one*

at a time, so it is our intention in each of these chapters, to give one example of a complete and practical illusion.

Indulging in few generalities, Devant explained the thinking behind his illusions, the necessary preparations and bits of manipulation, and the humorous lines of patter that he used. His advice was elegantly simple and sensible. Explaining his specific sequence for manipulating ivory billiard balls at his fingertips and causing them to multiply, Devant wrote,

> *The manipulator finds the temptation strong upon him to linger lovingly over sleights, passes and palms galore, whilst losing sight of the ultimate effect on the mind of his audience. We do not remember ever to have seen an illusion with billiard balls in which the effect was not blurred by this sort of thing instead of being made to stand out in relief like a clearly cut cameo. On being asked afterwards what the conjurer did with a billiard ball, the spectator probably replied, "Oh, all sorts of things."*

His offbeat, friendly humor became a cliché for the next generation of magicians, who copied his patter for their own performances. Urging a small boy up to the stage, Devant told him, "Make haste; don't hurry. That's right. Now come up here. Bring the other leg with you." Or placing a watch into a paper bag and handing it to the boy: "I do this myself because I do these things so gracefully, don't I? Like an elephant getting off a bicycle on a muddy day. Now will you hold the bag so and stay like that for about three-quarters of an hour, if you don't mind?"

In the end the book never changed the perception of magic. It was both too vague and too specific to be of use to the public. Audiences were amused by magic shows but weren't interested in analyzing them. *Our Magic* did become a revered textbook for magicians. Maskelyne had done his best to argue that magic was an art. Devant demonstrated that it could sometimes rise to the occasion.

• • •

John Nevil Maskelyne officially retired in 1911, leaving most of the important business decisions to his son, Nevil, and Devant. It should have been a smooth transition, but unofficially, the Chief's strong opinions continued to influence every program. He even lived in an apartment above the Maskelyne and Devant theatre in Langham Place.

The most serious complication for the company was Devant's growing popularity and success. In 1911, during the summer break in London, Devant accepted several music hall appearances outside of London. Will Goldston, a London magic dealer and the editor of a journal for magicians, selfishly urged him to stay at the Maskelyne and Devant theatre:

> *A rumor reaches us that David Devant has received and is considering a very tempting offer of a long Music Hall engagement. We sincerely hope that he will not yield to the temptation. Stay at the English Home of Magic. We London magicians [are] more discriminating [than] the average Music Hall audience. You are for us, Mr. Devant, not for them.*

Devant was a feature in the halls throughout Great Britain, with a full fifty-minute program of his magic. Despite Goldston's advice, Devant followed with another season on the road and included several of his illusions, mind-reading effects, comedic routines with children, and the dramatic sketch "The Artist's Dream." This had been Devant's first effect for Maskelyne, created almost twenty years earlier. For his music hall work he had improved it, speeded up the presentation, and presented the entire sequence in pantomime. In the sketch he portrayed an artist painting a large portrait of his deceased wife. He finished his work, covered the painting with a large piece of drapery, and fell asleep. As he dreamt, a Spirit of Mercy appeared to him, entering the room and drawing back the curtain over the painting. The image of his wife had left the background and was now standing in front of the canvas. Awakening, Devant reached out to her as she disappeared back into the canvas, once again a two-dimensional image. He turned to approach the ghostly Spirit of Mercy, who was now standing in the center of the stage. He reached to embrace her, and she disappeared in a flash. As the music swelled, Devant collapsed on the stage as if dead.

For the new climax of the sketch, Devant used the apparatus from his Mascot Moth illusion, rearranged within the setting of "The Artist's Dream." The music hall shows were lucrative engagements for the Maskelyne and Devant Company as well as Devant himself, but his growing success and his lucrative contracts meant that, ironically, he was able to spend less and less time on the small stage at St. George's Hall.

John Nevil Maskelyne had always been disdainful of music hall entertainments, considering them cheap and ordinary. He had disagreed with Devant over the inclusion of jugglers and acrobats, typical music hall fare, in the programs at St. George's Hall. His preference was for a more relaxed program, emphasizing slower presentations, elegant conjuring, or magic plays. But the success of music halls was signaled by the 1912 Music Hall Royal Command performance— variety performers invited to perform before George V and Queen Mary. It was at this command performance that Devant presented Thurston's egg trick, and his stardom was set in stone.

That proved to be a problem for the Maskelyne family. Since 1873 the Maskelyne name had meant magic in London. If Devant's fame brought new prestige to the Maskelyne and Devant Company, it must have inspired jealousy as well. The famous Maskelynes had been eclipsed by their junior partner.

Will Goldston, disappointed that Devant was now seldom seen in London, continued to pen long editorials honoring the magician. He even proposed that the theatre in Langham Place be renamed St. David's Hall. Devant became an expert at shrugging off these embarrassing compliments and getting down to work. As managing director, he still felt responsible for keeping St. George's Hall's program filled with new illusions. Often he introduced these effects at the hall before turning them over to other performers, like the Maskelyne sons.

Once, in conversation with a Scottish magician, Devant mentioned that he would pay money for a fresh idea for an illusion—the idea was everything, as far as he was concerned. The Scottish magician returned the next night and suggested that Devant make a motorcycle and rider disappear while the engine was rumbling and popping. Devant nodded and wrote the magician a check for 10 pounds. Even without a solution, he knew that the plot was a valuable one.

Months later Devant introduced Biff, the disappearing motorcycle and rider. When the curtains opened, the audience saw a large packing box raised off the stage on blocks. A motorcycle and rider rode on from the wings, circling the stage. The rider, adorned in leather riding boots, cap, and goggles, roared up a short ramp and into the box, which was made of vertical wooden slats. With engine idling, the box shook ominously. The end of the crate was closed, and it was slowly pulled into the air on ropes.

Meanwhile, Devant busied himself at the side of the stage with a strange sort of electric light. He insisted that his mysterious green lamp was a notable improvement on the X rays or theoretical "death rays" that had recently been in the headlines. He switched on his "D.D. Ray" and carefully aimed it at the side of the wooden crate, which was now high above the stage.

The suspended box continued to rumble, as exhaust fumes oozed from between the boards. The box was bathed in a circle of green light from Devant's lamp, when the engine suddenly stopped. The crate seemed to explode into its component parts, dropping planks of wood into an ever-increasing pile of loose timber on the stage. The empty framework swung quietly in the air. The motorcycle and rider were gone.

In June 1912, when Devant was playing the Empire Theatre in Newcastle, he motored over to the town of Hexham. There Devant visited a former employee, who told him that there was a conjurer playing in town. Devant was always curious to see a new magician, so that afternoon he went to the rented store that was serving as a makeshift theatre. Devant approached cautiously. The dingy Hexham storefront was a far cry from the sparkling music halls of his tour. Gazing up at the improvised sign, Devant noticed the oversized painted letters, which made him smile: "The Disappearing Donkey." It was a good idea for a trick, he thought. It had a nice, distinctive alliteration; it suggested a clear, interesting image in the mind of the audience, Devant nodded to himself. He could easily imagine it printed on a stone lithograph. As he took several steps further, he noticed the name of the magician on the top line, "Professor Charles Morritt Presents."

Devant froze as if he'd seen a ghost. Morritt, he had believed, was dead. It was many years since the grand old knight of British magic had been heard from—almost twenty years since his appearances in London, when he left Maskelyne's Egyptian Hall and arrogantly worked in opposition down the street. It was Morritt's departure that allowed Devant his first audition for Maskelyne. Like every other magician in London, Devant knew of Morritt's drinking problem. He hadn't been surprised when the rumor had quickly spread through London that Morritt was dead. Devant wondered whether this was an impostor in Hexham. Still, the very title, "The Disappearing Donkey," seemed particularly authentic, especially worthy of the ingenious Yorkshire Conjurer.

Devant hesitated and then rapped on the door. There was a rattle of activity inside, the sound of a bolt being thrown, and the door swung open in the midday sun. It was Charles Morritt. The same Charles Morritt. He was jamming on his coat, adjusting his high silk hat as he stopped to squint at his visitor. Morritt broke into a broad smile.

To Devant, he seemed like a ghost; the magician's translucent skin was now lined with age, but his back was straight, and his eyes twinkled with recognition. Devant was quickly ushered inside. Morritt was delighted to meet the new managing director of the Maskelyne theatre, and he teased him with his recollections of the Chief and the fickle London public. Devant was happy to rediscover this magician of his youth and clearly felt a debt to the seasoned professional.

As Morritt explained, despite the rumors of his demise he had been working continuously. After his productions in London and problems with his health, he returned to theatre management in the provinces and, when prospects were lean, engaged in various publicity tricks to earn a few pounds. The previous year, he told Devant, he had presented his old hypnotic stunt, a Man in a Trance, which was always good for a quick profit. In Glasgow he found a volunteer who agreed to be hypnotized for 13 days and 12 nights, remaining in a silent, unfeeling, cataleptic state. During that time members of the public could visit backstage and examine the man. It was a cheap attraction, Morritt shrugged, but it still sold tickets. When the chips were down, it always sold tickets.

"I've actually turned the corner now, with a good, solid string of effects—a quality program in the works," Morritt told Devant with a wink. Devant was surprised by the optimism of his host, who seemed as proud and comfortable in the dusty storefront as if he were backstage at the Coliseum. Devant noticed Morritt's frayed collar and cuffs.

"Would you like to see the Donkey?" Morritt whispered. Devant nodded. "The Donkey!" the old magician called out to his assistants backstage. Devant pushed aside several empty chairs, taking a seat in the center of the room, as Morritt tugged open the curtain.

On the stage stood an assistant wearing a white Pierrot clown costume. He held the reins of the star of the show: a common, stubborn, and wholly disinterested English gray donkey. His name, Morritt explained, was Solomon. He was a sort of genius of his race, the world's only disappearing donkey. Solomon contemplated his London visitor beyond the footlights with the perfect mixture of boredom and malice, batting his long eyelashes and responding with a twitch or stomp.

Morritt's Disappearing Donkey illusion

Just behind the donkey was a brightly painted wooden stable raised on legs. The front of the stable was closed with two wooden doors; the back was closed with a draw curtain. There were also doors in the sides. Morritt reached into the wings and picked up two wooden hoops, each about three feet wide, that had been covered with stretched linen. One of these hoops was hung on cords just behind the stable. Leaning forward into the lights, he pointed out to Devant how this hoop would form a barrier behind the stable, a sort of target to demonstrate that the donkey couldn't leave by jumping out the back. The second hoop was slid under the stable, eliminating the suggestion of a trapdoor in the stage.

With a long riding crop in his hand, Morritt urged on Solomon with compliments and entreaties that, with a blink, went ignored. The clown pulled on the reins. The donkey resisted, locking its legs, arching its neck, and kicking wildly. Inch by inch it was slid into the end of the stable. The clown quickly jumped out, leaving the donkey alone inside, as Morritt slammed the doors. Instead of the sound of footfalls, instead of the expected explosion of hooves on wooden panels, there was a sudden silence. "Open it up!" Morritt yelled to Pierrot. The doors were swung open, and the curtains pulled aside. The stable was completely empty, surrounded by the fabric hoops, which could still be clearly seen. The clown jumped into the stable, hinging up the roof to show that the structure was empty and unprepared.

Morritt bowed deeply, and Devant clapped for the old showman. The donkey had provided a masterful bit of showmanship, and audiences of 1912, not far removed from horses, donkeys, and mules, would have appreciated the intractable beast who was so perfectly uncooperative and then so suddenly, magically, under the wizard's control. "It's good, isn't it?" Morritt asked, climbing down off the stage. "Yes, Charlie, it's very good." In fact, the illusion probably mystified Devant, who might have realized what Morritt was doing, even if he didn't know exactly how. It seemed like Morritt had stumbled onto something really new. "I was just thinking," Devant continued, "how this would look at St. George's Hall."

As managing director, Devant was completely responsible for deciding what was onstage at the theatre in London. He was free to engage Morritt, his Donkey, and any of his other ideas. By hiring Morritt, Devant was able to place an energetic, inventive magician at the helm of St. George's Hall and ease much of his own burden. Politically, it was an interesting choice. Morritt was an old associate of the Chief, but his tastes were surprisingly modern. To Devant, Morritt was an ally, helping to counteract some of the old-fashioned choices of the Maskelyne family.

When Morritt first appeared at St. George's Hall in the summer of 1912, reviewers naturally recalled the good old days, commenting on Morritt's slightly nostalgic evening clothes, with his high, stiff collar and square-cut tailcoat. If John Nevil Maskelyne was pleased to see Morritt attracting an audience, he was also reminded of the Yorkshire Conjurer's stubbornness. Twenty years earlier at Egyptian Hall, Morritt had once been a loyal associate, but he then became an ungrateful employee and a competitor down the street, playing in opposition to Maskelyne and Cooke, grabbing headlines by offering to make the Tichborne Claimant disappear every evening.

The Disappearing Donkey became a favorite with the audience, and part of its popularity was the donkey itself. Many mentioned how impossible it seemed that the donkey could be so strangely cooperative. "With never so much as the sound of a departing hoof," one review commented, it was "as if the intelligent creature had discovered the secret of the fourth dimension." Morritt was careful to demonstrate that no one was concealed inside the stable at the beginning of the illusion. Then the clown led the donkey up the ramp and instantly jumped out again, leaving Solomon alone inside for the disappearance. Morritt only added to the mystery by claiming that he depended "on the donkey working the mechanism for the trick."

The donkey was the source of several adventures. Jasper Maskelyne, the grandson of the Chief, later wrote how one evening, just before it was due to step onstage, the donkey found an open door backstage and sauntered out into the night. At the last minute the magician discovered the escape route, and a squadron of stagehands and performers organized a search party as the show continued at St. George's Hall. They found the animal standing beneath a streetlamp, window shopping on Oxford Street, and escorted it back just in time for its appointment onstage.

A sleight-of-hand magician named Edward Victor was in the Maskelyne repertory company of magicians, which meant that he was occasionally called upon to present one of the feature tricks. One night he was performing the Disappearing Donkey. He took the animal through its paces, slammed it inside the stable, and then dramatically threw open the doors, pronouncing that it had disappeared. Instead, he found the donkey was still there, blinking back at him. Victor later explained to friends that a stagehand responsible for operating the apparatus had fallen asleep. He contemplated the situation and announced to the audience, "I promised to show you a disappearing donkey, so here I go!" He turned on his heel and walked off the stage.

Devant liked the illusion enough to rebuild it for his own show, and he presented it in his music hall tours with a donkey he named Magic. Today we have quite a bit of information about this trick. We have rough sketches of both Morritt and Devant performing it. Devant's version was almost exactly the same as Morritt's, but his stable had doors at the back instead of curtains. Devant's notes for his presentation have survived, and these include his stage directions about how the doors were shut and how the clown pulled the donkey inside.

There's also a hint at a secret. Devant's notes give the cues for the stagehands responsible for the magic. From those instructions, "two assistants beneath stage" were operating the apparatus. They raised a "fake" just before the donkey entered. *Fake* is a technical term used by magicians to indicate something that the audience actually looks at but camouflaged or prepared to look like something else. If the fake were raised, it probably meant that some sort of door or container was lifted or opened by the stagehands. As the stable seemed to be isolated in the middle of the stage, the assistants were concealed downstairs, below the stage, and performed their duties through some opening in the floor. The fake was then lowered again before the stable door was re-opened, and the illusion was completed. This also corresponds with Edward Victor's story of the sleeping stagehand.

Those are the clues. The audience was looking at some sort of construction that was camouflaged. It was raised before the donkey stepped inside, then lowered again so that the donkey seemed to disappear. But other than those tantalizing details, we don't really know how Solomon accomplished his trick. We don't know what the fake was or how the donkey moved around it. We don't know if the donkey ended up hidden onstage or backstage or beneath the stage.

It's rare for a stage illusion to remain such a secret, particularly a popular illusion that had been performed for a number of years and by several different entertainers. It probably indicates that technically, it was a very good trick—deceiving a number of magicians who watched it. If it had simply been a variation on another principle or a twist on an old secret, other performers would have recognized this and recorded it. Morritt once boasted to a friend, "There is no man [who] could make this illusion [unless] he actually measures it, so there is no fear of imitation." In other words, the inventor considered the secret quite exceptional, impossible to discern unless the apparatus were to be studied in detail.

At the same time, the fact that this illusion has remained such a secret is also evidence that it was probably not a great trick, neither so sensational nor dramatically different that competitors went out of their way to study it or question others about how it was done. Perhaps magicians had been fooled but not terribly impressed. In other words, there was something about the Disappearing Donkey that was just clever enough and not too clever—allowing it to slip through the cracks and remain a perfect mystery.

During his years back on the London stage, Morritt collaborated with Devant on several other interesting effects. One was titled Beauty and the Beast. A low, round table with open legs, like a large Moorish stool, was shown to the audience. A bell-shaped cage of gauze was shown, collapsed flat and empty. The gauze bell was then suspended on a cord over the table so that it covered the tabletop like an oversized beehive. Devant busied himself with another small flower trick and, moments later, turned his attention back to the gauze cage. Electric lights inside the gauze slowly began to glow, turning it transparent. The audience was amazed to see a brief scene being enacted atop the table. A princess approached a rose bush, ready to pick a flower. Lurking behind the bush, a bearlike beast lunged at her. To the surprise of the audience, the princess threw her arms around the beast and kissed it. This immediately transformed the beast into a handsome prince. The gauze bell was raised, showing the two actors. They stepped down off the table to take their bow.

Charles Morritt was also the creator of an illusion called Ragtime Magic. A wide tabletop, about waist-height, extended right to left across the stage. Standing behind the table at equal intervals were four men. The tabletop was thin, and the men's legs were visible behind the table. Each man held a framework box about the size of a small trunk, which rested on the table. Working with military precision, the four assistants rotated their boxes, opened them, showed them empty, slid them together and apart, and spaced them evenly across the table. Morritt blew a whistle, then reached inside each box to produce yards and yards of silk. These were the "rags" suggested by the title. Finally, all four boxes were lifted. Although the boxes were empty just moments before, now each contained a ragtime musician. The four Mystic Minstrels stood up, stepped off the table, and played several jazzy selections for the audience.

In many ways these illusions were similar to other concoctions of Morritt's and Devant's, with the same mix of commercial appeal and practical theatrics. Ragtime Magic played on the then-current recent craze for ragtime music, a good excuse to include the band in the per- formances at Maskelyne and Devant's theatre. Beauty and the Beast has the unmistakable touch of David Devant—the overlapping of large and small illusions into one scene, the fairy-tale characters, the the- atrical "vision," which appears as a hazy image behind the gauze and then turns out to be real.

Charles Morritt's contributions were clearly the secrets behind these illusions. It's now apparent that during his years away from London, in experiments in waxwork museums and storefronts, he was still liberally making use of optical principles. Devant explained how Beauty and the Beast was accomplished:

> *I daresay you have been able to guess the secrets of this illusion.*

Devant might have thought an explanation was hardly necessary to anyone interested in magic. As in many other illusions, it was done with mirrors:

> *In the first place two sheets of mirror glass are placed under- neath the octagonal platform. They meet at the top end, that*

is, the end farthest from the audience, and open out gradu-
ally towards the end nearest the audience.

In other words, a triangle of mirrors concealed a space between the
legs of the table, the basic theory used in Tobin and Stodare's Sphinx
many years before:

> *They are in fact open wide enough at that end for the prince*
> *to climb up through the opening provided in the stage,*
> *having climbed up on the top of the platform. (You must*
> *remember that there was nothing seen through the bell until*
> *the lights were put on inside.) The prince now hands the*
> *lady up.*

The actors started beneath the stage and climbed through a trap door.
Mirrors were necessary so they wouldn't be seen between the legs of
the table.

According to Devant, more space was gained through an additional
bit of camouflage:

> *The [table] legs not being quite enough to conceal the*
> *opening between the glasses, a small pair of steps is requi-*
> *sitioned, and these are put in front and conceal the extra*
> *space taken up. They are put carelessly sideways so that*
> *they should not be suspect.*

• • •

Devant made it sound easy, ordinary, old-fashioned. "I daresay you
have been able to guess the secrets of this illusion" was a particularly
disarming phrase. In fact, Devant was adept at concealing a great deal
by explaining it all, and his description of Beauty and the Beast hinted
at Charles Morritt's amazing discovery. The key phrase was that the
two mirrors met "at the top end, that is, the end farthest from
the audience, and open out gradually towards the end nearest the

audience." In other words, the mirrors were facing backwards and were at the wrong angle for a reflection.

If magicians had really read carefully and understood Devant's words, they might have thought it was a misprint. A mistake. Based on fifty years of optical illusions, it simply shouldn't have worked.

12
Houdini

It's not the trick. It's the magician.
—Harry Houdini

agicians only do certain things.

They can make things appear; they can make things disappear. They can cause an object to transpose from one place to another; of course, this is really the same as making something appear in one place while a duplicate object disappears somewhere else. They can cause an object to be transformed, becoming something else. Again, this is a variation of an appearance and disappearance.

Objects float. They can be destroyed, cut apart, or divided and then restored. They can be magically animated in some way, moving by themselves. One object can penetrate another. The magician can demonstrate something that seems to violate a natural law—like a living head or a ghost. Or the magician can simulate mind reading or psychic phenomena.

That's ten possibilities. Depending on the definitions, other magicians have reduced the possibilities to as few as seven or expanded them to nineteen, but it ends up being a surprisingly short list. Similarly, analysts have pointed out that there are only a handful of elemental plots in fiction, a dozen basic jokes, and eighty-eight keys on a piano.

But just as every story isn't worthy of being put on a stage, or every sentiment translated into lyrics, not every impossibility is suitable for entertainment. Great magic captivates an audience with a simple plot, a situation that offers a thoughtful challenge, provides conflict, and offers a distinct climax and a surprise. The very best effects have a sort of mythic connection with the audience, appealing because they combine symbols in an appealing way. That's why Walking through a Brick Wall, an illusion introduced by the British magician P.T. Selbit and later performed by Houdini, was captivating for audiences. It's why Biff, the Disappearing Motorcycle, was especially appealing. A motorcycle was noisy, a fast and dangerous novelty. The idea of containing and controlling it through magic seemed particularly impossible. Similarly, Charles Morritt's Disappearing Donkey was an attractive idea. Everyone knew that donkeys couldn't be handled, that they were stubborn and ornery.

When magicians invent their illusions, they usually follow a certain formula: think of something completely impossible, then figure out a way to apparently accomplish it.

David Devant clearly approached the job as a playwright or story-teller. To him the effect was everything. "I would find a means of doing the trick if I could get a suggestion of what to do." This was why he offered to pay for any novel effect and why he accepted the challenge to make a motorcycle disappear on the stage. Once he had determined a good, captivating image for the audience, he solved the problem by applying a method. It also meant that he treated secrets with a certain abandon, using the most convenient techniques to solve his problems.

One of those possible techniques used a mirror. The optical princi-ples first used by Thomas Tobin at the Polytechnic had become second nature to magicians by 1900: 45 degrees plus 45 degrees equaled 90 degrees. Tobin's kind of mirror illusion not only was useful to profes-sional magicians but had become abused and overused in sideshows and carnivals. In a typical ten-and-one attraction, a tent containing one strange exhibit after another, for the cost of a nickel you might have seen a living head on a table, a spider with a human face, a living half-lady or disembodied hand—all optical illusions dependent on Tobin's 45-degree mirrors. Unfortunately, in a sideshow the mirrors might not be clean, or the scenery might be carelessly arranged. Observant viewers could spot a telltale smudge or the sparkling edges of the glass.

Guy Jarrett, the American illusion builder who worked for Howard Thurston, became familiar with mirror illusions in typical sideshows. He knew they called for careful attention to detail, and he based his own stage illusions on the way audiences studied these effects, looking for discrepancies or noticing odd shadows or flashes of light. In his own illusions using mirrors, he concentrated on surreptitiously sliding them into place, then carefully removing them again. For example, the mirrors under a table might be raised through the stage, as the table seemed to be momentarily, accidentally covered by

another prop. In this way the mirrors were present only for the necessary seconds of the illusion, giving the performer greater freedom
around the apparatus and mystifying even the audience member who
was watching carefully.

Charles Morritt was a secretive showman in the old style. Unlike
Devant and Jarrett, he didn't write about his secrets and seldom spoke
about his approach to magic, but he left a string of ingenious illusions,
many of which can be analyzed. It's clear that his effects were being
evolved trick by trick, each secret fine-tuned for each new invention.
It was the opposite approach from Devant's. Morritt began with the
secret. He could find a good optical effect and then fit a clever plot to
it. In this way the tiny, necessary details of the secret were accom-
modated and disguised within the presentation.

It's the hard way to invent an illusion, a reckless way of backing
into the final product. But it's not impossible, and the results can be
amazing—think of a playwright who begins with colorful riffs of dialogue, then finds a story to contain them.

Morritt's evolving secrets began before the turn of the century, with
the wedge of mirrors in his cage illusion. It's worth looking at exactly

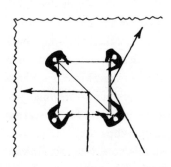

*Morritt's wedge of mirrors, the
view from the top*

what was happening in his illusions
and how Morritt tried to increase
the efficiency of each invention.

In Morritt's illusions, like the
four men holding the square board,
he used two mirrors to form a
wedge. One was set at a 45-degree
angle, which reflected a side wall of
scenery. The other mirror was set at
a 90-degree angle, projecting per-
pendicularly from the back wall of
scenery. One of those mirrors did
most of the work. The 45-degree angle mirror was wide enough that
someone could hide behind it, becoming invisible. But in order for this
mirror to reflect properly, Morritt needed to arrange a duplicate wall
of scenery at the side of the stage, carefully lighting it so that it would
match the scenery in back. The mirror figuratively "reached over" to

the side for its image, giving the impression that the audience was looking at the scenery behind the illusion.

The mirror set at 90 degrees didn't do anything except to seal up the wedge, so that the audience sitting at one side of the auditorium couldn't peer behind the 45-degree mirror and see the concealed assistant crouching beneath the board. Morritt must have realized that although this 90-degree mirror wasn't good at concealing much—it's hard to hide behind the edge of a mirror—the reflections in it were efficient. Morritt didn't need to provide additional matching scenery. This mirror perfectly reflected the back wall, "reaching" only several feet to the side, at a soft angle, in order to find a matching patch of scenery.

Hanging extra curtains around the sides of the stage and adjusting scenery and lighting was awkward and time consuming. The 90-degree mirror was much simpler to use, almost automatic in the reflection it provided. Charles Morritt recognized that an ideal situation would be to use a 90-degree mirror for his illusions—if only he could hide someone behind a thin edge of glass.

His solution was to angle the glass slightly, not as straight as 90 degrees, not as far as 45 degrees.

Somewhere between 90 and 45 degrees—the math ends there. The exact angle—depending upon the width of the theatre, the distance from the backdrop, the size of the mirror—can't really be specified. It can't be calculated, because it doesn't work, at least, not with the neat 45-plus-45-equals-90 perfection of Tobin's discovery. Morritt's oblique mirror only comes close.

But after years of experience with these principles, Morritt realized that he could make other adjustments in his apparatus, in light and color, in size and shape. Coming close would be good enough. His discovery was the work of someone who had studied the principles on stage, fretted over the details, and fidgeted with bits of looking glass before he went to bed for the night, searching for something new. It was as if he'd decided that one plus one didn't really have to equal two. He just had to make the audience think that it did.

•   •   •

In 1914 Morritt filed a patent in London, explaining an odd invention. It was a barrel that had a diagonal mirror fitted inside it. The patent papers were titled "Improvement in Apparatus for Stage Illusions":

> *The object of my invention is to provide an apparatus for use in an illusion at an entertainment by means of which the spectators, when looking into the open end of a cylinder . . . shall believe that they are looking into and through an appliance, which is quite hollow and empty.*

The patent drawing showed a round, wooden barrel. An oval-shaped mirror extended from the front edge opening, diagonally across the barrel, and ended at the opposite side by bisecting the back opening. Morritt suggested disguising the edge of the mirror with a series of slats to close the back end of the barrel.

His description claimed that the barrel would appear to be empty because, to someone looking into it, the half-circle of the back would be duplicated in the glass. Even more, the scenery beyond the open back would be duplicated, giving the viewer the impression of looking clear through the apparatus. If something were concealed in the wedge-shaped area behind the mirror, "rabbits, birds or the like," the barrel could be shown empty, and Morritt could set it on one end, reaching inside to produce the animals.

Technically, the barrel doesn't look empty. If the audience could have stopped to examine the reflections inside, they would have noticed that the inside shape of the barrel had been ridiculously skewed. The reflection made it look much larger on the inside than the outside; it also made it misshapen, much wider at one end than the other.

That's why Morritt's new idea for mirror tricks doesn't work.

In a sideshow setting the audience might have had time to examine the interior of the barrel and notice that the shapes were misaligned. But on a stage a good magician like Morritt realized how an audience used specific visual cues to judge that something was empty. By painting the interior of the barrel black, the sides could be deemphasized, blending together into a dark void. This would make the back circle much more visually important.

The mirror would also distort the circular end of the barrel; the reflected half-circle would go slightly oval. But the shape was just close enough to a circle to make this work. The audience wouldn't be able to judge a perfect circle and wouldn't notice the difference in shape.

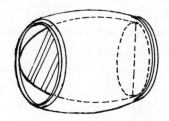

Most importantly, the mirror allowed the audience to look apparently through the barrel to the backdrop several feet behind it. Here the strange, oblique

Morritt's patent for a barrel with a mirror inside

mirror functioned deceptively. The audience actually ended up seeing the backdrop directly behind the open half-circle and another patch of backdrop, from several feet away, showing behind the reflected half-circle. Again, if the audience could study the image carefully, it would have noticed that in the reflected half, the backdrop wasn't quite flat. It was pitched at a slightly different angle. But a stage curtain of a continuous color or a regular pattern wouldn't betray this slight discrepancy. In the hands of Charles Morritt, the apparatus could be tipped forward to give the audience a quick view inside, emphasizing the bright color of the curtain behind it. If the result wasn't mathematically perfect, it was perfectly deceptive.

That's why Morritt's new idea was a brilliant illusion.

His patent noted that different shapes might be used, including a cylinder, "a truncated cone or a rectangular shaped elongated box." Morritt noted that he preferred "the shape of a truncated pyramid." Like many patents, it may have sought to protect the idea and still conceal certain details. More than likely, he never built this barrel. There's no record of his performing a trick with a barrel, and the task of determining the shape of that mirror, then fitting it inside and constructing the barrel around it, would have been daunting.

Despite the fact that Morritt had patented the secret, recording it in print, no magicians ever seemed to understand it. Maybe the weirdly elliptical mirror confused them or looked especially costly. Maybe they disregarded it because they couldn't actually tie the explanation to any trick that was being performed. More than likely, to any magicians who saw the patent, it just looked wrong.

That was also the problem with Devant's written description of Beauty and the Beast. It simply sounded wrong. In this effect, Morritt was also using his strangely oblique mirror—actually, two of them, arranged in a narrow, little wedge beneath the Moorish table. A small set of steps concealed the wide part of the mirrors. Members of the audience seated on either side could apparently see beneath the table, looking through the cutout legs, and see the backdrop behind the apparatus.

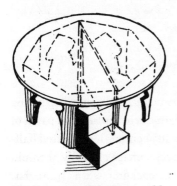

The oddly shaped legs of the table would have concealed the fact that the reflections were slightly askew. Again, the focus of the audience would have been on the curtains hanging behind the table. Another neat deception was the white, gauze-covered bell, which covered the table during the illusion. This was first seen collapsed into a flat circle of white fabric and leaning against the back of the table, which allowed the audience to think that they were looking through the legs of the table. It was a typical Morritt touch, a sign of his careful analysis and presentational details. As in his barrel illusion, the white gauze circle disguised the imperfections and was the ideal deceptive shape to be placed behind his oblique mirrors.

The Beauty and the Beast table, showing the mirrors

This imperfect reflection was a revolutionary idea. Tobin had plotted his deceptions as mathematical formulas, according to his architectural training. Morritt had discovered a way to squeeze his illusions from slight discrepancies. It was the work of a canny, experienced showman.

• • •

In September 1912 Houdini was at the height of his career. While touring in Germany, he introduced what would become his most famous, most ingenious white-knuckle escape, the Water Torture Cell.

Houdini had been planning the Water Torture Cell for at least three years and had devised it with Jim Collins, his chief assistant. It was a "mechanical escape" as opposed to a challenge: instead of getting out of borrowed straitjacket, handcuffs, or a wooden crate supplied by a local lumberyard, the Cell was a specially made piece of apparatus that could be examined by the audience and then used to contain Houdini in a potentially fatal manner. The Cell, which Houdini always called USD (for upside-down), was beautifully made of thick planks of polished Honduran mahogany. The front plate was one-half inch of transparent glass, surrounded by a gleaming, nickel-plated frame. It was just under five feet tall and about two feet wide, like an upright aquarium. The handles and locks were bright brass. From the moment the curtain swept open on the apparatus, it was surrounded by assistants in dark rain slickers, who occupied themselves with filling the Cell from a hose and mixing in buckets of hot water to raise the temperature inside the tank. The apparatus was beautiful and threatening; audiences contemplated it with the same weird awe that they might have felt for a guillotine.

Houdini stepped onstage in evening clothes. He took the spotlight to explain the apparatus and invite a committee to join him and supervise locking him inside:

> Ladies and gentlemen. . . . In introducing my latest invention, the Water Torture Cell, although there is nothing supernatural about it, I am willing to forfeit the sum of one thousand dollars to anyone who can know that it is possible to obtain air inside the Torture Cell, when I am locked up in it, in the regulation manner, after it has been filled with water. . . .
>
> In front, a plate of glass for self-protection. Should anything go wrong when I am locked up, as it's absolutely impossible to obtain air, one of my assistants watches

through the curtains, ready in case of emergency, with an
axe, to rush in, demolishing the glass, allowing the water to
flow out, in order to save my life.

Houdini dashed into the wings to change into a bathing suit and
robe. Lying on his back on the stage, his ankles were locked in a massive, heavy set of stocks, which formed the lid of the tank. When the
stocks were hauled into the air over the stage, Houdini was suspended, upside down, his blood rushing to his head.

Carefully, the assistants centered his head above the tank of water.
Houdini paused to take several dramatic deep breaths and then,
holding the last breath, gave the signal for the stocks to be quickly
lowered, plunging him inside. The audience strained in their seats or
stood to watch the procedure; it was obvious that every step of the
confinement was adding to the danger. Water surged over the top of
the tank and cascaded onto the canvas tarp that covered the stage.
When Houdini was fully inside the Cell, the assistants stepped in,
locking the stocks to the top of the tank. The escape artist could be
clearly seen through the glass front, helpless, with his head five feet
beneath the water and his hands unable to reach any of the locks on
the outside. A rectangular cabinet of silk fabric was pulled around the
tank, concealing it completely, and the orchestra ominously played
"Asleep in the Deep." The crowd settled nervously, monitoring the
faces of the assistants, the movements of the orchestra leader—
watching for any indication that something might be wrong.

One account of the performance commented that "something of a
thrill passes over the crowded theatre," and the audience waited
silently, expectantly. "A few more seconds and the curtains move,"
noted one reviewer:

We jump to our feet. Suddenly the curtains are torn asunder,
and Houdini leaps through them. He is dripping with water;
his eyes are bloodshot, a speck of foam is on his lips. But he
is free. And that, and only that, is what the audience have
been waiting for. "He's done it," "He's escaped," "He's free!"
There follows a great shout of general applause.

S.H. Sharpe, a British writer and theorist on the art of conjuring, was a notoriously tough audience. As a boy he saw David Devant and found his low-key, friendly approach to be only disappointing and ordinary. He felt that Charles Morritt had substituted bluff for real ability. But, Sharpe wrote, "the only magician whom I felt really came up to the label on the box was Houdini with his Water Torture Cell . . . a memory worth recalling."

His escapes made him a legend, but Houdini wanted magic tricks.

Despite his success with the Water Torture Cell, Houdini cast himself as a magician and purchased a number of effects that could be featured in a new show. It's clear that he had set Howard Thurston in his sights. Professionally, they were friendly acquaintances, but Houdini considered Thurston to be "posing" as the world's greatest magician. This assessment was reinforced by a warm, gossipy friendship that had grown between Houdini and Harry Kellar. Kellar was retired in Los Angeles—no competition—and treated Houdini as a son, praising him for his own work and complaining about Thurston's changes since he had taken over Kellar's business.

In assembling his show, Houdini solicited the help of his friend Will Goldston. A Liverpool magician who became London's leading magic dealer in the early 1900s, Goldston ran the Theatrical and Entertainments department of the A.W. Gamage store. He published books and magazines about magic, stocked the latest effects, and arranged to have stage illusions built to order. Goldston's position guaranteed that he knew everyone in the industry and all the latest news, but he had a dangerous way of revealing the latest professional secrets in his publications. Over the years he had boldly included accounts of the latest Maskelyne and Devant tricks, a rough diagram of the cherished Maskelyne and Kellar Levitation, and even several illusions that were still in guarded development by a famous music hall magician—Goldston somehow published these details before they were ever performed for the public. His ability to obtain current secrets and rush them into print was particularly cold-blooded, and Goldston's professional friends were naturally cautious of him.

Years later Goldston told a story about Houdini that might explain how Houdini ingratiated himself with Goldston and also protected his own turf. Goldston was preparing one of his annual compilations of tricks, but as the press deadline neared, he found himself lacking material. Houdini listened sympathetically, and the conversation turned to the new program that Devant had just introduced at St. George's Hall, featuring four extremely original and puzzling effects. As Houdini turned to leave, he told his friend, "You know, Will, every lock can be opened."

The next morning the postman delivered an anonymous package to Goldston, filled with beautiful diagrams—the secrets of Devant's four effects. Goldston naturally included them in his annual book. Devant was furious. He impulsively fired his assistants, then reconsidered and rehired them all. Years later, when the two men were on better terms, Devant asked Goldston how he had obtained the secrets. Goldston had to tell him that there was no good explanation—he suspected Houdini but the escape artist had coyly denied any involvement. The part that had particularly baffled Devant, he confessed to Goldston, was that the drawings reproduced the precise design of his wife's buttonhook. That buttonhook was used offstage, during a crucial moment in one of the tricks, to grasp a loop of thread.

Goldston later wrote,

> Houdini was a lion, snapping his jaws at all and sundry. He snapped them at Maskelyne, Devant, and myself, so jealous was he of his professional standing. To anyone who seemed likely to filch a share of his limelight, Houdini was a tyrant.

When he began plans for his own magic show, Houdini asked Goldston for "an illusion inventor who can keep a secret." Goldston considered the request carefully and recommended Charles Morritt, who had just returned to London with a string of new mysteries at St. George's Hall. Goldston considered Morritt "the greatest master of mirror illusions since Pepper," and seemed to have particular respect for the Yorkshire Conjurer as one of the old guard—Goldston's admiration meant that he politely avoided putting any of Morritt's secrets in print.

• • •

Houdini and Morritt arranged their meetings in Britain between performances, stepping out into the alley behind the theatre so they could talk privately. They made an unlikely pair. The American escape artist was earning the top salary in music halls, but he was an unremarkable figure offstage, an angular little man dressed in rumpled clothes with a flat, porkpie hat. Houdini tended to talk in sensations, snarling about his competition or imitators, boasting of his potential. Morritt, who earned a modest salary even with Maskelyne and Devant's company, was tall and elegant, dressed in a frock coat and high hat. Morritt nodded slowly and fingered his cigarette, the very picture of a magician, as Houdini nervously paced circles around him. But they found an instant connection. Morritt's style of magic, inventive and flashy, was perfectly suited to Houdini's taste. Over the course of several meetings, Morritt quickly dazzled Houdini with a string of new ideas, sensations he had dared not offer to anyone else— not to Maskelyne or Devant, not even to Thurston in the United States. Even better, Morritt was enthusiastic about Houdini's plans and offered to explain everything Houdini didn't know about stage illusions: what kind of scenery to order, the efficient way to organize band calls, what to tell the electrician, how to pack the props so that the delicate mirrors wouldn't break.

Houdini was excited about the thought of performing real magic, and he eagerly filled out the show with historic effects. He purchased the show of the British magician Hermalin and bought Buatier deKolta's final creation, his legendary Expanding Die illusion, from Goldston.

DeKolta had introduced the Die when he toured the United States. He began by walking onstage with a small valise and telling the audience that it contained his wife. At the conclusion of his show, he reached inside the case and removed a large black die, about eight inches square, with white spots painted on it. He placed the die atop a low, thin table—really just a square board on four short legs—and stepped away from it. The die quickly expanded in a fraction of a second, with a strange lopsided motion. It swelled in three dimensions at the same time. As it settled again, it was nearly a cubic yard.

DeKolta returned to the giant die, lifting it off the table. Beneath it was his wife, calmly sitting cross-legged.

The famous Die trick was an incredible piece of machinery, comprised of telescopic tubing and powerful expansion springs. Goldston had acquired the Die after deKolta's death in 1903, and Goldston's wife, a music hall performer named Leah Laurie, presented it for a short time. But it was a delicate piece of apparatus, requiring constant adjustment and a full hour of careful preparation before every show. Houdini paid top dollar for it—it had been renowned as the famous deKolta's crowning achievement—and took lessons to learn the methodical steps necessary for each performance. Goldston double-crossed his friend by including drawings of the full secret in his next book, an ostentatious, expensive publication called *Exclusive Magical Secrets*, which was bound in leather and equipped with a lock to secure the front and back covers, supposedly indicating the enormous value of the descriptions inside. After negotiating for the legendary deKolta effect, Houdini fumed when he discovered that the Expanding Die was no longer his exclusive secret.

From a Paris magic dealer, Houdini purchased copies of two of Robert-Houdin's most famous effects, the trapeze automaton named Antonio Diavolo and the Crystal Cash Box. He never presented the automaton; it required too much repair in order to make it ready for a performance, but Houdini did use the Crystal Cash Box, a pretty, little glass coffer, in the opening of his show.

These Robert-Houdin effects were strange choices, to say the least, only several years after Houdini had pointedly rewritten magic history by casting Robert-Houdin as a dangerous villain and ridiculing his lack of creativity. One of Houdini's biographers saw the purchase of Robert-Houdin's effects as "a primitive hunter gorging on his slain wolf to ingest its power." It was typical Houdini, an example of his confusing love–hate passions, which exhausted so many of his associates.

During July 1913, as Houdini toured Europe, he was shocked to open a telegram reporting the death of his mother, whom he had idolized. He quickly returned to New York, canceling his performances. He was inconsolable in his grief.

When he resumed his contracts in Europe late that year, his escapes were as popular as ever, but Houdini was especially restless, intent on performing his "Grand Magical Revue." He premiered the experimental program in British cities through the spring of 1914: Barrow-in-Furness, Dover, and Nottingham. It was made attractive to theatre managers by being packaged in a "split-week" of features: On Monday through Wednesday he featured the popular Water Torture Cell; Thursday through Saturday was the "Grand Magical Revue" starring Houdini, "the Supreme Ruler of Mystery."

A representative Houdini inspiration was Money for Nothing, his bombastic version of the classic coin-catching routine. T. Nelson Downs had become a feature in vaudeville with his careful sleight of hand with coins, but for Houdini it was quantity, not quality, that mattered. He would produce five hundred gold sovereigns from a cloth bag. Goldston remembered that Houdini enhanced the trick with a publicity stunt. He hired detectives to accompany him after each performance to a local bank, where he made a great fuss about depositing his fortune of magically created money. The story generated a newspaper story the next morning, free advertising for the show. The same money was quietly withdrawn again for the next performance.

Good-Bye Winter was Houdini's title for Morritt's disappearance of a person atop a stack of tables. Hello Summer was Morritt's production of a lady from a pyramid-shaped box, a variation on his barrel trick. In Lady Godiva a lady and a pony disappeared. Houdini closed the show with Metamorphosis, his popular trunk illusion from his earliest shows. The famous deKolta Die was presented only a few times. Houdini's "Grand Magical Review" played probably a dozen performances.

The advertising insisted that the show would "prove Houdini the Greatest Magician that History chronicles." Houdini added his own hyperbole, handwritten in the margins of one playbill for his files, claiming that his revue was "said by all the great English critics to be the best mystery show ever presented . . . an almost original program." Actually, he found that audiences, critics, and theatre managers were impatient if he didn't deliver his trademark escape act. Other magicians were more suited to coin tricks and magic cabinets; Houdini's blustery style left little room for finesse.

Houdini opened his show with Robert-Houdin's Crystal Cash Box, the little glass box bound with gilt metal that was suspended by two ribbons over the stage. Picking up a number of coins, Houdini seemed to toss them toward the box. They disappeared in his hands and reappeared, seconds later, rattling inside the swinging box. It must have been a lovely illusion in Robert-Houdin's tiny Parisian theatre, but Servais LeRoy, the Belgian magician who knew Houdini well, thought that it had been "quite lost with Houdini." As the opening effect to the "Magical Revue," "no one ever saw the coins and few even heard their arrival in the glass box," according to LeRoy. Houdini bullied his way through the tiny trick, oblivious to the effect it had on his audience. "It was somewhat difficult to realize that a great showman should entirely fail to see this; possibly it was that eternal belief in himself."

LeRoy believed his friend simply wasn't suited to performing magic:

> His illusions were anything but subtle. Using other men's ideas, he was unable to improve on the original and was forced to let it go at that or produce something still weaker.

Houdini's "almost original" "Magical Revue"—comprised mostly of Morritt, Robert-Houdin, and deKolta inventions, was, as Will Goldston recalled, an "utter and complete failure." Houdini packed up the effects and shipped them back to America. "If the English want escapes, they can have them," Houdini harrumphed to Goldston, "but I am determined to give a good magical show before I die."

Like Goldston, many magicians found Houdini to be a difficult, prickly acquaintance, wary of any competition. But Morritt and Houdini seemed to share a real friendship. Houdini considered Morritt "the finest inventor of illusions in the world." Morritt liked the American, who was never afraid of a big idea.

One evening in England, as Houdini prepared for a music hall show in his gray-enameled dressing room, Morritt arrived to discuss possible illusions and share the latest gossip. He set his high hat in a corner of the dressing table, fell back in the easy chair, and threw one leg over the other. He complained about the Maskelynes' leaden touch with their shows and analyzed the wartime business in the music halls.

As Morritt took the last puffs on his cigarette he leaned forward and caught Houdini's eye in the mirror. "Of course . . . if you really want to make headlines with your magic," he started. Houdini, preparing for his first performance that evening, was thumbing a line of rouge on his cheeks. He paused and looked back at Morritt's reflection, listening closely. "You shouldn't bother with little tricks, rabbits, pigeons. Make an elephant disappear!"

Houdini cut him off: "It'd be worth thinking about if it could be made practical."

"Oh, it's practical. I've got a very efficient way to do it, one of the nicest props I've ever devised."

"Maybe, but that's just the apparatus. It's not possible to troupe with a live elephant. It's too expensive."

"I didn't say it was easy. I said that it's an idea for the man who wants to make headlines."

Morritt might have intended his suggestion to startle or impress. But Houdini realized that the magician sitting in his dressing room had a way to actually accomplish the illusion. Both were experienced performers at the top of their careers; both knew that a vanishing elephant would be impossibly ambitious, preposterous, impractical. It was also a great idea.

It was such a great idea that another inventor had already had it.

13
Jennie

*Maybe you think I've only talked about things
that happened long ago. You know, history.
Well, magic is history.*
—Guy Jarrett

hen magicians are looking for publicity, they turn to big tricks. The Great Lafayette toured with a lion around the turn of the century. Horace Goldin matched him with a tiger. Thurston vanished a horse in his magic show, and when he decided that the trick wasn't enough of a draw, he returned the next season with a vanishing automobile.

Magic only works on the scale of a human being which, in my mind, means that it involves something between the size of a collar button, which a performer can hold in his hand under someone's nose, and an elephant, which he can stand next to and still be seen, giving the impression that he's actually involved.

Television should be the perfect medium to showcase the collar button—it can make small, beautiful manipulative magic accessible to an audience. But television has always survived on drum-banging exaggeration to attract a large viewing audience, so magic on television went through a long phase during which it emphasized big tricks.

Ever since the 1950s, magicians have made an uneasy truce with television. In order for any performing art to survive, it has to have visibility on television. Music, dance, opera, and even juggling and puppetry: For better or worse, they all have to be made to work on television. The difficulty with magic is a natural suspicion of TV technology. Viewers could easily imagine that special effects or editing were responsible for the tricks. To counteract this, most magicians have sought to be scrupulously honest in their approach, carefully photographing their illusions with long, continuous shots to point out that the camera did not cut away, or working in front of a live audience to guarantee that all the magic was really happening in front of their eyes.

The most monumental miracles on television rely on the fact that the view of the audience can be contained and controlled. Through a lens the magician can be framed in the foreground, and the Statue of Liberty placed in the background—roughly translated to the same size. The conceit is that this sort of enormous trick can be reduced to a human scale.

Over the years I've designed a number of enormous tricks specifically for television specials—including the idea and secret for disappearing the Statue of Liberty, an entire herd of elephants, the castle at
Disneyland, a B-2 bomber, and a tour bus. These illusions enticed
people to watch magic on television, and they made the reputations
of several popular magicians. But there's a disappointing quality to any
magic on television, a futility in direct proportion to the size of the
miracle. In fact, magic doesn't really belong on television. Even
if the performance can be bolstered by disclaimers—"no trick
photography"—and surrounded by cheering audiences, it suffers
because it's tough to talk a remote audience into being impressed.
Ultimately, there's no substitute for sitting with a group of people, just
several feet away from a really skilled magician, agreeing to surrender
a measured amount of logic, being led through some fascinating
impossibility, watching closely.

Sometime around 1916, when Morritt and Houdini were still wondering whether they could really make an elephant disappear, Guy Jarrett was clearing his throat in the office of R. H. Burnside.

"This derby will represent the elephant," he began quietly. Jarrett
was dressed in paint-splattered trousers and squinted through wire-
rimmed glasses; he wasn't a performer and felt uncomfortable trying
to impress the director of New York's Hippodrome theatre. Jarrett
positioned the hat on a small, wedge-shaped platform in the middle
of his model wooden stage. "Here's the cast," he said, waving his fingers at a row of tiny cutout figures, "and here's the queen."

"The what?" Burnside snapped. "I thought this was about an
elephant."

"I see it as a production number. You know: one of your Hipp specialties with the king, the queen, the nobles. Hundreds of people in
costumes."

Burnside rolled his eyes. Jarrett was there speaking to Burnside only
because his good friend Clyde Powers was a Hippodrome stage manager. Through Powers, Jarrett had teased Burnside with a telegram
stating, "Startle press and public alike by vanishing an elephant."

Burnside invited him to present his idea but wasn't interested in the technician telling him how to direct his shows. "Sure. Let's get to the trick."

Jarrett crouched at the edge of his four-foot model, pulling a series of threads. "The curtains drop," he said, as two squares of red silk fell in front of the hat. "The cast moves forward to see what's happening. The queen commands them to watch. And in five seconds . . ." He pulled two more strings. There was the sound of something sliding and the sound of something clicking. The silk curtains were pulled up, and the hat was gone. "Now, don't worry—the orchestra will cover any sounds."

Burnside got up from his chair slowly, keeping his eyes on the model as he backed against the wall in his office, standing on tiptoe. Jarrett realized that the director was now pretending he was in the balcony. He still couldn't see where the hat had gone. "And you think we can do this at the Hippodrome?" Jarrett looked up and smiled. He knew he had him. "Well, *I* can do this at the Hippodrome. I've done a lot of this for the best magicians in the world, for the finest Broadway shows. I know what I'm doing."

After the 1913 season with Thurston, Jarrett had settled in New York, working behind the counter at Clyde Powers's magic shop, creating material for professional magicians and vaudeville acts, and building props and special effects for Broadway shows. Like everyone on Broadway, he'd heard that the Hippodrome was in trouble, that producer Charles Dillingham and director R. H. Burnside were desperate for features.

In fact, the Hippodrome had been a preposterous idea from the moment it opened its doors in 1905. The original developers, Fred Thompson and Skip Dundy, conceived it as a Manhattan follow-up to their fanciful Luna Park at Coney Island, and indeed the Hippodrome was more of an amusement park than a theatre. It covered an entire city block on 6th Avenue between 43rd and 44th Streets. The enormous auditorium seated 5,200 people in two balconies and a dress circle. The stage, nearly the size of a football field, could hold 600 performers, or the stage flooring could be withdrawn hydraulically to show a gigantic tank of surging water suitable for diving displays, water ballets, or simulated storms at sea. A favorite Hippodrome trick was to have an army of extras march into the water and never emerge; it was accomplished with a wide diving bell that took them to a back-stage exit. The size of the Hippodrome made audiences gasp; the impracticality of it brought its producers to their knees. Thompson and Dundy had lavishly adorned the interior of the theatre with smooth marble pachyderm heads, intending them to signify good luck. Instead, they just signified "white elephant."

The opening production told the story: Act One was titled "A Yankee Circus on Mars," which conveniently allowed for a three-ring circus on the stage, a full-sized tent, flying spaceships, and a view of the Martian Court, inhabited by hundreds of dancers. Presumably, this wasn't enough. Act Two was titled "Andersonville," which re-created a Civil War battle. In fact, the famous Hippodrome stage looked empty unless hosting a battalion of dancers or a cavalry unit.

The theatre regularly employed a corps de ballet, clowns, horses, and the Powers' Elephants, a troupe of performing pachyderms (the elephants' owner was no relation to Clyde Powers). Jarrett knew that elephants were available, the stage was the right size, and the necessary technology wouldn't be a problem.

Jarrett's model stumped Burnside. The producer pointed at Jarrett's miniature stage as he stubbed out his cigar. "It's interesting. Leave the model, and we'll consider it."

Jarrett didn't move. "Actually, Mr. Burnside, I won't leave the model . . ." His voice trailed off. Burnside got the idea.

"You're going to have to trust me and leave the model here. I've been in this business a long time."

"Me too. I don't leave models, and I don't believe in Santa Claus." Guy Jarrett threw a canvas cover over the model and pushed it toward the door. Burnside watched him walk out.

Meanwhile, the Maskelynes had tired of David Devant. They resented his stardom and his control over the company. Devant's salary in music halls was impressive, as much as 325 pounds per week. It was much more than he could earn at the St. George's Hall in London. In turn, the Maskelyne and Devant Company realized more money when Devant worked music halls, as part of his contract paid profits back to the company. Still, the Maskelynes were embarrassed when he played in the London area, offering his show for pennies a ticket, when on the other side of town, St. George's Hall was struggling to hold an audience. One board member commented that Devant was "too expensive a luxury for St. George's Hall."

The Chief, John Nevil Maskelyne, was officially no longer on the board of directors of the company, but he certainly made his opinions known through his son Nevil. They didn't like Devant's choices. They didn't appreciate his new illusions, which had been designed to entertain only the public, preferring more restrained mysteries, "things which would puzzle conjurers themselves." They thought that the entertainments at St. George's Hall felt like music hall programs and wanted their original format of magic plays. Devant resisted, convinced that the plays were expensive, slow, and old-fashioned.

As long as Devant's choices were attracting audiences to the theatre and his music hall tours were adding to their bottom line, the Chief could only complain in philosophical terms. But two forces conspired against David Devant.

The first was the Great War. On October 4, 1914, the first German bombs were dropped on London. St. George's Hall offered matinee shows and avoided some of the problems of nighttime blackouts, which severely affected the business at most West End theatres. Morritt managed the touring company during this time and also battled with the Maskelynes, rearranging the program so that the slower magic plays were buried in the middle of the evening. Morritt's tour did well in the provinces, but he realized that, much like Devant, his profits were keeping the theatre in London afloat. Morritt wrote to a friend,

> St. George's Hall has not drawn, in fact they are doing so bad
> . . . owing to the war that they think of closing down; all the
> artistes and staff there are on half salary. Our show in
> the provinces [has] made money all along the line, big busi-
> ness in fact. We have kept the London Hall going.

With the continuing war and the diminished business, the Maskelynes calculated that Devant was now costing them money, as they needed to hire a managing director for St. George's Hall while he worked in music halls.

The second problem was Devant's declining health. He postponed his 1915 music hall tour on the advice of his physician. Increasingly, he was depending on long vacations to soothe his nerves and prepare him for his tours. Devant naturally assumed that his ailments were caused by overwork.

The Chief, suspecting that Devant would be supporting St. George's Hall less and less, stepped in. Maskelyne contacted Charles Morritt, informing him that his services as a performer were no longer required. When Devant heard this, he realized that his authority as managing director was being overruled. In the spring of 1915, Devant's and Maskelyne's attorneys attempted a settlement. By June, Devant had been completely bought out of the company, and the business was renamed Maskelynes Ltd. The official announcement explained that Devant had chosen to concentrate on his music hall appearances.

There's no question that Devant had modernized the shows at St. George's Hall and had, on many occasions, rescued the Maskelyne company with an infusion of creativity, insightful choices, and cash. But there came a time when the battle had become personal, and nothing could repair the disagreement; even Devant's successes were perceived as thumbing his nose at the venerable Maskelyne family. As the partnership dissolved, Devant was not seen simply with jealousy but was imagined as an arch villain. The Chief wrote to a friend,

> *I have succeeded in getting rid of Devant entirely. It has been a costly business for me but it is money well spent. The reputation of the entertainment was almost ruined and I expect to have a tough job to retrieve the success. . . . If this dreadful war would end I think all would be right.*

● ● ●

Charles Morritt promptly rented a theatre in the Royal Polytechnic, across Regent Street from St. George's Hall. He shared the bill with the American magician Carl Hertz, opening the "Morritt and Hertz Mysteries," with daily matinees at three o'clock. The show offered "the Greatest Combination of Mystifiers the World Has Ever Seen," with a mix of music, variety, and magic that seemed a discomforting competition to Maskelyne. Morritt served as producer, director, and star. He produced ducks and flowers, repeated his old mind-reading favorites, and made his famous donkey disappear. For the finale of the show, he presented a new invention called Tally Ho! A large cabinet that was draped with yellow silk curtains was opened, shown empty, then quickly closed. The audience heard shouts and pistol shots from inside the cabinet. Opening the front, Morritt revealed "an entire fox hunt": two huntsmen on foot with rifles, a hunting dog, and a lady in green velvet riding on the back of a live horse.

The Polytechnic show wasn't successful. The theatre was a long, flat concert hall. The scenery was cheap, and the assistants were not properly rehearsed. By most reports, they gave away as many tickets as they sold. Morritt soldiered on for several months and also presented Tally Ho! at a nearby music hall, magically producing the popular jockey Tod Sloan. By November, Morritt finally closed the show at the Polytechnic and headed back to the provincial halls, seaside resorts, and museums. Mind-reading, hypnotism, or illusions: Morritt's versatile repertoire had been crafted from years of experience.

John Nevil Maskelyne, the grand old man of British magic, didn't survive the Great War and never saw the business return to his theatre. The war had drained performers, musicians, technicians, and, ultimately, audiences from every London theatre. St. George's Hall returned to the old format, featuring magic plays. As before, the company was partly supported by a profitable music hall tour by Nevil Maskelyne. Through 1916 he toured with the illusion called the Haunted Window, which was, ironically, one of the many inventions David Devant had introduced at St. George's Hall.

On May 1, 1917, as the Chief was presenting his plate-spinning routine, he made two slight mistakes, failing to keep the porcelain basins spinning, which was uncharacteristic of him. He finished the show, taking the part of the "Witch in Will, the Witch and the Watchman," the original magic play from 1873 that had started his career in London. After the curtain fell, late that night he was diagnosed with pneumonia and pleurisy and confined to his bed in the flat above the theatre.

His sons, Nevil and Archie, filled in for the following weeks, appearing onstage and managing the theatre. On May 18, 1917, John Nevil Maskelyne died. He was 77 years old. His theatre closed for two days, the day he died and then again on the day of his funeral—the family's sign of respect for the founder. The Maskelyne theatre of magic had been a London institution for 44 years, and the next generation of Maskelyne magicians was determined to continue the tradition.

David Devant continued to play in Britain's music halls. The years after St. George's Hall should have been the most successful of his career; he was certainly at the height of his fame. Through 1918, however, magicians noticed a certain stoop-shouldered shuffle and an occasional tremor in his left hand. For his many fans, who remembered the strong, elegant performer commanding the stage at St. George's Hall, charming each audience with his broad smile—"All Done by Kindness"—the sight was particularly uneasy.

Late that year he was performing a Lesson in Magic, one of his favorite tricks, which he had created many years before to amuse a party of his daughter's friends. A small boy was invited onto the stage and told that he would be taught a trick, using a handkerchief from a man in the audience. The handkerchief underwent a bewildering series of changes. It became torn strips, a long, white streamer, and then was discovered inside a lemon. The handkerchief was cut, mangled, and burned before finally being found inside a wine bottle, safe and sound.

Halfway into the routine, as the audience laughed at each predicament, Devant merrily rattled through his patter; it was a performance he had given thousands of times. "Hold the handkerchief as I'm holding mine," he said, and the audience grew oddly silent. Devant looked over at the small boy, who was smiling back at the magician and surprisingly shaking the handkerchief wildly at his fingertips. Devant was confused by the small boy's response until he happened to look down at his own hand, holding his own handkerchief. It was twitching uncontrollably.

He announced his retirement the following year.

It was Houdini who made the elephant disappear.

Dillingham and Burnside's Hippodrome shows continued with their random formula of disconnected spectacle and oversized vaudeville; all had vaguely accommodating titles like "Hip-Hip-Hooray," "Happy Days," "Good Times, Better Times," and "Everything." The 1917 edition, "Cheer Up," featured a marching chorus of soldiers, hundreds strong, who paraded through a recreation of Union Square to the Statue of Liberty, where an enormous troop steamer packed with soldiers sailed past the New York skyline. In a jungle setting Powers' Elephants danced; at a rural train station, a full-sized locomotive chugged across the stage, delivering boxcar-loads of hoboes to perform a medley of old favorites. Then a series of American heroes marched onstage to music by Sousa, while overhead an enormous eagle was festooned with electric lights. Diving horses performed for the crowd, diving girls disappeared into the waters, and for the finale all of Coney Island was recreated on the Hippodrome stage.

Houdini joined the company in January 1918, just four months into the run, and became the feature of "Cheer Up" for nineteen weeks, matinees daily. It was the longest engagement of his career. It was billed "The Vanishing Elephant, with the famous mystifier Houdini."

Naturally, Jarrett always felt that the idea had been stolen from him, that Dillingham had called in Houdini and urged him to work out the illusion. "There are so many people that would rather steal a thing and even make a bum of it, rather than pay for it. They just have that feeling in them," Jarrett wrote. Joe Lee, a press agent and a friend of Houdini's, claimed that the idea had been suggested as Houdini and

Burnside stood in the wings, watching the performing elephants in "Cheer Up." Burnside jokingly suggested that Houdini should make one of the elephants disappear. Weeks later Houdini called and said he was ready to try it.

If that conversation really occurred, both Burnside and Houdini had been playing games. Houdini might have been motivated by his rivalry with Howard Thurston, who was rumored to be proposing spectacular ideas for the Hippodrome show: an auto race or a disappearing horse. Houdini was looking for a trump card. But we also know that Charles Morritt had already suggested the Vanishing Elephant to Houdini, and it was Morritt's illusion that was ultimately presented on that stage. More than likely, several people had the same idea at the same time. Both Jarrett and Houdini realized that the Hippodrome was the perfect place to stage this illusion, and by the time Houdini spoke with Burnside, he had his game plan in mind.

When it came to his spot in the program, Houdini's magnificent bravado was on display. He began by walking out on the massive stage and performing one of the smallest tricks in magic, the Needles.

Armed with a dime's worth of needles and a spool of thread in his vest pocket, Houdini preferred this trick for impromptu shows, when he was called upon to perform in a newspaper office or at a banquet. It was an old trick, probably originating in the Orient, and Houdini had learned it in his dime museum days. He invited a small committee onstage to supervise, asking for doctors or other professional men. The Great Leon, a vaudeville magician and a friend of Houdini's, brought his son to the Hippodrome to see this show. Sitting in the balcony, looking down at the tiny man in the black frock coat who was standing at the edge of the immense Hippodrome stage, Leon's jaw dropped. "Look at that son of a gun, he's really gonna do the Needle Trick."

Houdini opened his mouth wide, asking the committee to assure themselves that he had nothing concealed inside. Pulling several packets of needles from his pockets, he placed bundles of loose needles at his lips and appeared to swallow them, dozens and dozens at a time. "You'll notice that I swallow them eyes first, so they can see where they're going." Throwing his head back and opening his mouth, he asked the committee if they could see the needles anywhere. They confirmed that his mouth was empty. Reeling off yards of white thread from the spool, he quickly gobbled this as well.

Dramatically, Houdini cleared his throat, winced, coughed, and removed the end of the cotton thread from his mouth. He slowly pulled until a sparkling needle was revealed dangling from the thread. Several inches farther along, another needle, then another and another, until all the needles were revealed, perfectly threaded along the long string that stretched across the stage.

The Needle Trick was a favorite of Houdini's, and it was said that at the Hippodrome he used an impressive 200 needles and 60 feet of thread; still, it simply couldn't be seen by most of the audience, except for the occasional sparkle of a needle in the spotlight. Performing it was a test of Houdini's pantomime skills and forceful personality. "They knew there were needles," according to Leon, "because Houdini told them so."

Then a drumroll, and Jennie entered, a full-grown Asian elephant that was part of the Powers troupe. Houdini wrote his own account of the trick for a magician's journal:

> *I introduce her as the first known Vanishing Elephant. She weighs over ten thousand pounds and is as gentle as a kitten. . . . The elephant salutes me, says good-by to the audience by waving her trunk and head . . . and gets a big laugh, for the good-natured beast lumbers along and I believe she is the best natured elephant that ever lived. She certainly is very fond of me.*

Sime Silverman described the show in *Variety*:

> *The elephant was led upon the stage by its trainer with Houdini watchfully standing by. Houdini made the elephant do a little magic by making a piece of sugar disappear. In the immediate vicinity was a "cabinet" that would not fit an ordinary stage, [for] Houdini's four-legged subject. The assistants turned the cabinet around. It only required fifteen of them to do it.*

Houdini continued:

> *I use a cabinet about eight feet square, about twenty-six inches off the floor; it is rolled on by twelve men. I show all parts, opening back and front.*

Of course, he'd conveniently left off one dimension, the longest one. More than likely, the cabinet was about eight by eight feet on one end, and fourteen or fifteen feet long. The cabinet resembled a small box-car and was painted like a big circus wagon. On any other stage, the apparatus would have seemed enormous, but on the Hippodrome stage, it was simply a big box. Houdini wrote:

> *The elephant walks into it; I close the doors and curtains— doors in the back and curtains in the front.*

Once the elephant had been led up a ramp, the doors were closed behind it, and the box was given a quarter-turn by the assistants, rotating it on its heavy casters so that one end faced front. There was an oval opening in the front, covered with iron bars and a curtain

Houdini's Vanishing Elephant at the Hippodrome

inside. Houdini opened the front curtains, allowing the audience to see inside. It was inky black. Suspiciously black. The assistants ran to the back of the cabinet, opening two half-circular doors, allowing the audience to look through the cabinet to the curtain some fifteen feet beyond it. According to Sime Silverman in *Variety*,

> *One would swear he was looking at the backdrop directly through the cab. . . . No elephant. No trap. No papier mache animal. It had gone.*

Houdini boasted,

No special background, everything is in bright light, and it
is a wonderful mystery for an elephant to be so manipulated.
They move so slowly.

Houdini bowed, and the curtains swept closed on the scene, which
the Hippodrome program had called "The Most Colossal Disappearing
Mystery that History Records." But as the audience contemplated the
illusion, most of them were disappointed. Clarence Hubbard, who
reviewed it for a magician's magazine, noted:

The Hippodrome being of such a colossal size, only those sit-
ting directly in front got the real benefit of the deception.
The few hundred people sitting around me took Houdini's
word for it that the "animile" had gone—we couldn't see
into the cabinet at all!

Just like the Needles, it had only been a trick because Houdini told
them it was a trick.

Magicians agreed that the Vanishing Elephant was a completely unimpressive trick. Servais LeRoy thought that Houdini's illusion was
"perfect in [its] utter weakness." The standard joke at the time among
Houdini's contemporaries was that three men wheeled the cabinet
onto the stage. The elephant stepped inside and disappeared. Then
twenty men stepped out from the wings in order to wheel the cabinet
offstage. Where did the elephant go?

Of course, Houdini was not actually guilty of this mistake, but it
was a snide comment on his carelessness with magic and suggested
that the elephant ended up simply hiding inside the box. That was the
Great Leon's best guess. The box was large on the end, and the circular
opening that the audience was looking through was quite small. "He
could hide a whole damn circus in that box," Leon told his son. Perhaps the elephant was lying on the floor, and the audience was looking
over her, or she was standing to one side inside the box, hidden by a
dark piece of scenery.

There's no question that the proportions of the Hippodrome and the impractical size of the apparatus accentuated its faults. The stage was wide, and Houdini's cabinet was long and narrow, so only a thin strip of the audience, sitting directly in front, would have appreciated that the cabinet was empty. If the cabinet had been of a manageable size, it could have been opened and then pivoted to the right and left, giving everyone an opportunity to see into it.

Houdini countered any criticisms with his own self-congratulations:

> It is the biggest vanish the world has ever seen. It is a weird trick. In fact, everyone says, "We don't see enough of it." They are so busy watching for false moves that though the trick takes seven or eight minutes, it appears like a few seconds.

He knew that the real value of the illusion was its publicity. A few thousand saw the illusion each night, but millions had read that Houdini had made an elephant disappear. That put Houdini in a new category. According to *Variety*, he was no longer the premier escape artist but was now "the Master Magician." Houdini eagerly wrote to his friend Harry Kellar, surprising him with his news:

> Have been saving [this illusion], but it is just as well it is brought out [for] my debut in America as illusionist. So, I am still in the ring.

• • •

A rough calculation shows that during the run of "Cheer Up," nearly a million people must have seen Houdini make Jennie disappear. But there are few good accounts of the illusion and no authoritative explanations. Audience members and technicians were interviewed. Authors, magicians, and historians have offered various theories. No one can really explain why Jennie couldn't be seen inside the cabinet. Like Morritt's Disappearing Donkey, somehow the secret has been lost. A number of magicians believed that the two illusions were closely related, and some even suggested that the Elephant was a larger version of the Donkey trick. But the descriptions are of two completely different pieces of apparatus, of different sizes and shapes, which were used in completely different ways.

Several years later Houdini revived the Vanishing Elephant illusion just down the street at the Times Square Theatre to promote a film. The new elephant, named Baby, was notably smaller than Jennie and less impressive inside the big box. At the Times Square Theatre, Houdini boldly introduced the effect by calling for all the scenery in the theatre to "strike"; as all the drapes were lifted, the audience was staring at the bare brick wall and steam pipes of the theatre. It was a dramatic presentation, and at the smaller Times Square, where more people could see inside the cabinet, the illusion must have looked more impressive.

As magicians must hide their secrets in plain sight, it's strange for such a famous illusion to remain a mystery. Stage magic has always been a gradual evolution of principles, so it should have been simple for Houdini's peers to recognize elements that hinted at the solution. But magicians have only managed to rule out possibilities. Houdini probably didn't use a trapdoor; the cabinet was raised off the stage floor on large wheels. Mirrors seem to have been impractical, being much too large; besides, in the wide Hippodrome auditorium, some spectators would have been staring at their own reflections. It also seems unlikely that Jennie sneaked into the nearby curtains; there were no curtains at the Times Square Theatre.

The mystery of Houdini's Vanishing Elephant led to the gnawing conclusion that magicians were genuinely fooled. It might have been a great illusion disguised as a bad illusion. It probably involved Morritt's innovative thinking, waterlogged by Houdini's ordinary performance.

Guy Jarrett was convinced that his idea for the Vanishing Elephant would have been better. It probably would have been. His suggestion was to use an enormous table onstage, equipped with mirrors, like Tobin's original Sphinx illusion. All the scenery surrounding the table would be carefully arranged for the reflections. The elephant would stand on the table and be covered with a tent. The action of the scene allowed the mirrors to be secretly pushed up through the stage, so they would be beneath the table for only the few necessary moments—as the elephant was being lowered by an enormous elevator.

If he had done it, the illusion would have been a masterpiece of stagecraft. That's why Jarrett so resented losing out to Houdini's unimpressive trick:

> *So, [Burnside and Houdini] did that stinky vanish of an elephant. People become disgusted when their time is taken up with such foolish stuff, and particularly if they had paid money to get in and expect to see something. It was so lousy that I was never curious about it.*

Perhaps Houdini's trick was foolish or even stinky. But, of course, Guy Jarrett was a professional stage technician and an inventor of illusions. He was just pretending when he said that he wasn't curious about it.

14
Sensations

*Let them steal my inventions, and I will
always be a step or two ahead of them.*
—P. T. Selbit

The magician and author Henry Hay noted that the decline of the waistcoat has affected magic more than the invention of communications satellites. It might be romantic to say that magic is timeless. It is actually just oblivious to new ideas, fashions, or trends. The permutations of Devant's and Morritt's inventions seem interchangeable, just variations on a formula. Although both made a suffragette appear and disappear, Devant made a German soldier shrink to a tiny chocolate man, and Morritt produced a group of ragtime musicians, they were just trying to attract crowds.

"Topicality" for magicians was seldom more than this sort of simple veneer, a character in a costume, or a title that sounded interesting on a poster. Magicians were concerned with tempting audiences to the theatre. Politics or controversy was merely a lucky accident.

On a gray December morning in 1920, a small group of people assembled at St. George's Hall to watch the audition of a new illusion.

P. T. Selbit, a tall, slender British magician with sharp features, stood at the side of the stage in his tuxedo, rubbing his hands together, waiting for a cue. From a seat on the aisle, Nevil Maskelyne nodded to him. Selbit began, speaking in a resonant bass voice and adopting the nature of a scientific lecturer.

"Ladies and Gentlemen, it gives me great pleasure to demonstrate a modern mystery and a scientific marvel, the inexplicable problem of solid through solid, which I shall demonstrate this evening by attempting to . . ." his voice rose dramatically as he spoke the word "attempting," then a long pause as he looked over the dozen men who formed his audience, ". . . saw . . . through . . . a . . . woman!"

The pianist in the pit began to play, and the curtain opened. Onstage was a plain, unfinished pine box, roughly the size and shape of an upright coffin. Selbit introduced Jan Glenrose, his main assistant, who was wearing a pretty patterned dress with delicate ruffles around the neckline. He then invited several men from the audience onto the stage to serve as a committee. Jan was tied with ropes around her wrists, ankles, and neck. As she backed into the wooden box, the ropes were threaded through corresponding holes in the box. The lid was placed on the box, and the hasps locked. The box was lifted by Selbit's assistants and placed across a horizontal stand of plain boards. The men from the audience held the ends of the rope taut, stretching out the lady in the box and restricting her motions inside.

Selbit picked up a strip of plate glass, about four feet long and slightly less than a foot wide, pushing it through a vertical slot in the lid of the box and down through the bottom. It seemed as if the glass must have passed through the lady's chest. This was repeated with two similar sheets of glass, through her waist and between her legs. The spectators rewarded Selbit with a smattering of applause, which echoed in the cold theatre.

But Selbit was just warming up. Two rectangular blades of steel were passed horizontally through the lady at her neck and hips. Selbit explained that the wooden box had been divided into eight separate sections, which he carefully demonstrated by placing a cigar box atop the large wooden coffin and moving it between each steel and glass partition as he dramatically counted, "One . . . two . . . three. . . ." The wooden box had been barely large enough to contain the lady and certainly didn't provide enough room for her to twist or wriggle around inside.

The piano player switched to a dramatic march as Selbit pulled the strip of glass from the center of the box. An assistant entered with a long, two-handled crosscut saw, which glistened in the stage light. Selbit warned the men to pull tightly on the ropes, ensuring that the lady was stretched out inside. Placing the saw at the midpoint of the box, across the lady's waist, two assistants began sawing. With each stroke the saw rasped and roared through the thick pine planks, dropping sawdust on the stage below. Inch by inch it descended, until it had clearly reached her body. The sensation was visceral, and Selbit had managed to suggest that the audience was witnessing an insane crime. With several more purposeful strokes of the saw, it ripped through the bottom board, clattering to the wooden framework beneath the box.

Selbit stepped in, unlocking the hasps at the top of the box and opening both halves of the sawed lid to peer inside. An expression of concern played across his face, and then he looked up and broke into a broad smile. He pulled a scissors from his pocket, cutting the ropes free and allowing the lady to be lifted from the box to take her bow.

For some reason Selbit's performance failed to impress Nevil Maskelyne. Maybe the dreary, clinical audition caused him to underestimate the drama of the illusion. Maybe he resisted the grisly, overtly suggestive nature of the effect. Perhaps Maskelyne simply couldn't anticipate the public's interest. Few did.

A group of agents from Moss Empire, watching the same tentative premiere, huddled in a corner of the auditorium and decided that Selbit had the new sensation for their music halls.

Sawing through a Woman was one of magic's few incendiary successes. It turned out to be the perfect product for the decade that would be later said to "roar": impulsive, aggressive, and thrilling.

The feverish interest in the effect took many magicians by surprise, and Selbit had a difficult time holding onto, then managing, its success on the stage—the same way one might stoke a modest flame and suddenly discover a raging inferno. With the perspective of time, there seems to have been a hidden subtext or meaning behind this fourteen-minute music hall turn. Selbit had come up with the right idea at the right time.

Selbit was born Percy Thomas Tibbles in London in 1881. As a boy Percy was an amateur magician, also serving as an apprentice at a silversmith shop near the London Pavilion. One day he discovered that the basement at the silversmith's was being rented out to Charles Morritt, who was secretly building and rehearsing his latest trick—this would become his cage illusion. Percy picked the lock, sneaking into the workshop to study the apparatus every evening when Morritt left. Years later he confessed that whenever he sat in the audience and watched Morritt's cage, "we have always felt a parental interest steal guiltily over us."

Tibbles worked as a journalist, writing for a theatrical paper and later editing a handbook and periodical for magicians. He changed his name, reversing it, to Selbit and performed a fashionable act of coin and card manipulations. Shortly after he began working in music halls, he calculated that audiences wanted to see something exotic and mysterious. For several years he worked under the name Joad Heteb, impersonating an Egyptian magician by wearing dark grease-paint, a black, stringy wig, and a gold robe.

Selbit was an especially creative magician and also a restless entre-preneur. He always seemed to be in a three-point stance, ready for the next new idea that would, like a starting pistol, propel him again through the music halls. In an effort to make the most of these cre-ations as quickly as possible, Selbit employed other magicians, fran-chising his ideas, with multiple productions playing different theatres.

In 1910 he toured with an amazing effect called Spirit Paintings, which was first suggested by a magician named Dr. Wilmar. In Spirit Paintings, Selbit showed a number of large blank canvasses, which were examined by members of the audience. Two canvasses were selected, marked, and placed face to face inside a frame. A powerful electric lamp behind the canvasses backlit them so that the white can-vases glowed on the darkened stage.

A committee of spectators then chose the name of an old master and concentrated on that name. Colors slowly materialized on the illuminated canvas, becoming brighter and sharper as the audience watched. When the painting seemed fully developed, Selbit slid both canvasses from the frame and opened them up, showing the com-pleted artwork. It had been painted in the style of the selected artist.

Wilmar had acquired the weird Spirit Paintings effect from an Omaha, Nebraska, magician named David P. Abbott. Abbott had discerned the secret when he visited with the Bangs Sisters, two Chicago mediums who were famous for producing paintings during their séances. As usual Selbit gave the presentation a number of amazing touches. Airbrush work was little known at the time, and the final paintings, rendered in rich, bright colors with an airbrush, were exhibited in the lobby of the theatre after the performance. The audience was astonished to notice that there were no brushmarks on the spirit paintings.

From the sublime to the ridiculous, Selbit's next creation was the Mighty Cheese, a large, flat wheel of cheese about eighteen inches across. It was "the strongest cheese on earth," he told the audience. The cheese stood on its edge instead of falling over, and it seemed impossible to wrestle the cheese to the ground and pin it flat against the stage. A number of men from the audience were invited to take on the cheese. As they pushed against it, it slithered and twisted out from under them, skittering across the stage and sending the men flying.

Henry Bate, Devant's mechanic, made the Mighty Cheese for Selbit. It was a hammered sheet metal case that enclosed a large, heavy flywheel. Backstage before the show, the concealed flywheel was attached to a stationary bicycle that had been specially modified. A healthy stagehand pedaled frantically until the wheel was humming at well over a thousand revolutions per minute. When the cheese was slid onto the stage, the whirling flywheel served as a gyroscope, holding the cheese upright as the men pushed. Selbit guaranteed laughs by adding two confederates to the performance. They seemed to be merely volunteers from the audience, but the magician could rely on them for the most hilarious, acrobatic attempts to wrestle the cheese to the ground.

Selbit toured for Maskelyne and Devant in 1912 and 1913, presenting Devant's Window of a Haunted House illusion in music halls and American vaudeville. The following season, he introduced the illusion of Walking through a Brick Wall at St. George's Hall. When Selbit performed it, he introduced a lady in a long, fashionable dress, who apparently passed through the wall. In 1914 Houdini copied the illusion at Hammerstein's Roof Garden in New York. Houdini's presentation was much more dramatic because he walked through the wall himself, perfectly complementing his reputation as an escape artist.

But the Sawing illusion was Selbit's greatest creation, one of the most famous illusions ever created. After the audition at St. George's Hall, it was first shown to an audience on January 17, 1921, at the Finsbury Park Empire. The Sawing was an immediate sensation. Reviewers commented on the "bloodthirsty . . . hair-raising" spectacle. Selbit responded with a flurry of publicity stunts, including ambulances parked at the theatre and auditions for potential victims. Between performances Selbit's men carried buckets from the stage door to the front of the theatre. As crowds watched, the men poured murky red liquid into the gutter. "Perhaps the artistically inclined may affect to scoff at this type of magic," one review noted, "but there was no possibility of doubting that it pleased a large audience at this particular presentation."

The English company of the Grand Guignol had just opened at London's Little Theatre on September 1, 1920. Not surprisingly, writers compared Selbit's thrilling illusion to the famous French theatre of horror, the original Grand Guignol. The *Daily Express* wrote that Selbit's illusion provided a perfect plot:

> *An infuriated husband finds letters addressed to his wife—*
> *they are signed respectively George and Henry. A saw is taken*
> *from the sideboard, [the wife] is promptly cut in half, and the*
> *respective portions, packed in brown paper parcels, are dis-*
> *patched with best wishes to George and Henry. This delectable*
> *morsel might be sheer joy to the Little Theatre audiences.*

The famous Grand Guignol shows first premiered in Paris in 1897. The theatre was a claustrophobic little space of fewer than three hundred seats in the rue Chaptal. It had originally been built, over a century earlier, as a convent, and the gothic wooden angels, long pews, confessional booth, and vaulted ceilings added to the weird atmosphere inside the theatre and made the productions seem especially sacrilegious.

Oscar Méténier, who developed the *rosse* play—literally, a "vicious" play—created the formula for Grand Guignol. The evening consisted of four to seven short plays. Some were no more than fifteen minutes in length. They were arranged as a sort of vaudeville, interspersing society comedies or farces with *rosse* plays, which dealt with low-life subjects, such as crime, murder, rape, and torture. The formula was called "hot and cold showers," a fast-paced mixture of surprise and dread in the style of the best roller coasters. The audience never knew what to expect. Grand Guignol became famous for its horror plays, which were shockingly depraved and grotesque. When under the control of playwright André de Lord and producer Camile Choise, these plays were often accompanied by elaborate, bloody special effects: burned flesh, gouged eyes, stabbings, and decapitations. It wasn't uncommon for one or two members of the audience to faint on any evening, and the cobblestone alley adjoining the theatre was often filled with hyperventilating spectators.

Today the Grand Guignol is remembered for influencing the impressionistic, shadow-filled horror films of the 1930s and the bloody, nothing-left-to-the-imagination slasher movies of the 1960s. The actual theatre achieved its greatest success and widest public curiosity in the years just after the Great War, when road companies were mounted in London and New York. The London production featured the established recipe of exaggerated violence, terrifying madness, and demented sexuality. Moralists and censors roundly attacked it.

During the war Europe had witnessed the slaughter of a generation: over ten million killed and twenty million wounded. The veterans returning from the front were disfigured, shell-shocked, and burned by mustard gas. The war had not only made the public conscious of technological horrors and death but desensitized them to these subjects. Entertainment in general had become fiercer and nastier. The Grand Guignol and Selbit's new illusion were two examples of the same phenomenon. Writing many years later on the decline of magic, Will Goldston blamed the First World War:

> *Magic has suffered a good deal. The Great War turned the world, and people's ideas, topsy-turvy. The demand in entertainment, after the war, was for noise and excitement. Those magicians who were able to adapt their programs to meet the new condition did well, but they could not re-establish magic in all its old prestige.*

Goldston didn't name the magician responsible, but it is clear that Selbit's Sawing established the new conditions. Unlike the Grand Guignol, no blood was shed on Selbit's stage, and the finale revealed a happy ending, the lady restored in one piece. Still, the illusion teased audiences with the same thrills of violence that were making headlines at the Little Theatre. Selbit's stark apparatus, just a long, thin packing box and some ropes, felt less like music hall conjuring than a maddening, Grand Guignol–style crime in progress.

• • •

Within months of its debut, Sawing through a Woman had started a war among magicians.

Horace Goldin was an American illusionist who had specialized in sensations—shooting an assistant out of a cannon and into a nest of trunks hanging over the audience's head or making a tiger disappear. Early in his career Goldin had become famous for presenting trick after trick in rapid succession, without stopping to speak. "Silence is Goldin," joked Selbit, who felt that the American magician was setting a dangerous precedent.

Photographs of Goldin show an unlikely figure for a magician—just the opposite of Selbit. All his life he was round and fleshy, with an oversized nose and thinning hair. But in motion, Goldin had mastered the dashing, graceful gestures of a swashbuckler, and his act emphasized this constant momentum, an attractive mix of color and spectacle. He was well known as an inventive magician and created a number of popular effects. On June 3, 1921, several months after Selbit's sawing premiere, Goldin introduced his own illusion at the Society of American Magicians' annual banquet at the McAlpin Hotel in New York. He called it Sawing a Man in Two. Goldin placed a hotel bellboy inside a box—his hands and feet protruding from the ends—and sawed through the center of the box.

The premiere at the McAlpin Hotel was suspiciously hurried, and magicians realized that Goldin had quickly assembled his clumsy trick to capitalize on Selbit's latest success. Goldin made several mistakes that night. For example, he used a bellboy as a victim, rather than an attractive lady. The apparatus used was oversized and crude. The finished product wasn't terribly deceptive and failed to excite the audience.

Many magicians at the McAlpin Hotel thought Goldin's trick was merely a curiosity. But Howard Thurston, watching from the audience, realized that it could be a great illusion. Thurston wanted the apparatus rebuilt in his Long Island shop, and he quickly approached Goldin with a proposal. Goldin would allow Thurston to turn the prop over to Harry Jansen, a well-known magician and apparatus builder. He would improve the trick, building a deceptive, finished prop for Goldin. In exchange, Thurston would add the illusion to his touring show.

The most important element in making money with the trick was time. Both Goldin and Thurston knew that Selbit would be arriving soon in the United States.

The improved apparatus included several elements suggested by Jansen. Now it was on a thin table rather than a heavy platform. And the victim's head protruded from one end of the box throughout the effect, giving the audience a clear view of her. Instead of using a plain wooden box, the new prop was brightly enameled, with panels painted with fleurs-de-lis or stenciled Egyptian motifs. It was purely visual, substituting a bright cartoon version of a crime (Sawing a Woman in Half) for a horrifying, dark suggestion (Sawing through a Woman). Thurston introduced it in his own tour in 1921. Goldin filed a patent for the illusion and launched his assault on the Keith vaudeville circuit in the summer of that year. Goldin was featured in the largest cities; smaller cities saw the illusion presented by one of Goldin's associates, Servais LeRoy, Jansen, Kalma, Joe Dolan, or Henry Marcus.

Goldin systematized the publicity stunts. Ambulances would tour the streets with signs advertising "We are going to Keith's in case the saw slips." Uniformed nurses stood in the lobbies; advertisements solicited local carpenters, doctors, and surgeons to assist and brave local girls to offer their bodies. Goldin supervised every element of the advertising, insisting to theatre managers,

> Sawing a Woman in Half actually transpires in full view of the audience. They are shown the two separated parts of the woman in plain view. Therefore, please, at no time in your press material, billing, slides or other publicity refer to it as "An Illusion." By doing so, you merely take away from its sensational value.

Each magician added his own touches. Thurston's presentation made stars of his volunteers by secretly cueing them through the comedy. The magician played the part of host, the dapper man in the tuxedo who was bemused by the mayhem onstage.

Thurston began by inviting a group of spectators onto the stage:

> I will now show you the unsolved mystery of sawing a young lady in two parts, and for this evening's performance I will allow a committee of persons to come onto the stage to try to discover the secret. You have my permission to examine every part to discover the secret and tell it to the audience. Anyone may come. You ladies come along with the men. Now let us have all the boys and girls.

The people were arranged in a half-circle around the apparatus. The table was shown, and doors in the box were opened wide, showing that nothing was concealed inside. Thurston introduced his assistant, Eileen, holding a crystal ball in front of her eyes and hypnotizing her. She was lifted into the box, and her head protruded from one side of the apparatus, with stocks locked around her neck. Her feet were pushed through and locked in stocks at the other end. Eileen's hands were pushed through holes in the end of the box near her face.

> One of you gentlemen, come this way. Place your hand on her forehead. Don't caress her. Touch her. One of you gentlemen, hold her feet.

Thurston held up a long, polished stainless steel crosscut saw and struck it with a mallet; it gave out a keening wail. One of the small boys from the audience dashed off the stage, running back up the aisle to his seat.

Thurston turned his attention back to the men at each end of the box.

> Now you may hold her hands. You have hold of her hands, haven't you!

The man shrugged.

> *You know, there are some that have more experience than others. You have hold of her feet?*

This man also seemed doubtful, telling Thurston, "I think so."

The magician stopped, turning all his attention to the man holding the lady's feet:

> *I want to prove something to you. Let go. I will prove to you that these are perfectly good feet. George, let me have the scissors.*

Thurston's main assistant handed him a pair of scissors. A number of newspaper exposures of the Sawing illusion had guessed that mannequin feet were substituted for the lady's own feet. Thurston played upon this suspicion. He snipped the toe away from the lady's stockings, showing her wiggling toes.

> *Now you can tell that they are all right. See that they are alive. Hold them carefully. Now, one thing to do. Cut her in two parts, equal parts. The slightest slip of this saw may prove fatal to the young lady. Ready. Saw!*

Thurston's assistants pulled the saw back and forth, slicing through wood strips at the middle of the boxes. As the saw reached the lady's body, her head turned right and left with each stroke of the saw. The audience laughed nervously, and Thurston stopped to admonish the men holding each end of the lady.

> *Gentlemen! The object of this is to prevent the body from straining the saw. I asked you to hold firmly so the saw does not twist the body, and should there be an accident, every one of you is equally guilty. And especially you!*

The sawing continued, but as the saw reached the bottom of the box, the lady let out a scream. The committee from the audience scattered, running back to the steps and up the aisle to their seats. This left one man, holding the lady's feet. He looked over nervously at the magician, pulled out his handkerchief, and mopped his brow.

Thurston placed a large metal blade in the box, sealing up the path of the saw. A second blade was slid alongside the first, but halfway down it seemed to catch on something. Thurston tried to push the blade down and failed. He turned to the man at the lady's feet:

Young man, draw her feet out.

Following instructions, he pulled sharply on her feet, and the blade fell into place with a thud. This was too much for the man, who let go of the lady's feet and ran back to his seat like the other spectators before him. Thurston called up the aisle after the spectator:

Don't go! Don't go!

But he couldn't be coaxed back to the stage. The lady wiggled her hands, then her feet. The two half-boxes were pulled apart, showing a gap of about two feet. It certainly seemed as if the lady had been cut into two pieces. Thurston stepped up on the table, walking between the boxes. Thurston's assistants turned the table completely around, showing the lady's head, hands, and feet, all very real and separated at the opposite ends of the table. To prove the point, they even lifted one of the boxes completely off the table.

A very curious experiment in mental suggestion. Play the mystic music.

The orchestra took its cue, starting a waltz as the boxes were pushed back together again. Thurston removed the blades, unlocked the stocks, and opened the box, showing the lady was now back together in one piece, reclining in the empty cabinet. She was lifted out and stood on the stage. Thurston snapped his fingers, awakening her as the orchestra played its final chord.

• • •

Selbit arrived in New York in September 1921 and signed with the Shubert's vaudeville circuit. He quickly sued Goldin over what he considered the appropriation of his effect but lost when it was determined that Goldin's Sawing was a different illusion. In a pre-emptive strike Goldin had registered many possible titles for the act with the Vaudeville Manager's Protective Agency, boxing Selbit into a corner. Selbit discovered there was one prospective title still available, the Divided Woman, which was how he was forced to bill the act.

W.C. Dornfield, a popular magician during the 1920s, saw Selbit's first performance in America and told me over a half-century later how impressed he was with the British magician. At the conclusion of the act, Selbit thanked his committee onstage by giving each man a pretty metal charm, a golden saw with Selbit's name engraved on it. Dornfield was introduced to Selbit afterwards and congratulated him on the illusion but advised him not to use the phrase "golden saw," as it sounded like an advertisement for his rival. Selbit took the advice.

Variety wasn't especially impressed and didn't find the original to be any better than the imitation:

> Selbit lectures the act [and] takes his presentation very seri-ously, it seems. . . . This one might aptly be titled Sawing a Box in Half, for it omits the principal punch of the Goldin presentation, in which the woman's feet and head are seen while the saw apparently passes through her body.

The British magician had a difficult time after Goldin's head start in the United States, and the Shubert vaudeville circuit, a new enter-prise, didn't have the prestige of the Keith-Orpheum theatres. Selbit organized his own group of magicians, who took the act around the world, but he found many cities in America blocked to him; Goldin's army of magicians had anticipated his every move.

Compared with Goldin's illusion, Selbit's version was less visual and more serious and intellectual. Magicians took sides in the battle.

Guy Jarrett, who admired the most sophisticated, deceptive illusions, felt that Selbit's illusion was "a mystery" but Goldin's Sawing "did more to ruin magic than any other damager. . . . it sickened the public." More than likely, it was the cartoonish aspect of Goldin's trick that Jarrett resented. David Bamberg, Theo Bamberg's son, who worked with Selbit in the United States, felt that

> *Selbit's version was more baffling, but Goldin's more spec-*
> *tacular. Goldin finally won the battle. It was a spite war and*
> *the only ones to make any money were the big shots who*
> *controlled vaudeville. They made a fortune.*

The success of the illusion led to more and more imitations. American magicians such as the Great Leon, Linden Heverly, Claude Alexander, and David Swift made their claims for the idea. By November 1921 Thayer Magic Company of Los Angeles advertised the illusion in magicians' trade journals. They sold it for $175 or plans in a book for five dollars. Goldin bristled at the copies and, ironically, spent most of his profits dashing to court, attempting in vain to enforce his patent or stop other magicians.

It was almost impossible for any magician to legitimately claim the Sawing in Half illusion as an invention, because the idea for the illusion had been described in Robert-Houdin's book, first published in 1858. Robert-Houdin claimed that Torrini, his mentor in magic, created the illusion. In *The Memoirs of Robert-Houdin*, Torrini described his presentation:

> *At my summons, two slaves brought in a long and narrow*
> *chest, and a trestle for sawing wood. Antonio seemed to be*
> *terribly alarmed, but I coldly ordered the slaves to seize*
> *him, place him in the chest, the cover of which was imme-*
> *diately nailed down, and lay it across the trestle. Then,*
> *taking up the saw, I prepared to cut the chest asunder.*

Torrini sawed the box into halves and then separated the two pieces, covering them with a large cloth. When the cloth was removed, the audience was shocked to see two pages, dressed exactly alike, one on each box. He had sawed a man into twins.

More than likely, there was no Torrini and no mid-nineteenth century Sawing illusion, but Robert-Houdin's account—fact or fiction—had been read by every magician.

Another popular American book, Hopkins's *Magic*, was published in 1897. It gave an account of many classical illusions, optical effects, and stage special effects. A paragraph in the book described a comic illusion, which had been seen in New York several years earlier:

> *A clown throws himself on a sofa and is cut in two by a harlequin. One part of the sofa with the body remains in one part of the stage while the other part of the legs and feet (which are all the time vigorously kicking) disappear through a wing at the other end of the stage. The action is very sudden and the effect startling.*

Author and magician John McKinven has discovered that the clowns were the Hanlon Brothers, a popular troupe of acrobats, who presented elaborate, spectacular shows filled with effects. The show was called "Superba." And while the Hanlons might not have intended the effect as a magic illusion, many magicians were aware of the description in Hopkins's *Magic*.

In many ways Selbit's effect seems to have been derived from Robert-Houdin's account. Goldin's illusion may have been inspired by the Hanlon Brothers. It's hardly worth discussing the secret of the Sawing in Half illusion. Various books, advertisements, or pamphlets have recorded the basic deceptions. Sometimes the lady avoided the path of the saw, or a tricked blade was used. Sometimes a set of false feet or a second person had been introduced into the box. The elements that made the performances memorable and mysterious were the important doses of presentation—funny, threatening, or challenging.

Since the original versions, there have been dozens of variations.

Goldin's later variation used a large circular saw and no box at all—
just the lady sliced in half like a log. Jarrett created his own version,
using a box so pointedly small and confining that the lady could not
twist out of the way. In the 1960s the South American magician
Richiardi returned the illusion to its Grand Guignol origins; as a
motorized saw sliced through his daughter, a long splatter of blood and
viscera stained the backdrop and the magician's white hospital robe.
At the conclusion of the illusion, the two halves were reassembled in
a perfunctory manner. Groggy and pallid, the lady was lifted away
from the saw as the audience murmured to themselves, wondering
what they had just seen.

All the confusing false starts and historical precedents indicate that
Selbit's great idea was to saw a woman in half in 1920. One important
ingredient in his successful recipe was 1920. The other was a woman.

Before Selbit's illusion, it was not a cliché that pretty ladies were
teased and tortured by magicians. Since the days of Robert-Houdin,
both men and women were used as the subjects for magic illusions.
Victorian gowns often made it unrealistic for a lady to take part in an
illusion or be pressed into a tight space. A lady might look especially
uncomfortable if she were given some necessary task onstage, like
crawling atop a table or crouching inside a box.

During the early 1900s, as a shapely leg became not only acceptable
on the stage but admired, it was fashionable to perform magic with a
cast of attractive ladies. An important consideration was the size and
flexibility of the assistants. An illusion built around a lithe woman was
considerably more deceptive than one built around a boy or a man.

But beyond practical concerns, the image of the woman in peril
became a specific fashion in entertainment. When Selbit introduced
the Sawing in 1921, one of his earliest publicity stunts was to offer
Christabel Pankhurst twenty pounds a week to serve as a permanent
sawing block for his illusion. Christabel and Sylvia Pankhurst,
together with their mother, Emmeline, had been leaders in the British
woman's suffrage movement.

From 1905, when the Women's Vote Bill failed in Parliament, the cause of women's suffrage became known for its radical and sensational techniques. Emmeline Pankhurst warned that the goal would require violent means. No longer could women, or the cause, be thought frivolous. Hunger strikes, arson, bombings, and window smashing—blocks and blocks of storefronts at a time or the prime minister's residence—became established techniques for nearly a decade. In 1907 the suffragettes tussled with London police for five hours, and fifty-seven women were jailed as a result. In 1908 both Emmeline and Christabel were jailed after a hundred thousand suffragettes stormed government buildings. Emmeline, like many in the cause, made a dizzying routine of her jail sentences. A hunger strike, once inside, granted her release. But according to Parliament's newly passed Cat and Mouse Act, upon regaining her health outside, she was once again jailed to complete her sentence. Emmeline was jailed twelve times in twelve months.

The frightening militancy attracted attention. However, when war was declared in 1914, Emmeline Pankhurst urged an end to the protest so that British women could support the war effort. The contributions of women, at home or in factories, were vital and earned respect from the government. Without the benefit of further riots or hunger strikes, the first suffrage bill was passed just one month after the Armistice in 1918.

More than two years later, when Selbit challenged Christabel and Sylvia Pankhurst, he was challenging the women who had faced off with the government and frightened society with their goal. His joke was a reminder of the previous decade of tumult, the memory of which the Great War had not erased. "What a chance for Selbit!" a review concluded. "To be able to say he has actually 'sawn off' the redoubtable 'Sylvia'!"

By 1921 society had realized a number of important changes. The world had lost its innocence, and the crusading ladies had forfeited their innocent charms. Selbit was in a position to unwittingly capitalize on these changes, stumbling upon a dramatic fantasy that made headlines around the world.

•   •   •

Selbit returned to England early in 1922, disgusted by his court battles in America. He turned his attention to new ideas. His following
illusions included Destroying a Girl, Growing a Girl, Stretching a Lady,
the Indestructible Girl, Crushing a Woman, and Broadcasting a
Woman. Selbit wasn't a misogynist but, anxious to continue the success of his Sawing, followed with a series of weird torture illusions.
Some of these effects were quite ingenious, but none reached the popularity of the original.

Selbit's trademark style involved standing at the side of the stage
like a professor, providing a running commentary as the assistants
handled all of the apparatus. It sometimes left the magician with little
to do. When Selbit introduced Crushing a Lady, he was excited by the
response. Eager to send out multiple productions, he called Oswald
Rae, a talented magician who was one of his associates. "We've hit
pay dirt on this one, Ossie," he reported. "You open Monday with it
in Birmingham. I'm sending over the script now so you can learn it.
Dolly and the boys have done the illusion. All you need to do is show
up for the band call, and they can fit you into the presentation."

The apparatus was packed and shipped, the assistants set it all up
and took the band through their cues, but Oswald Rae arrived late for
the rehearsal in Birmingham. As he pushed his way through the stage
door, he saw the large, colorful apparatus for Crushing a Lady being
wheeled into the wings. "Don't worry," Dolly told him. "We had a
good rehearsal. Do you know the script?" Rae nodded. "Just stand at
the prompt side through the action, and we'll take care of it."

For the first matinee that day, Rae watched the action, timing his
words carefully. Dolly reclined inside of a large wooden box, surrounded by inflated balloons. Another heavy chest, of a size to nest
just inside the first one, was raised on a block and tackle. Two men
crouched inside this chest, filling it completely. Slowly, the smaller
box was lowered inside the larger one. The balloons burst, one by one,
under the pressure. The boxes were opened to show that Dolly had
disappeared, apparently flattened beneath the chest. The process was
reversed, and she reappeared.

After that performance, Oswald Rae met Dolly backstage. "Percy's got a good one, doesn't he?" she asked him. "Yes, he does. I have to admit, it puzzled me." Dolly offered to walk him over to the apparatus and show him how it was done. "No, don't. Let me watch it a bit more." Ossie later told a friend that he performed Crushing a Lady for a full week, two performances a day, and still had no idea how it was done.

After the success of the illusion, the Maskelynes couldn't deny the appeal of Selbit's Sawing illusion and arranged with the inventor to present it at St. George's Hall. But when Clive Maskelyne performed it, they chose a more innocent title, Matter through Matter. The Maskelynes were attempting to hold onto the old traditions of conjuring. They never understood that the teasing horror was the secret of the illusion's intrigue.

The Sawing illusion roared through the music halls and vaudeville theatres for several seasons before playing itself out. Selbit had made a clean break from the Golden Age mysteries that had been defined by the Maskelynes since the 1870s. No longer was magic "All Done by Kindness," as David Devant had once advertised. Those days were over. Those magicians were disappearing.

15
Keeping Secrets

Magic cannot stand still. It must either advance with the times, or fall behind.
—Nevil Maskelyne

In retirement Harry Kellar didn't garden or build ships in bottles; he rebuilt the ton and a half of steel and bronze that constituted his famous Levitation of Princess Karnac. He studied the most efficient winches, tested wire samples, supervised the machine work on each tiny bolt and spring, and tried out a new technique to pass the hoop over the lady. Once Kellar was happy that he had assembled the perfect apparatus for this effect, he packed it away in oversized trunks painted with the name *Kellar*, and stacked the trunks in his Los Angeles garage. It was as if he was about to begin another tour. In truth, he didn't know what to do with the improved levitation. Kellar never actually entertained the idea of performing again, but he'd spent a lifetime building magic and wrestling with each technical problem. He couldn't stop.

Harry Kellar died in Los Angeles in 1922, when he was 73. He'd lived long enough to become the grand old man of American magic—toasted, honored, and consulted.

Just over four years later, Kellar's friend Houdini died unexpectedly while in the middle of a tour. Houdini's 1925 show consisted of three separate acts. The first act was Houdini's return to magic, including a number of mechanical props, Robert-Houdin's crystal coin box, and two of Morritt's mirror illusions, the production and disappearance of two assistants. In the second act of the show, Houdini featured his escapes, including his famous Water Torture Cell. The last act consisted of exposures of fraudulent Spiritualists, an exciting lecture in which he demonstrated how people were fooled in the séance room.

Not surprisingly, Houdini's magic was the least impressive part of the formula, but the Spiritualism exposures brought him a great deal of valuable publicity and filled the theatres. The elaborate show had been hard on Houdini, who was suffering from a broken bone in his foot when the show reached Montreal. A student from McGill University visited Houdini in his dressing room. He had heard Houdini boast of his highly developed abdominal muscles and inquired if the escape artist thought he could take his punch. Houdini nodded in agreement but was caught off-guard by the young man's sudden flurry of blows to his stomach. The escape artist shrugged off the injury, but two days later, when the tour arrived in Detroit, Houdini was in terrible pain with a raging fever. Houdini's appendix had been ruptured. Doctors operated but discovered they were too late; there was no cure for peritonitis. He lingered for several days in the hospital and died on Halloween 1926. Houdini was fifty-two years old.

In the 1952 movie *Houdini,* starring Tony Curtis and Janet Leigh, Hollywood suggested its own ending to the Houdini story. The film portrayed his dying in an attempt to escape from the Water Torture Cell. But the real Houdini took few chances and never failed at any escape. It was much more typical of the man that his death was caused by a boast, a misunderstanding, and arrogantly toughing out an injury.

Nevil Maskelyne died in 1924. According to his son Jasper,

> *My father was a wonderful electrician. He taught himself to be a master illusionist, but his heart never thrilled at the glitter of the footlights or the clatter of an appreciative audience.*

The management of St. George's Hall was turned over to the following generation, three of Nevil's children: Noel, Mary, and Jasper. Jasper, the youngest, was a popular magician and a smooth performer, with patent leather hair and a neat, upturned mustache. But the business had changed dramatically, and the family struggled to produce magic revue shows through the 1920s and '30s. Most magicians felt that the Maskelyne shows suffered from a lack of originality and couldn't compete with the changing fashions in entertainment.

In 1933 the little gray and gold theatre, St. George's Hall, which had once hosted the Davenport brothers and was the home of David Devant's greatest creations, was sold to the British Broadcasting Company (BBC), which used it for radio broadcasts. Celebrating the sixtieth anniversary of Maskelyne shows in London—its last year in the business—the family transferred the Christmas magic show to

the Little Theatre, the intimate auditorium that had thirteen years
earlier hosted the blood and mayhem of the Grand Guignol.

Charles Morritt, the "Man of Mystery," found business difficult
through the 1920s. He managed a dance hall in Bristol and planned new
features for his act. Ironically, it was his reliable money-making scheme
for meager times, a Man in a Trance, that gave him so much difficulty.

In October 1927 he performed in Halifax, Yorkshire, at the Victoria
Hall, sharing the bill with the film of the week. A local resident,
William Ingham, nicknamed Billy Fish, had been recruited to "volunteer" for the stunt and would remain hypnotized for a week. Morritt supposedly gave him lessons on how to appear hypnotized, how
to lie motionless in a coffin, how to endure needles poked through his
flesh, and how to be awakened on the stage. If spectators arrived to see
the man, he hastily jumped into the coffin and resumed his "trance."
Once they left, he found time to secretly take his meals. At the end
of the week, Morritt would awaken the man, then solicit donations
from the crowd, pleading that the man had been unable to work
during the duration of the trance. These donations were then split
between the magician and his accomplice.

A policeman from Halifax followed Morritt to the following town,
Pudsey, where he saw the latest Man in a Trance. The policeman
examined the man in the coffin, tickling his feet and lifting his eyelid
to touch his eyeball. The man winced, exposing the deception. Morritt and his assistants were arrested.

In November the 68-year-old showman was brought to court and
charged with obtaining money under false pretenses. Morritt
protested the nature of the charge. "It is a technical point of law," he
wrote to a friend:

> He signed an agreement with me that he was to receive one
> half of the collection, and the remaining half was to go in
> expenses. I went on the stage two nights and said to the
> audience that there is going to be a collection for the man.
> It was simply an oversight on my part. Had I said he is to

*receive half the collection then there would have been no
charge. [The expense] comes to little more than half. I did
not get one penny. . . . The whole case is blackmail.*

In the middle of preparing a defense, Morritt was taken to the hospital and endured two operations for intestinal problems. His legal and medical problems completely strapped him. P. T. Selbit and Will Goldston came to his aid, raising money to support him for his trial. When the case was tried in January 1928, Morritt was prepared with press clippings about his hypnotic abilities, the contract with Billy Fish, and evidence of the policeman's blackmail. Morritt insisted that the performance was genuine. Billy Fish changed his story several times, suggesting that he was in a trance for at least part of his time in the casket and felt "dazed and funny."

The total contribution from the audience had been slightly less than twenty pounds (almost one hundred dollars), and one by one, the witnesses agreed that they had not been defrauded, that it was "a good show for the money." Only three complaints against Morritt remained, for contributions totaling six pence. When Morritt's counsel pointed out that he was now being charged with obtaining six pence under false pretenses, "with no evidence of false pretenses," the case collapsed, and Morritt was declared not guilty on all counts.

Morritt's victory was a technicality. He went to work with his niece, a fortune-teller at a seaside resort. His health never returned and he spent the next five years in Morecambe, Lancashire, hospitalized with tuberculosis and was then confined to the Isolation Hospital in Chorley. Morritt made several efforts to complete his autobiography but was disheartened when he lost the manuscript.

He kept his secrets. When Houdini's brother Theo wrote to him, explaining that he had inherited Houdini's props and asking for technical details of the illusions, Morritt was firm, insisting that he wouldn't put the secrets on paper. "I would explain them personally, because it is not for me to describe them by writing." Morritt never disclosed how his donkey, Solomon, disappeared or how his friend Houdini had managed to hide the elephant. Charles Morritt—the Yorkshire Conjurer and the master of mirror illusions—died on April 10, 1936, of pulmonary tuberculosis, long forgotten by magicians.

• • •

Howard Thurston's touring production, billed as "the Wonder Show of the Universe," reached a high point in the late 1920s. It was long and lavish, presented in three acts with a cast of over twenty onstage.

As always, Thurston began the show with his famous card manipulation. Then the rest of the program included:

> The Levitation of Princess Karnac. The dream in mid-air of the dainty Princess Karnac surpasses the fabled feats of the ancient Indian Sorcerers. She floats over the stage and vanishes like a fading cloud.
>   Sawing Through a Woman (by Public Request)

Thurston's stepdaughter Jane, a pretty blonde, tap-danced and sang "My Daddy's a Hocus-Pocus Man."

> The Mystery of the Vanishing Whippet Automobile, with seven beautiful girls vanishes on a brilliantly lighted stage.
>   The Indian Rope Trick—First Time out of India

In one of his smallest tricks, Thurston showed a glowing electric lightbulb in a lamp on one side of the stage. He picked up a canary, placed it in a paper bag, and instantly made it disappear. The lightbulb flickered and went out. Inside the clear glass bulb was the live canary. Thurston removed the bulb and broke it open with a hammer, setting the bird free.

> Do the Spirits Return?
>   The Girl and the Rabbit
>   Iasia, A Woman Vanishes at the Dome of the Theatre, Over the Heads of the Audience. Where Does She Go?

After saying goodnight to the various children in the audience who had assisted him during the performance, the curtains opened on Thurston's cast, now dressed in beautiful white clown costumes. Thurston stepped to each person, producing thin fountains of water, which sparkled in the spotlights like strings of diamonds. The foun-

tains appeared at the tip of a wand or the points of a folding paper fan.
He picked up a fountain, moving it from place to place on the stage—
placing it on the toe of an assistant or on the cap of another. He coaxed
a fountain to dance along the edge of a sword and balanced another
stream of water atop a spinning wheel. Holding half a coconut shell
in his hand, Thurston caused gallons of water to gush from it. A lady
floated atop a spray of fountains, revolving in graceful arcs as colored
lights played on the scene and the curtain fell.

But "the Wonder Show of the Universe" was far too expensive to
stage during the Depression. In 1931 Thurston began sharing the bill
with feature-length talking movies, performing as many as five one-
hour shows each day. It was grueling work for Thurston, who was over
sixty years old. Even in these shorter shows, he insisted on presenting
his best material, which required cutting trapdoors into the stage
floors and installing the elaborate system for the famous Levitation.

In October 1935, after a difficult day of performances in Charleston,
West Virginia, Thurston and several members of his company went to
a restaurant for a sandwich and a bottle of beer. He stood up to put on
his coat and collapsed onto the floor from a stroke. His show was
packed and shipped back to New York as Thurston recovered; he was
making plans to begin touring again, when he died on April 13, 1936,
just three days after Morritt's death.

It's now generally understood that David Devant's illness, officially
listed as "paralysis agitans," was a progressive, debilitating result of
syphilis. After he retired, Devant taught several of his routines to a
younger magician, Claude Chandler, and together with P. T. Selbit,
Devant proposed a new show for St. George's Hall, suggesting three
new illusions. But the Devant and Selbit show was rejected as too
expensive for the Maskelyne family.

In 1928 Devant's wife, Marion Melville, died as a result of alco-
holism. By that time Devant's affliction had left him unable to walk or
control his hands. A former missionary named Will Curtis served as
secretary and nurse for Devant. At a Christmas party in 1929, Devant
saw the performance of a young conjurer named Francis White and

asked to be introduced. White felt queasy hearing that this legendary performer, who other magicians now called "Master," was in his audience. After the show he was taken to the empty concert hall, where he found Curtis with Devant, a sad, crumpled figure in a wheelchair.

But Devant was positive and complimentary about White's act. He invited the young man to his home for tea and promised to teach him his famous billiard ball manipulations. Devant was unable to use his hands. When the lessons began, White was surprised to find that Devant gave the halting instructions and Curtis, the quiet nurse by his side, picked up the ivory balls and demonstrated each manipulation perfectly. During his years with Devant, Curtis had taught himself to act as the Master's hands.

Devant wrote his autobiography in 1932 and then, four years later, dictated the deceptions used during his long career, which were assembled in the book called *Secrets of My Magic*. The title page noted:

> *In which are disclosed for the first time the Secrets of some of the Greatest Illusions of this Master of the Art of Magic.*

It was probably not a book he had wanted to write, but the project became an economic necessity. He padded it with material from earlier books and tricks contributed by his colleagues in magic. One chapter contained Morritt's recollections of his early career. The center chapters of *Secrets of My Magic* were filled with simple, elegant descriptions of his famous illusions—the Mascot Moth, "The Artist's Dream," and the strange mirrors under the table in the illusion called Beauty and the Beast.

In order to promote the book, several explanations of his tricks were excerpted and published in *The Windsor Magazine* in December 1935. The article was called "Illusion and Disillusion" and was introduced with a strangely pessimistic remark on life from the great magician that must have indicated Devant's years of frustration:

> *At some time or other we have all decided that life is one long disillusionment. It is a platitude and like all platitudes it seems that each of us discovers it anew. The illusions of*

*childhood are shattered one by one until our eyes are widely
opened and we look for a catch in everything. A full appreciation of this fact and the ability to take advantage of it are
the chief assets of the magician.*

The *Windsor Magazine* trick exposures, in a journal for the public,
were in violation of the rules set forth by The Magic Circle, a presti-
gious British organization of magicians, which Devant had helped to
found in 1905. He had been the first president of The Magic Circle and
donated his library to the club. The Circle wrote to Devant, regis-
tering the violation of rules and asking for an explanation.

Devant had faced a similar situation in 1908, when he was at St.
George's Hall and published a series of tricks for beginners. But in 1936
he seemed particularly confused to be involved in this controversy. He
insisted that *The Windsor* was a dignified journal and his article was
merely a promotion for his upcoming book. He told one reporter,

*The tricks I exposed were my own so I did not think that I
had broken any rule. I owe it to posterity to give the world
my secrets before I die. I don't think I shall live much longer.
The Magic Circle seems to think that the mechanics of a
trick are the secret of its success. In my view it is only the
artistry of the performer that can make it magic.*

The Council of The Magic Circle was caught in a bind. It was obliged
to enforce the club rules but horrified to be facing off with the great
David Devant. All magic clubs felt a need to crusade against "exposure"; it has always seemed to be a grand, important cause to amateur
magicians. In 1935 the Quaker Oats Company had published a series
of simple "tricks you can do" for children, and The Magic Circle was
hotly debating these exposures in the same terms as Devant's magazine article. Sidney Oldridge, a magician who had served on the board
of directors at St. George's Hall, wrote a letter decrying the witch-hunt:

*Regarding Quaker Oats, Ltd, I imagine the extent of the
damage they will suffer may be that some members of the*

Council will delete these particular oats from their breakfast menu. I hope this may not oblige Q.O. to put up their shutters.

[Devant] was the most popular magician in the world, out by himself as an exponent of the art. Apparently, all this is forgotten now, in the days of unfortunate ill health, when least in a position to retaliate, he has been subjected to insult by the very society for which he did so much. After all is said and done, how could magic have survived without "exposures"? No, a nation without history does not survive [and] neither does an art without public records and "exposure."

But any club is a little world of fantasy, and club rules are the hard-and-fast attempts to legislate and guarantee that fantasy. The world's greatest magician had decided that his secrets were not the essence of his magic. The club was determined to save David Devant's secrets from David Devant. The council's decision was to expel the magician for breaking his trust:

We are extremely sorry for Mr. Devant and sympathize deeply with him in his affliction, but surely neither that nor the high, almost unique position attained by him in the world of magic can be any excuse. [The] older members knew what his name really meant at the height of his fame, as the present generation cannot of course know, but if the Rules are to mean anything at all, no other decision could have been reached.

• • •

Guy Jarrett never liked Thurston's show. He always remained bitter about their season together and thought that the "Wonder Show" had slowly degenerated into a magic show for children, "a pretend show" filled with flashy, silly tricks:

Magic, which is one of the arts, and one of the best entertainments for the great intelligent public, has suffered terribly. In fact it has been murdered.

Jarrett's business had dissolved with the onset of the Depression; vaudeville was dying, and magicians had no need for his material, especially his unusual, contrary ideas about how magic should be presented. "There is no place for my knowledge except in a book," he wrote.

Although Guy Jarrett had resolved to write his book on magic, he couldn't figure out how. He wasn't a good typist. He didn't have the money to have a book printed and couldn't interest a publisher in his idea. After all, he'd spent his career in the workshop, and his reputation was known to only a small group of professional magicians.

But Jarrett had plenty of time and patience. He bought a hobbyist's printing press, a cast-iron six-by-nine-inch Kelsey Excelsior, which sat on his workbench, and a case of foundry type, the tiny lead letters that could be assembled into lines. Throughout 1936 he spent evenings at his basement shop at 40th Street and 10th Avenue in New York hunched over his press, writing the book by assembling it one letter at a time. When he was finished with page one, he locked the type onto his little press, inked the rollers, and printed his pages by pressing down on a spring handle, which rolled ink over the plate and then pressed each sheet against it.

> *I say my book is just different. I have invented and built more real illusions than the combined output of all the magicians in America, and will describe at least twenty of my greatest effects in this book. I will write for you my associations with the notables of the theatre. There will be plenty about magicians and what of their future.*

After printing page one, he broke apart the individual letters, cleaned off the ink with sprits, re-sorted the letters into their type case, and began composing page two.

The Kelsey Excelsior was so small that Jarrett needed to assemble the signatures of the book, folding each sheet and turning it inside out as the pages were printed. Each piece of paper went through his press four times.

The process took him the better part of 1936. Jarrett wrote about

his illusions for the Thurston show, including the tiny Bangkok
Bungalow. He described how he produced twenty-one people
from a small wooden cabinet about the size of a phone booth in
the "Greenwich Village Follies" and teased readers with a description of his new and improved Sawing in Half illusion. Jarrett recalled
his meeting with Devant and how he made Bela Lugosi disappear
at the climactic moment in the Broadway play "Dracula." He also
explained why Thurston's show was a collection of junk, how
Houdini didn't know anything about magic, and roundly cursed
magicians—he abbreviated the word as "magi"—for their lazi-
ness, their lack of creativity, and for underestimating the "great intelligent public":

> Magi of the last twenty years doing illusions have been ter-
> rible. Not bright enough to invent good illusions, and devoid
> of business sense to buy good ones, the stuff they've pre-
> sented has no element of mystery.

After 106 pages dense with type, opinions mixed with secrets, high-
flying idealism mixed with deflating pragmatism, Jarrett decided that
he was finished. On the last page of his book, he wrote:

> This is a hell of a good book. I just read it. I invented the
> tricks, built the tricks, made the drawings, set the type,
> printed the book, and will bind the book. All out and over.

He hard-bound each volume in thick blue buckram and printed the
title, *Jarrett Magic*, on the spine. When he was finished, he probably
had slightly more than 200 books, which he advertised in a journal for
magicians:

> *Jarrett Magic and Stagecraft*
> *$5.00*
> Terse, pithy, no prolixity, no pictures of magi and bla bla.
> Read my book and cease being just a "drug store magi-
> cian" with an apologetic delivery "doing at tricks" and get

*sense into your head, become an artiste with a real stage
manner. Be a real entertainer.*

*This book is not for the Y.W.C.A., and rhetoricians and
purists attempting to read it will suffer violent poisoning.*

• • •

Magicians have an uneasy, debilitating relationship with secrets,
which they know to be priceless and worthless at the same time. The
actual devices might be simple and crude and only of value as tools for
a larger goal. Leonardo da Vinci was obsessively secretive about his
techniques for mixing paints. Today it seems silly because we realize
that no formula for pigment or mineral spirits would allow anyone to
paint like da Vinci. In 1905 Devant was delighted by the clever, simple
mechanism of the Mascot Moth because it allowed him to create a
marvel. At that time, the tiny trapdoor and sliding tube had been
admired by John Nevil Maskelyne as "the trickiest trick" he had ever
seen. By 1936, when Devant described the illusion in *The Windsor
Magazine,* it had been over fifteen years since he had performed the
illusion. He claimed that "its secret strips it of glamour and romance
and leaves behind nothing but disillusion."

The combination of the Depression, the popularity of motion pictures,
and the decline of vaudeville and the music hall had conspired against
live entertainment. There were fewer opportunities for magicians. Some
had designed acts to be small and efficient, so they could be easily trans-
ported, and quickly set up to share the bill with movies or on the dance
floor of a nightclub. For magicians like Thurston, who had proudly built
up his show larger and larger over the years, this wasn't a possibility.

A generation of great magicians had been guarding their precious
illusions. But by 1936 the business had changed, and there was no
market for these mysteries. Unable to perform their illusions, the
magicians were left with only the secrets. Devant decided that
they could be written about and sold, these last remnants of the art.
Jarrett was given the opportunity to analyze and critique them. Morritt decided that secrets should be discarded and ignored—stoically
kept as secrets until the end.

Was this ultimately a sign of their worthlessness or of their value? What's the value of a secret if it has no power to intrigue? Magicians must pretend that every secret is vital, which is always the first deception of a magic show. Throughout his career, Devant had insisted that the secrets were unimportant and the real art of magic was in the presentations. Some magicians have thought that this was disingenuous, that Devant's attitude was a way of focusing the attention on the performer and denying the devices and inventions that had brought him success. Could there be a magician without secrets? Could secrets really be incidental to a magician's popularity?

Today it's impossible to deny the value of Devant's secrets. There's almost no visual record of him as a performer, just short bits of trick films, which allow us to see a flickering image of the magician in action. We can't evaluate his voice or mannerisms or personality onstage; we can only guess at his expertise with the subtle movements that would have been necessary for his illusions. We recognize Devant's achievements through his secrets. We see him as an artist not because we can study his paintings but because he's left us the globs of paint from his palette. It's a poor substitute for his real achievements: looking at a mix of colors and trying to imagine how beautiful any individual painting could have been.

Most magicians dismissed Jarrett's book. It was expensive and difficult to decipher, filled with misspellings, abbreviations, and confusing diagrams. Jarrett's penchant for preaching and criticizing was considered offensive. Most magicians wanted tricks they could easily perform, instead of Jarrett's expensive, elaborate stage effects, which were now out of fashion.

In the middle of Jarrett's text, he explained the story of his Vanishing Elephant at the Hippodrome over twenty years earlier. He explained how Burnside was first interested in his idea and then double-crossed him, calling in Houdini. Jarrett dismissed Houdini's trick, describing how unimpressed the audience was and how large the box seemed in comparison with the openings in the ends. He concluded with a tiny, rectangular illustration and two simple sentences:

*Probably it was a mirror. Take a little mirror and set it on
my drawing and you see it works, quite an ingenious idea if
there was any trick to be made with it.*

It seems that most magicians missed those sentences. A few who
read them carefully quickly dismissed them. Anyone who looked at
Jarrett's diagram knew that it wouldn't work.

But, coincidentally, the diagram revealed the fourth version of
Charles Morritt's idea that "didn't work": the patent with the barrel,
Beauty and the Beast, Ragtime
Magic, and Houdini's Vanishing
Elephant. In two sentences Guy Jar-
rett had connected the dots.

Houdini's Vanishing Elephant
was a rectangular version of Morritt's barrel. The solution perfectly
matches most descriptions. When
the trick started, the cabinet was
facing sideways. The elephant
entered from one side, led behind
the wedge of the mirror inside. The
back doors were then locked behind

*Looking into Houdini's
Vanishing Elephant cabinet*

the elephant and the cabinet given a quarter-turn, bringing the narrow
front toward the audience.

The front was opened, and the two half-circles were then opened in
the back. Actually, the audience saw only one semicircular door open.
The other door was merely a reflection of the first door. Jennie was
hidden behind a large mirror.

The cabinet would have been about eight by eight by fourteen feet,
with a mirror close to eight by fourteen feet. The inside of the cabinet
needed to be inky black to disguise the odd angles and walls, forcing
the audience to focus on the circular openings. There's a wonderful
optical illusion created as the back doors are opened; because the
mirror is at an angle, the doors seem to open at two different rates,
the reflection moving slightly later than the real door moves. It would
have looked disarming and deceptive on a stage.

This secret also explains all of the faults of the illusion. The black interior gave many in the audience the impression that there were false panels or compartments hidden in the dark sides, or that the elephant was lying in the bottom. The illusion works best—that is, the distortions are least—as the mirror approaches 90 degrees from the backdrop. At most British music halls, with long, narrow auditoriums and deep stages, the illusion could have been effective. In the Hippodrome, the auditorium was wide. The cabinet was long and narrow, which meant that people seated at the sides couldn't look inside.

A logical solution would have been to open the cabinet, then pivot it from side to side, swinging the front so that the whole of the audience could see inside. This couldn't be done in Houdini's trick. First, the weight of the elephant made it difficult to move the cabinet quickly, even on casters. And once the back circle was opened, reflecting the curtains or the brick wall behind the cabinet, the cabinet couldn't be moved. Turning the cabinet would give the impression that the vertical folds of the curtain or the rows of bricks moved toward each other and converged—disappearing into their own reflections. This would expose the illusion. Houdini was forced to open the cabinet, keep it in place, and take his bow.

Magicians continued to ignore Jarrett's explanation. In the 1960s authors Walter B. Gibson and Morris N. Young, both experts in magic, collaborated on a book analyzing Houdini's secrets. They wrote that Jarrett

> decided that maybe the cabinet had a mirror, running from the edge of the opened front curtain back to the very middle of the hole in the back door. Thus people were supposed to see an upright semicircle, plus its own reflection, making a full circle in all. All very good, except at the Hipp, with people looking into the cabinet at so many odd angles, a lot of viewers would have been looking squarely at the mirror and getting a reflection of the auditorium, while others, whose line of vision was close to parallel with the mirror itself, would have seen only part of a hole in the back of the cabinet. Keeping Jennie safely behind such a mirror would

*have been a problem of its own and swinging such a huge
and cumbersome appliance into place could have proved
still more difficult. So we can count the mirror out because
it was never in.*

The authors had perfectly talked themselves out of the solution.
First, the size of the mirror was not a problem, as Pepper and Tobin
had proven half a century earlier. Jarrett, an expert in building stage
illusions, had suggested using large mirrors for his own disappearing
elephant trick. In Morritt's cabinet the mirror didn't really have to
swing or move. The elephant would be led into the wedge-shaped
hiding place with wooden walls and a mirror applied on the opposite
side of one of the walls. It's a mistake to think that the elephant is
inside the cabinet alongside an enormous, delicate piece of glass. The
wooden wall would be between the two, and the elephant wouldn't
have an opportunity to get close to
the polished surface of the mirror.

They were similarly wrong about
the angles at the Hippodrome. It's
true that the stage was wide,
but the "safe zone" of the cabinet
can be plotted. By simply blocking
off a short section of the mirror
closest to the audience—for
example, painting a strip of it
black—the offending reflections
could be eliminated.

*Houdini's Elephant cabinet,
the view from the top*

Jarrett's nonchalance about the idea helped to keep the secret. He
had feigned a disinterest in Houdini's trick, and we're not even sure
from his ambiguous description whether he saw the illusion in person.
Also, Jarrett carelessly recommended the worst way to demonstrate
the secret. By putting a mirror on his drawing, the floor plan was
transformed into a weird trapezoid shape, demonstrating how all of
the angles inside seemed to go haywire.

• • •

Was this secret worthless or priceless?

After all, generations of theatre audiences have been told that many magic tricks are done with mirrors, even if they don't quite understand how these illusions are created. Morritt simply discovered how to use a different angle. Could it be considered a new creation if the angle changed from 45 degrees to 30 degrees, to 26 degrees?

The secret of the Vanishing Elephant might have been the ultimate achievement of a magical scientist, an illusion that was seen by hundreds of thousands of people and deceived them all. Except for Morritt's mysterious patent, the principle had been almost completely concealed, existing only in tentative hints. Charles Morritt died before Guy Jarrett explained the illusion in print, but he would have been delighted to know that his illusion had not only fooled the best of them but continued to confuse and mystify magicians. They thought it simply looked wrong because they couldn't recognize the geometry. They didn't understand the tweaks and twists of a clever old showman.

It was obviously a vital secret for Harry Houdini. He was able to accept Burnside's challenge and present the largest illusion in the world. Even if audiences found it uninteresting, the illusion became part of Houdini's legend, a colossal achievement destined for history. No longer was he merely the man in the bathing suit, locked underwater, or nailed in a box. It was Morritt's illusion that helped to earn him the reputation he had sought, standing alongside Robert-Houdin, Kellar, Maskelyne, and Thurston in the pantheon of magicians because of a single feat. Houdini was the man who made an elephant disappear.

Ultimately, it was a secret worth fighting for, a secret that a handful of great magicians considered important. They recognized what it suggested, a principle of optical science that could be adorned and disguised as magic.

For a few minutes on a stage, it could create the image of something impossible. For a short period of time, an entire audience could watch and wonder. They could puzzle over a fantasy and remind themselves what it felt like to encounter something unexpected and wonderful.

"Resolute imagination is the beginning of all magical operations," according to the philosopher Paracelsus. "Because men do not perfectly believe and imagine, the result is that arts are uncertain when they might be wholly certain." To the great magicians these sorts of secrets have always represented potential and have always been priceless.

In 1937 David Devant had become too helpless to live at home and was accepted in the Royal Hospital and Home for Incurables at Putney in southwest London. Will Curtis followed him there as his personal nurse. Magician Francis White, working behind the scenes at The Magic Circle, had extracted a promise that the Circle would reinstate Devant after a respectful period of time. The club offered the Master an honorary lifetime membership in 1937, which he was proud to accept.

One day, when Horace Goldin was visiting Devant at Putney, Devant remarked that, being in the hospital, he no longer had a chance to see any magic. Goldin made secret arrangements to perform a show for the patients, surprising Devant and Curtis. The Magic Circle quickly formalized these shows, which were presented annually for Devant's birthday.

At one of the early Magic Circle shows, White performed a small trick in which a steel rod was apparently pushed through a square of glass. A reporter from the *Sunday Express* took pictures of White performing the trick, and the next day the magician was surprised to find his photo in the paper next to an embarrassing headline, "The Trick That Baffled Devant." White knew that his trick could not have fooled Devant. It was a simple parlor amusement that used a secret from one of Devant's own illusions. He quickly contacted Curtis to insist that he wasn't responsible for the article and asked him to convey his apologies to the Master.

"Please don't worry about it," Curtis said. "I'll tell you a secret, if you promise not to betray it: It was Mr. Devant who gave the story to the reporter. You know, Francis, he's been very grateful for all your help. He had nothing else to give you, except a bit of free publicity."

David Devant died in 1941. For many years, The Magic Circle continued the annual magic shows at Putney in his memory.

16
Encore

I sometimes make mistakes.
The donkey never does.
—Charles Morritt

ne piece of the puzzle still didn't fit: the Disappearing Donkey.

Over many years, researching various illusions and using them on the stage, I flattered myself that I had a real feeling for Charles Morritt's mysterious inventions. I could identify a logical, step-by-step evolution of his principles. I knew what kind of optical secrets Morritt was using in his magic before the Disappearing Donkey; I knew what he was using after this illusion. I assumed that I should be able to connect them together in a neat progression; all I needed was the missing link.

After all, from a magician's point of view, there are plenty of clues to the secret. For example, there were the circular, fabric-covered hoops that were placed around the stable—one hanging behind it, one slid beneath it. The circle was a design motif that formed a sort of fingerprint for Morritt's oblique mirror. He used circular shapes to disguise the slight distortion caused by the mirror. For me, the circle had become like the black "X" in the Stodare and Tobin mirror illusions, a clue pointing to the edges of the mirror.

I could also sense the necessary flaws in the illusion, the little inconsistencies that would have been necessary for the secret to reveal itself. For example, in Devant's presentation the illusion began with the doors of the stable closed. The hoop was hung on cords behind it, and the doors of the stable were opened, giving an audience a view thorough the apparatus to the hoop.

But the neatest way to hang the hoop behind the cabinet, the most theatrical way, would be to open the cabinet wide at the start of the trick, before the donkey entered, then step behind it and, with the audience watching closely, suspend the hoop on the two cords. In other words, it would be more natural to show them the action than to tell them about it. To me it felt like there was some optical effect involved, something that looked right at specific moments but was concealed when it looked wrong by someone's stepping behind the stable.

The Disappearing Donkey couldn't be the simple illusion that Houdini's Vanishing Elephant was. The cabinets were of completely different shapes and opened in different ways. Houdini's apparatus was long and narrow, opening only on the small ends. Morritt's cabinet was wide and could be opened completely—the front, the back, and at least one end—for the entrance of the donkey. The shape of the Disappearing Donkey was much better suited to most stages.

And then there was an especially annoying fact, recorded in every account of the illusion. At the conclusion, as the doors were opened and the stable was empty, the assistant who was dressed as a clown would jump inside the stable, showing that it was empty and pushing open the hinged roof to show that the donkey was really gone. If anyone had dared to jump into Houdini's cabinet, they would have bumped into a mirror or, at the very least, been duplicated by a reflection.

Over the years I collected a thick green file of documents on the illusion, including sketches, articles, reviews, and interviews conducted with Morritt. I filled pages in notebooks with sketches of the apparatus, trying to reconstruct the sight lines of the audience and the size and shape of the prop. No illusion is perfect. If it were perfect, it wouldn't be an illusion. There are always inconsistencies or tiny hiccups during a presentation that necessarily result from the secret. A good inventor knows how to disguise these flaws within a presentation. A good performer can smooth over these flaws so that they seem logical and motivated. I was hoping that, seventy-five years after the Disappearing Donkey, I could diagnose some of these flaws and pry them open to reveal Charles Morritt's mysterious secret.

My friend Alan Wakeling retired in 1987. He had had a long career, first as a performing magician and then as a consultant, inventor, and director of magic for television shows, theme park attractions, and Las Vegas and corporate shows. One day shortly after he retired, I arranged to have lunch with him and drove to his home outside Los Angeles.

When I arrived, I presented Alan with a special puzzle. "If you're looking for something to do in retirement," I started, "I thought you might enjoy going through this file." I wasn't really hoping to fool Alan. He must have realized that any work he did on the Disappearing Donkey was actually a favor for me, not merely for his amusement, but Alan graciously accepted the assignment. I had gone through the file, removing all of my own sketches and speculations. "I'm not going to tell you what I think," I explained to Alan. "Just read the descriptions, look at the evidence, and tell me where the donkey went." Alan might have been the most experienced man in this field. I realized that he was the perfect person to notice something that I'd been missing.

Alan was born in Los Angeles in 1926 and learned about magic through the usual route, from an assortment of ineffective magic kits and dog-eared books in the public library. In Los Angeles, Alan worked as an assistant to Peter Godfrey, one of the last magicians to work at St. George's Hall in London. Godfrey later moved to Los Angeles and became a film director.

The 1950s wasn't an auspicious time for magicians. There were no big touring shows and few opportunities for performers. Alan became a nightclub magician. He's always joked about how he had idealized these sorts of performances: "The chandelier, the polished black dance floor, a spotlight illuminating the single performer in an elegant tuxedo." Of course, it wasn't like that at all. The clubs were cramped, the agents were crooked, and the jobs were catch-as-catch-can. Magic acts weren't popular. He couldn't get in the office if he told the agents that he was a magician. So, early in their career, Alan and his wife, Helen, developed an act of beautiful sleight of hand with Chinese fans. When asked what kind of act they performed, Alan told them it was a "novelty act." He counted on the fact that when agents finally realized it was magic, they'd be sold.

Alan survived by his creativity. He devised a series of amazing acts with cocktails, with numbers, or with bright, colorful illusions decorated like they'd come from the center ring of a circus. One of his specialties became an artistic version of the classic billiard ball act, slowly producing five large white balls at his fingertips as he sat on a tall barstool. He created his own version of Selbit's famous Sawing illusion, using a beautiful oak box and performing it on a dance floor inches away from the audience. Among Los Angeles magicians, Alan quickly developed a reputation as "one of the best-kept secrets in magic." He created effects and directed routines for nightclub magicians Channing Pollack and Marvyn Roy as well as special material for Mark Wilson, a popular television magician in the 1960s and '70s.

There are only a few of us who invent and design magic—it's a pretty small field—so when I arrived in Los Angeles in 1981 to work for Doug Henning, I was the new kid, and Alan was the seasoned professional. By that time he'd earned an amazing reputation. Experienced magicians loved Alan Wakeling illusions because they were elegant and theatrical, arranged like a series of perfectly composed images. Alan never really lost the sensibility of a performer. Like the dancer who becomes a choreographer and knows instinctively how the audience will receive each step, Alan's inventions were designed to make the performers look their very best.

Over the years Alan and I had collaborated on a number of illusions, and I'd always admired his ability to solve problems quickly. That's why I was a little concerned when I didn't hear anything from Alan about the Disappearing Donkey. I thought he'd forgotten about it.

Then one day when I arrived to pick him up for lunch, I was surprised to find the green file folder sitting in the middle of his table. I pointed at it. "What do you think?"

Alan cleared his throat and straightened his glasses. "Well, I have to tell you: That's an interesting problem," he said very quietly. He slid the file toward me, and I was disappointed by what looked like a casual gesture of defeat. "Whatever he was doing back then, it's not the way you'd do it today. It doesn't have the feeling of a modern illusion, the proportion. You know, those old illusionists tried to get as much as possible from a prop." I nodded, realizing that he was building up to something.

"One thing for sure," he continued. "There were two clowns." That wasn't what I expected to hear. It didn't really make any sense. "Okay, Alan, why do you say that?"

"Because you wouldn't dress that assistant as a clown unless you were doubling him for someone else." I knew that in Alan's circus act he used clown makeup to create a pair of look-alike assistants; this was one of his important secrets.

"But why would he need two clowns?" I asked.

"No idea." Alan picked up the file and handed it back to me.

"Maybe it had something to do with a mirror," I suggested, looking for evidence of Morritt's famous discoveries. "Was he matching reflections in a mirror? There has to be some reason."

"Oh, I'm sure that there was a very important reason, but I don't know what it was. No, that sort of reflection doesn't make any sense. Besides, there weren't mirrors in the cabinet, because the clown jumps inside at the end. But I know he needed a second clown. The secret involved two identical clowns."

I left with the green file under my arm. The problem was not whether Alan was right or wrong but the reminder of something that should have been obvious; Morritt's illusion wasn't just a matter of optical principles or hiding places. Part of the secret was the finesse of the presentation, the tiny feints and deceptions that enhanced the performance and surrounded the geometry like a fog. Two clowns? It was as if Alan had whispered to me, "I think you need to pay attention to Morritt's bow tie." Was it a suggestion that could really help me?

Alan was certainly right about the style of the illusion. I knew ways that I could make a donkey disappear in a box. Alan probably knew several different ways. But that wasn't the point of the exercise. We were trying to figure out how Morritt had done it, based on the principles that were in use in the early 1900s, the secrets he was familiar with, and the fashion of magic being created and performed then.

Magic's doldrums during the 1950s and '60s forced magicians to reevaluate the art. A small group of innovators, including the popular performer Robert Harbin in England and Alan Wakeling in the United States, designed illusions that didn't require curtains, lights, and stages but could be performed in a cabaret or a nightclub. Admittedly, these experiments were only possible when magicians had time, which is a nice way of saying that they weren't always working.

Guy Jarrett's philosophies of design were appreciated by later generations of magicians. Avoiding the big, cumbersome boxes used by the old-fashioned magic acts, the new goal was to carefully design illusions by taking into account the size of the assistant. Props were built smaller and smaller to deceive the eye. Some illusions were actually adjusted to particular female assistants the way that a suit of clothes can be tailored to fit a specific body.

At the turn of the twentieth century, magic props had been built from thick planks of white pine, painted with layers of enamel paint. The secret doors, flaps, and catches were coarse and oversized, guaranteed to work in the humidity of the south or the cold of the north, designed to be thrown inside crates and jostled on the train to the next city. But by the 1960s magic craftsmen like John Gaughan refined magicians' props in artistic ways, using a variety of materials and creating more delicate, sophisticated apparatus.

Fifty years earlier Howard Thurston would have been shocked at these ideas. His goal was to fill the stage with colorful production value. A big box was thought to look "emptier" than a little box. A large piece of apparatus could be painted with lots of attractive colors and enormous patterns. Even more importantly, these oversized, overbuilt props could accommodate any sized assistant from season to season during Thurston's many tours.

Today the fashion would be to make the donkey stable as small as possible and to use the proportions of the illusion as part of the visual deception. By modern standards Morritt's prop feels too large and too complicated.

According to Devant's notes on his presentation, the stable was closed up except for one door on the side. Then, just before the donkey was about to enter from that side door, the magician gave "a signal" and "the two assistants beneath stage now raise[d] the fake."

I realized that taking a donkey through a trapdoor down through the stage was impossible. Devant toured the music halls with the illusion. Morritt performed it outdoors in Brighton. The equipment necessary for this sort of trapdoor—an enormous mechanism installed in each stage—would have been beyond the capacity of any touring show or seaside stage. Every account of the illusion remarked on the speed of the disappearance and the absence of any hoofbeats, suggesting that the donkey had not gone very far.

More than likely, the men under the stage were simply operating something inside the cabinet. Perhaps holes were drilled in the floor. Ropes were passed through the legs of the cabinet, and the men, pulling on these ropes, were able to raise and lower the fake. Devant used just this sort of operation in several of his illusions at St. George's Hall. It meant only that the fake was large and heavy, requiring a special arrangement so that it could be moved. It also meant that the cabinet was truly isolated in the center of the stage, far from any curtains.

Devant's notes also mentioned that the "performer is listening for the lowering of the fake. Directly he hears it down, he opens the doors." In other words, as soon as the fake was down, the visual illusion was complete, and it could be shown to the audience.

I began applying various principles used by Morritt throughout his career, but nothing completely explained where the donkey was hiding. His wedge of mirrors didn't fit inside the cabinet. It couldn't work below the cabinet. But when I tried it *behind* the cabinet, something amazing happened. It suddenly looked familiar.

Morritt boasted about his donkey, insisting that his particular gray neddy was responsible for working the mechanism of the trick by itself. But this was clearly part of his deception. Jasper Maskelyne, the Chief's grandson and of the last generation of Maskelyne magicians, wrote a colorful account of the family called *White Magic*. The book isn't easy to find and isn't widely read. It's filled with the usual magician's exaggerations and secrecy, but Jasper stumbled when he attempted to recount the anecdote of the donkey's escape backstage. I arranged another lunch meeting with Alan Wakeling.

"Have you ever read Jasper Maskelyne's book about his family?" I asked. "I didn't know Jasper Maskelyne wrote a book about his family," he said.

"I'm going to read you something that you're not going to believe." I opened the book to page 146 and began:

> We were presenting a trick with a donkey, but the donkey
> disappeared before its time. An agitated magician came

running up. "My donkey's disappeared!" he gasped. "Some fool's left the door open at the back, and the damned beast has vanished. We're due to go on in five minutes. What shall we do?"

I hastily said a word to the stage-manager and, assisted by two clowns in full make-up, raced out into Langham Place to try to trace the lost quadruped. I was presently joined by no fewer than five policemen, and we presently ran him to ground nearly half a mile away. . . . The donkey, escorted back to the theatre by the five constables, two clowns and myself, arrived in time to be included as the penultimate turn of the evening.

"Two clowns—how about that?" Alan said. "Now I suppose we really have to figure out why."

The answer was in Morritt's presentation. Reviewers were amazed when Solomon the donkey was left alone inside the stable. They naturally expected the worst from the animal and were astonished to find that it had been so neatly manipulated. But the revelation of two clowns meant that the donkey was never actually alone. The trainer of the donkey—probably not a performer—was made up as a clown. Another assistant, of the same approximate size, would look identical in the same makeup and costume.

As the trainer led the donkey onto the stage, the duplicate Pierrot clown was hiding somewhere in the stable. The donkey was pulled into the stable, and then seconds later the matching clown jumped out again, giving the impression that the animal was alone inside. The audience waited for the donkey to start kicking or lunging for the doors. They didn't know that the trainer was still with Solomon, leading him quietly to his hiding place. Solomon was no super-donkey but had to be handled with the requisite attention and coercion. In fact, Morritt wasn't simply making a donkey disappear. He was making a clown appear and then making a clown and a donkey disappear.

●   ●   ●

Imagine that a shelf was behind the stable and just large enough for the donkey to stand on. It was concealed by a large mirror, which slanted over it. The mirror formed the angled roof of the container.

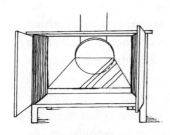

*Looking into Morritt's
Vanishing Donkey cabinet*

The front edge of the mirror was concealed along the floor of the cabinet. The back edge of the mirror bisected the round muslin hoop horizontally.

Here's a good way to think of it. You can see the Disappearing Donkey in a mug of coffee. As you drink a dark-colored liquid from a mug, there's a point at which the edge of the liquid reaches the diameter of the circle at the bottom of the mug. Look straight into the mug. The liquid angles down to the front edge at your lips. The surface of the dark liquid is the mirror. It provides a nearly perfect reflection of the back circle, only slightly distorted because of the angle of the liquid.

The actual apparatus behind the donkey's stable would take on a particular trapezoidal shape. This is because of the audience's sight

*The hinged mirror and
container to hide the donkey*

lines. Morritt wouldn't have wanted people seated at the extreme sides to have a view of the sides of the container. By making the container wedge-shaped, these sides wouldn't be visible.

Now imagine that this mirror could be raised and lowered like a clamshell. Men beneath the stage, pulling on ropes, could hinge it up so that the donkey could step inside. The mirror would then be lowered against the side of the donkey, hiding it from view.

In other words, Solomon was standing beneath a mirror.

The reason it had looked familiar to me was that it was the same basic secret as Morritt's original cage trick. A wedge of mirror was concealed behind the apparatus; the mirror could open to hide someone inside of it. For the Disappearing Donkey, Morritt had tipped the wedge on its side. If the mirror were at an angle less than 45 degrees—say 35 or 40 degrees—it would reflect a higher patch of the backdrop, rather than need a separate bit of curtain for the reflection. The Disappearing Donkey was really the missing link in Morritt's string of inventions, the idea that was halfway between his early mirror effects and the later illusions using the oblique mirror and the circular shapes.

It also reminded me of an old theatrical effect that was described in an 1875 French book of stagecraft, J.J. Moynet's *L'Envers du Théatre* (The Theatre Inside Out). Moynet described a nineteen-century French production that included a view of the Chinese countryside. The effect was accomplished with large plates of mirror, arranged horizontally across the stage and tipped up slightly toward the audience. A cutout shoreline was at the top edge of the glass. When the shoreline was reflected in the glass, it gave the perfect impression of a lovely, placid lake. There were very few books on theatrical special effects at the time, and a magician like Charles Morritt may have seen this description. Perhaps the Chinese lake effect evolved into the hoop and the mirror that were behind the Disappearing Donkey stable.

I decided to test it out on a donkey. I met Jerie Garbutt, who lived a few blocks from me in Southern California and happened to be raising three Sicilian donkeys. I placed my model on the table in her backyard, explained what I knew about Morritt's trick, and asked if I could measure her donkeys to see if it would work.

I stepped over the fence to measure Burrito, an excitable jack with a pretty, apricot gray–colored coat. He was unhappy with the rattle of my tape measure. Jerie was able to supply commendable insights into a donkey's way of thinking. "If he's about to kick," Jerie warned me, "you'll first see a twitch. It's better to throw yourself close to the donkey rather than back away. It's like the crack of a whip. Much more painful at the end of the arc." That wasn't what I wanted to hear. Fortunately, Burrito confined his protests to wheezes and stomps.

"I don't exactly understand," Jerie said. "You're a magician, right?

Aren't you interested in performing this trick?" It was hard to explain the distinction, that this was just research. After all, magicians perform, don't they? "I think we should do this," she told me. "I have a donkey. You can build it, and I'll be responsible for the training."

Alan Wakeling agreed. "I think you should perform it. You've been working on this trick for years. When are you going to have another opportunity like this, with a donkey just down the street?" Alan was studying my little model, waving his fingers above it to test how the mirror reflected the background. "You're never going to know, really know, what Morritt was thinking, until you put it in front of an audience. It's not going to be magic until someone sees it."

I'm not a performer, but I knew that I'd have a sympathetic audience at a convention in the fall of 1995, the Los Angeles Conference on Magic History. A small group of us had organized the convention every two years to discuss the people, apparatus, craftsmen, and deceptions that had been used in the past. Willie Kennedy built the apparatus, based on my diagrams. Jerie Garbutt suggested another of her donkeys, Midget, for the part, a pretty, dark brown female donkey. For the record, donkeys are not stupid. As Jerie pointed out, they're pretty smart. They are not as easily scattered or confused as horses. They are single-minded and relentless, which sometimes translates into stubbornness and sometimes is a virtue.

Once again Alan was right. If it's calculated in a notebook, it ends up being geometry. If it's written or researched, it might be history. When people are watching, it has the potential of being magic. The real art is only complete in the mysterious pact between a performer and the audience. On November 11, 1995, I stepped onstage to show a hundred fifty magicians an illusion that had been lost for seventy-five years. As I cleared my throat, I noticed that Alan was sitting in the front row:

> In all of the world, there is only one. Ladies and gentlemen, it gives me great pleasure to introduce the famous Disappearing Donkey.

Jerie Garbutt has since told me how impressed she was with her donkey that night. Before the doors of the theatre opened, Midget was impatiently scratching the ground, nibbling plants, and surveying the area with suspicion. She seemed poised for trouble. As soon as the spotlight found her and the music began, however, she pricked up her ears, looked straight ahead, and made a perfect entrance, walking with determination onto the stage. A friend of mine in the audience, an actor, later commented on how unexpected and odd it is to be in a crowded room when a large animal enters, how strangely electrifying it feels. Morritt had a good idea. Donkeys are funny. When Midget moved with determination, her attitude seemed funny. When she balked and resisted, it was even funnier.

> It would be a very clever donkey indeed who could jump through this hoop without making a tear in the linen. I'm going to surround the cabinet using these two hoops, while all of you keep an eye on it. Take this hoop to the back of the cabinet and hang it from that loop of ribbon.

I handed the first hoop to an assistant, who stepped behind the closed stable. It wasn't actually hung from the ribbon. It was attached to the ribbon and then slid into a bracket behind the top edge of the mirror. In this way the hoop was suspended at the precise angle and position for the illusion. Meanwhile, I slid the second hoop beneath the stable.

We opened all the doors. The illusion looked perfect, with the fabric hoop hanging behind the apparatus. The stable was closed up again.

> There are also two doors in each side. That's for the performer's entrance.

How does a modern wizard keep such a secret? More than likely, the information was lost in the fits and starts that defined Charles Morritt's career. It was overlooked as the style of magic began changing. Devant had hinted at part of the principle in his book. A patent had described the principle in more detail. But Morritt's cre-

ation was never appreciated because it was intuitive, not mathematical. As a formula or a diagram it fails, and for decades it failed to con-
vince professional magicians. The discovery needed to be massaged
into place, using cabinets and red plush drops, imagined in train cars
between Leeds and London, hammered from splinters of wood and
pieces of mirror. It was the work of a new kind of alchemist, the
optical wizard, looking for gold within a series of infinite reflections.

Midget was led into the cabinet, and we secretly lowered the mirror
over her.

> *That's it. Open it up!*

The cabinet was opened wide. Midget had disappeared, or at least it
looked as if she had disappeared, the circle of fabric forming a deceptive target for the audience's attention.

> *The donkey is gone, ladies and gentlemen. The donkey is
> gone!*

A few great magicians—determined performers who wouldn't
merely tell a story but persevered in their efforts to demonstrate the
most wonderful fantasies—have always realized that these ephemeral,
temporary miracles could be restorative for their audiences. They listened for the brief pause between the end of the trick and the start of
the applause—the split second when the entire audience shares a gasp
of genuine amazement. At that moment there's always been an hon-
orable quality in illusion.

Acknowledgments and Notes

I'm grateful to my associates in magic, who share my interests and have shared their research into these subjects as well as supporting my own research. To Mike Caveney, author and collector, and John Gaughan, craftsman and collector, I'm particularly grateful for years of friendship and assistance. Thanks, in general and not insignificantly, to David Berglas, Don Bice, David Britland, Claude Crowe, Patrick Culliton, Anne and John Davenport, Rick Davis, Anne Davenport, Edwin Dawes, Tim Felix, Charlotte Hargreaves, Richard Hatch, Ricky Jay, William Kennedy, Bill Liles, Jay Marshall, John A. McKinven, Patrick Page, Sue and Pete Pudduck, John Salisse, Helen and Alan Wakeling, and Peggy Youngs. I'd also like to recognize the contributions of a number of friends who are, unfortunately, no longer with us: Jeffrey Atkins, Talky Blank, Leslie Cole, Werner C. Dornfield, Walter Gibson, Harry Hahne, Doug Henning, Bob Lund, Frances Ireland Marshall, Jane Thurston Shepard, Vic Torsberg, T. A. Waters, Peter Warlock, and Orson Welles.

Thanks also for the many years of support from my family, Harry and Sherri Steinmeyer, Sue and Stewart Church, Grace Steinmeyer, and my late father, Harry W. Steinmeyer.

For helping to make these various adventures and explorations into a book called *Hiding the Elephant,* thanks to Tim Onosko for his suggestions and my agent Jim Fitzgerald. I'm grateful to my good friend William Stout for the deft portraits that adorn the chapters, and to Mike Caveney for the use of photographs from his collection. Through this process I've been fortunate for the support I have received from the folks at Carroll and Graf, especially assistant editor Keith Wallman and my editor, Philip Turner, who has offered wonderful insights in translating my world into the real world. And many thanks to editorial director Joy de Menil and Justine Taylor at William Heinemann for their encouragement and enthusiasm.

Finally, I'm especially appreciative for the help of my wife, Frankie Glass. Although she's far too knowledgeable on these subjects to really be unbiased, her critical suggestions and encouragement have been essential to this project.

Chapter 1: Overture

I've assembled the account of Houdini's illusion from several sources, borrowing the words from Houdini's own account in *The Sphinx* magazine, a journal for magicians, March 1918, and Clarence Hubbard's account in the same issue. Houdini's biographies all mention his elocution, in particular Milbourne Christopher, *Houdini, the Untold Story* (Thomas Y. Crowell, New York, 1969) and Kenneth Silverman, *Houdini!!!* (Harper Collins, New York, 1996). The best account and comparison of contemporary accounts of the illusion is in Patrick Culliton, *Houdini Unlocked* (Kieran Press, Los Angeles, 1997).

The challenge from the *Daily Mirror* has been recounted in these books. I'm grateful to my friend Bill Liles, who has examined the actual *Mirror* handcuffs and speculated on Houdini's ability to pick the lock.

Servais LeRoy's remarks on Houdini were quoted in Mike Caveney and William Rauscher, *Servais LeRoy, Monarch of Mystery* (Magic Words, Pasadena, California, 1999). Orson Welles shared his memories of Houdini's show during conversations with me in the early 1980s in Hollywood. Welles also remembered meeting Houdini before the show, when his father took him backstage to the magician's dressing room. Young Orson explained to Houdini that he was learning magic. Houdini instructed him in the rudiments of the Pass, a difficult maneuver with a pack of cards. As Orson juggled the cards in his hands, attempting to follow Houdini's lead, the magician told him, "Never perform anything before an audience until you've practiced it a thousand times." At that moment the dressing room door burst open, and Jim Collins, Houdini's chief assistant, informed his boss, "We just got the new lamp trick from Conradi." "Great—put it in tonight!" Houdini fired back.

David Bamberg's memory of that precise lamp trick is from David Bamberg, *Illusion Show* (Meyerbooks, Glenwood, Illinois, 1991). Doug Henning performed the Conradi Lamp on his 1981 NBC television special; the prop was owned and restored by John Gaughan, and despite its reputation, it looked great on our show. Vic Torsberg's memories are from my conversations with him in Chicago during the late 1970s.

Walter Gibson told me about Thurston and Houdini in a conversation at his home in Eddyville, New York, in 1980. Thurston's routines are a vivid memory for several of my good friends in magic, including Werner C. Dornfield, Gibson, John McKinven, and Welles. Thurston's backstage mantra was recounted in a conversation with Jane Thurston; his approach to his audience was also described in Dale Carnegie, *How to Win Friends and Influence*

People (Pocket Books, New York, 1981). Thurston's routines are reconstructed from a transcript of his patter in Maurine Christopher and Jim Steinmeyer, *Howard Thurston's Illusion Show Work Book II* (Magical Publications, Pasadena, California, 1992). The Levitation patter is from Maurine Christopher and Jim Steinmeyer, *Howard Thurston's Illusion Show Work Book* (Magical Publications, Pasadena, California, 1991).

Chapter 2: The Ghost

Barnum's remarks on ghosts are from Phineas Taylor Barnum, *The Humbugs of the World* (Carleton, New York, 1866). The Dion Boucicault play "The Corsican Brothers," or "The Vendetta" (1852) was first produced at the Princess's Theatre. The history of the play is described in Richard Fawkes, *Dion Boucicault* (Quartet Books, London, 1979). The Corsican Trap was explained in Percy Fitzgerald, *The World Behind the Scenes* (Chatto and Windus, London, 1881). A good description of the exchanges and action of the play is indicated in A. Nicholas Vardac, *Stage to Screen* (Harvard Universtiy Press, Cambridge, 1949). I had a chance to examine parts of a Corsican Trap as it was being removed during the restoration of the Tyne Theatre in Newcastle upon Tyne.

I spoke on the developments of Pepper's Ghost at the Magic Collector's Association convention in May 1999, and this talk was first published in a limited edition as *The Science Behind the Ghost* and later included in Jim Steinmeyer, *Two Lectures on Theatrical Illusions* (Hahne, Burbank, California, 2001). The two sides of the story are explained in Henry Dircks, *The Ghost* (Spon, London, 1863), and Professor Pepper, *The True History of the Ghost* (Cassell, London, 1890). I've also used biographical information on Dircks from a talk by Edwin A. Dawes, "The Story of Pepper's Ghost and the Spectre Drama," delivered in November 1995 at the Modern Mystic League, Blackburn. The exhibits of the Polytechnic are explained in Richard D. Altick, *The Shows of London* (Belnap Press of Harvard University Press, Cambridge, Massachusetts, 1978).

The story of Pepper and Queen Victoria is quoted in Edwin A. Dawes, *The Great Illusionists* (Chartwell, Secaucus, New Jersey, 1979). The conversation between Dircks and Pepper has been reconstructed based on the accounts in Dircks's and Pepper's books. Pepper described the visit from Faraday.

Dircks included his 1858 address and quoted the section from Porta, along with his argument that his invention was different. Pierre Séguin's patent was sent to me through the courtesy of French magicians Jacques Voignier and

Pierre Albanese and was reproduced in Jim Steinmeyer, *Two Lectures on Theatrical Illusion.*

David Lano's story appeared in David Lano, *A Wandering Showman, I* (Michigan University Press, Ann Arbor, 1957). The fact that Lano could lie "head-up" or "head-down" in the oven without noticing the difference means that it was flat, which indicates that the glass overhead was tipped 45 degrees. The imitations of Pepper's Ghost are described in Thomas Frost, *Lives of the Conjurers* (Chatto & Windus, London, 1881).

Robin's career is described in Edwin A. Dawes, *Henry Robin, Expositor of Science & Magic* (Abracadabra Press, Balboa Island, California, 1989), and Christian Fechner (translated from the French by Stacey Dagron), *The Magic of Robert-Houdin: An Artist's Life* (Editions F.C.F, Boulogne, France, 2003.) Robin's claims were made in Henri Robin, *L'Almanach Illustré le Cagliostro, Historie des Spectres Vivants et Impalpables, Secrets de la Physique Amusante* (Pagnerre, Paris, 1864). Some of this material was translated and discussed by Henry Ridgely Evans, *History of Conjuring and Magic* (International Brotherhood of Magicians, Kenton, Ohio, 1928) and Henry Ridgely Evans, *The Old and New Magic* (Open Court Press, Chicago, 1909). Evans tended to favor Robin's claims, but these were disputed by S.H. Sharpe, *Conjurer's Optical Secrets* (Mickey Hades, Calgary, 1985), and S.H. Sharpe, *Salutations to Robert-Houdin* (Mickey Hades, Calgary, 1983). Robert-Houdin also disagreed with Robin's claims, as described in Jean Eugene Robert-Houdin (translated by Louis Hoffman), *The Secrets of Stage Conjuring* (Routledge, London, 1881). The history of these inventions was included in Sidney W. Clarke, *The Annals of Conjuring* (originally serialized in *The Magic Wand*, 1924–1928) (Magico, New York, 1983).

Pepper's Ghost survives today in several different forms, and the basis of the invention has been used in Teleprompters and heads-up displays in automobile dashboards and fighter jets. It was even used for several years in video arcade games to combine black-and-white monitor images with colored backgrounds. The use of a "beam-splitter," as the half-silvered glass is often called, was for many years an important element of film special effects, used to combine images on one frame of film.

Chapter 3: A New Type of Magic

Ira Davenport's remark was quoted in Harry Houdini, *A Magician Among the Spirits* (Harper and Brothers, New York, 1924).

The Name on the Paper trick, which I used as an example, can with a bit of creativity be assembled from secrets in the first English book that includes conjuring, Reginald Scot's *A Discoverie of Witchcraft*, first published in London in 1584. Any modern magician would have an easy time recreating this illusion, using a variety of possible methods.

For the story of the Davenports, I've used Houdini's *A Magician Among the Spirits* as well as the facsimile edition of Houdini's original draft, Harry Houdini, *A Magician Among the Spirits: The Original Manuscript* (Kaufman and Greenberg, Washington, D.C., 1996). Comparisons of these two books demonstrate Houdini's literary efforts and his reliance on editors and ghostwriters.

The Davenports' career has also been described in Milbourne Christopher, *Mediums, Mystics and the Occult* (Thomas Y. Crowell, New York, 1975); Henry Ridgely Evans, *The Old and New Magic*; Sidney W. Clarke, *The Annals of Conjuring*; and John Mulholland, *Beware Familiar Spirits* (Charles Scribner, New York, 1938). Particular insight into their early career was provided in Barnum, *Humbugs of the World*.

I've also assembled my account by using descriptions in Edwin A. Dawes, *The Great Illusionists*; Christian Fechner, *The Magic of Robert-Houdin: An Artist's Life*; David Price, *Magic, A Pictorial History of Conjurers in the Theatre* (Cornwall Books, New York, 1985); and Charles Waller, *Magical Nights at the Theatre* (Gerald Taylor Productions, Melbourne, 1980).

My account of the Fox sisters is from Milbourne Christopher, *Mediums, Mystics and the Occult*, and Harry Houdini, *A Magician Among the Spirits*. Houdini quotes Margaret Fox's confession and the account of her New York lecture.

The story of Boucicault's London séance is in Richard Fawkes, *Dion Boucicault*. The brothers' success and imitators in Paris is discussed in Christian Fechner, *The Magic of Robert-Houdin: An Artist's Life*. Their séances and the French riot were described by Jean Eugene Robert-Houdin, *The Secrets of Stage Conjuring*.

There are various accounts of the brothers' secret. The use of slack behind their backs was mentioned by William E. Robinson, *Slate Writing and Kindred Phenomena* (Scientific American, New York, 1898), and this sort of rope escape later evolved into an effect known to magicians as the Kellar Rope Tie. Houdini mentioned the slack gained by tying both of them in *A Magician Among the Spirits*.

Pepper's remarks are quoted from Professor Pepper, *The True History of the Ghost*.

Chapter 4: A Formula for Invisibility

Stodare's quote is from his souvenir book, Colonel Stodare, *A New Handy-Book of Magic* (A. Nimmo, London, 1865).

Vic Torsberg performed around the Chicago area for many years and was well known to Chicago magicians from the 1930s through the 1970s. He also assisted Harry Thurston, a Chicagoan who was Howard Thurston's brother, in his ill-fated attempt at a magic show and used to share great stories about this adventure and Harry Thurston's ineptitude.

I spoke on the evolution of mirror illusions at the Magic Circle Collector's Day, May 2001, and this talk was first published in a limited edition as *Discovering Invisibility* and later included in Jim Steinmeyer, *Two Lectures on Theatrical Illusions*.

The historical patents are referenced in Terence Rees and David Wilmore, *British Theatrical Patents* (Society for Theatre Research, London, 1996), and the ghost inventions were also discussed by Sidney W. Clarke, *The Annals of Conjuring*.

Proteus was explained in Professor Hoffmann, *Modern Magic* (Routledge, London, 1876), and in the article by Edmund H. Wilkie, "Optical Illusions," in *The Magician Annual, 1907–08* (Will Goldston, London, 1908).

The information on Thomas Tobin is from his obituary in the *Proceedings of the Ninth Annual Meeting of the Polytechnic Society of Kentucky* (Louisville, Kentucky, 1887). After an unsuccessful tour of the United States with Pepper in 1872, Tobin settled in Louisville, teaching chemistry at Central Kentucky University. He died there of consumption at age 40.

Colonel Stodare's career and the Sphinx were recounted in Edwin A. Dawes, *Stodare: The Enigma Variations* (Kaufman and Company, Washington, D.C., 1998). The story of the fingerprints on the mirror was quoted in John Braun, *Of Legierdemaine and Diverse Juggling Knacks* (Salon de Magie, Loveland, Ohio, 1999). The story of the paper pellets is from Jean Eugene Robert-Houdin, *Secrets of Stage Conjuring*.

The Oracle of Delphi was described in Edmund H. Wilkie, "Optical Illusions." The dates and sequences of these inventions have been based on the front-page advertisements in the *Times*.

John Maskelyne's quote is from an interview, "The Great Wizard of the West," from *English Illustrated Magazine*, January 1895. Devant's quote is from David Devant, *Secrets of My Magic* (Hutchinson, London, 1936).

The history of J.N. Maskelyne and his theatre was assembled from Milbourne Christopher, *The Illustrated History of Magic* (Thomas Y. Crowell, New York, 1973); Milbourne Christopher, *Panorama of Magic* (Dover, New York, 1962); Sidney W. Clarke, *The Annals of Conjuring*; Edwin A. Dawes, *The Great Illusionists*; George A. Jenness, *Maskelyne and Cooke, Egyptian Hall, London, 1873–1904* (published by the author, Enfield, Middlesex, 1967); Jasper Maskelyne, *White Magic: The Story of the Maskelynes* (Stanley Paul, London, 1936); and David Price, *Magic: A Pictorial History of Conjurers in the Theatre*. I've also used a brief autobiographical article, "My Reminiscences," which appeared in the January 1910 *The Strand* magazine.

J.N. Maskelyne's first cabinet was described in Edmund H. Wilkie, "Optical Illusions." The evolution and script for "Will, the Witch and the Watchman" was reproduced in S.H. Sharpe, *The Magic Play* (Magic Inc., Chicago, 1976). Sexton's lecture was discovered in a small book by my friend John A. McKinven, published by J. Burns of London, and was reproduced in John Braun, *Of Legierdemaine and Diverse Juggling Knacks*. The improved Maskelyne Cabinet was diagrammed in Will Goldston, *More Exclusive Magical Secrets* (The Magician, Ltd., London, 1921).

In 1997, for the Los Angeles Conference on Magic History, we resurrected "Will, the Witch and the Watchman" for our audience of magicians and enthusiasts. I took the liberty of revising the script since the original was filled with elaborate Victorianisms, puns, and character types. However, with the help of John A. McKinven, I retained the action of the play, the characters, situations, and magic. Our cast included a number of talented magicians and actors, including John Carney, Don Bice, Patrick Albanese, Lesley Lange, Craig Dickens, and Jim Piper. My friend Rolly Crump designed the poster and scenery. It was a good education in magic, and with some "dusting off," the play survives the years well. It was ingeniously arranged to favor one good actor, who played the part of Miles, the Watchman, allowing for other characters to enter and exit, providing the magic. The idea of having spectators seated on the stage, watching from various angles and eventually incorporated into the action, seems oddly modern and disarming. Our production was described, with photos, in the December 1997 issue of *Magic: An Independent Magazine for Magicians*.

The story of Psycho was described in John Gaughan and Jim Steinmeyer, *The Mystery of Psycho* (John Gaughan and Associates, Los Angeles, 1987), where I discussed the changes in Clarke's credits and his contribution to the *Encyclopedia Britannica*. Pole's article appeared in the January 1876 issue of *McMillan's Magazine*. The articles cited are from "Magic, White," by J.A. Clarke, *The Encyclopedia Britannica*, 9th edition (Adam and Charles Black, Edinburgh, 1875–1889), and "Magic," by J.A. Clarke and J.N. Maskelyne, *The Encyclopedia Britannica*, 10th edition (Adam and Charles Black, The Times, Edinburgh, 1902–1903). I had a chance to examine Psycho in the Museum of London, through the courtesy of John Salisse and Colin Sorensen. Maskelyne severely reworked Psycho before it reappeared in 1910; my own theory, explained in *The Mystery of Psycho*, is that he was attempting to make it play chess! John Gaughan owns Kellar's Psycho, and I was able to operate it backstage in its first "restored" performances, in 1987.

The Stollery and Evans trunk was described in Henry Ridgely Evans, *The Old and New Magic*; John Braun, *Of Legierdemaine and Diverse Juggling Knacks*; and Will Goldston, *Sensational Tales of Mystery Men* (Will Goldston, Ltd., London, 1929). Goldston believed that the trunk might not have been tricked, as he wrote in Will Goldston, *A Magician's Swan Song* (Long John, Ltd., London, 1934). This theory was put forward by Ellis Stanyon, *Stanyon's Serial Lessons in Conjuring* (Kaufman and Greenberg, Washington, D.C., 1996).

DeKolta's creations were described in Will Goldston, *Exclusive Magical Secrets* (The Magician Ltd., London, 1912); Will Goldston, *The Magician Annual, 1909–1910* (Will Goldston, London, 1910); and Peter Warlock, *Buatier deKolta: Genius of Illusion* (Magical Publications, Pasadena, California, 1993). DeKolta's lack of finesse onstage was described by Theo Bamberg to Robert Parrish, author of *Okito on Magic* (Magic Inc., Chicago, 1952).

The quote about the bedstead was made to Devant and noted in John Braun, *Of Legierdemaine and Diverse Juggling Knacks*. The temperamental disappearance of the large piece of cloth was discussed and discouraged by Louis Hoffmann, *More Magic* (George Routledge and Sons, London, 1890).

Chapter 6: Two Wizards

Morritt's quote is from a letter written to Will Goldston, through the courtesy of Claude Crowe. I wrote about Morritt in Jim Steinmeyer, *Art & Artifice and Other Essays on Illusion* (Hahne, Burbank, California, 1998). A good description of his energetic performances is found in Charles Waller, *Magical Nights at the Theatre.* The silent code is discussed in S.H. Sharpe, *Conjurer's Psychological Secrets* (Hades Publications, Calgary, Alberta, 1988) and Hercat, *Latest Sleights* (Dean and Sons, London, 1906).

The early biographical information is based on a Morritt article contributed to David Devant, *Secrets of My Magic.* At the end of his life, Morritt was working on an autobiography, but he lost the manuscript. It seems as if this short chapter included in Devant's book is the one remnant that survived. Accounts of Morritt's performances can be found in George Jenness, *Maskelyne and Cooke, Egyptian Hall.* I've also used playbills from my own collection.

Morritt's caricature and the description of his drinking appeared in the February 13, 1894, issue of *Ally Sloper's Half Holiday*, and I found it in an article by Stanley Collins, "F.O.S. Portrait Gallery," *The Magic Cauldron*, no. 14, December 1964. The Orton story is from Douglas Woodruff, *The Tichborne Claimant: A Victorian Mystery* (Farrar, Straus and Cudahy, New York, 1957), and the March 10, 1894, and April 14, 1894, issues of *The Graphic* (London). Information on the Ardlamont mystery and Scott, "The Missing Man," is from William Roughead, *Classic Crimes* (New York Review of Books, New York, 2000). Roughead also saw Morritt's hypnotic cross-examination of Monson and mentioned Morritt's troubles at the Eden Theatre.

Devant's story is explained in David Devant, *My Magic Life* (Hutchinson, London, 1931), and David Devant, *Secrets of My Magic.*

Morritt's Man in a Trance is quoted from a playbill in my collection.

Devant described his history with animated photographs in *My Magic Life.*

Chapter 7: Father and Son

Robert-Houdin's famous quote is from Jean Eugene Robert-Houdin (translated by Professor Hoffmann), *Secrets of Conjuring and Magic* (George Routledge and Sons, London, 1878). The description of his Orange Tree is taken from the English translation of his memoirs, Jean Eugene Robert-Houdin (translated by Lascelle Wraxall), *Memoirs of Robert-Houdin, King of the Conjurers* (Dover, New York, 1954). Like most of Robert-Houdin's stage creations, the Orange Tree was technically a *false automaton*, which means that it appeared to be animated by a clockwork motor but was actually operated by an assistant offstage using pull-strings. My friend the magic craftsman John Gaughan has reproduced the Orange Tree as a genuine automaton, operated by a mechanism. Ricky Jay performed it in his show "On the Stem," which was directed by David Mamet and produced at the Second Stage Theatre in New York through 2002 with a new accompanying routine of sleight of hand. I worked on this show, including this particular effect with John and Ricky.

The information on Robert-Houdin is taken from his own books, including his *Memoirs;* Christian Fechner, *The Magic of Robert-Houdin: An Artist's Life;* and S.H. Sharpe, *Salutations to Robert-Houdin* (Mickey Hades International, Calgary, Alberta, 1983).

For Houdini's early career, I've used the accounts by Milbourne Christopher, *Houdini: the Untold Story;* Patrick Culliton, *Houdini Unlocked;* and Kenneth Silverman, *Houdini!!!* The Maskelyne letter to Houdini is quoted in John Fisher, *Paul Daniels and the Story of Magic* (Jonathan Cape, London, 1987). Houdini's remarks on addressing an audience are from Walter B. Gibson and Morris N. Young, *Houdini on Magic* (Dover, New York, 1953).

I've quoted from Harry Houdini, *The Unmasking of Robert-Houdin* (The Publisher's Printing Company, New York, 1908), as well as the original magazine articles, collected in Harry Houdini, *Conjurer's Monthly Magazine* (Kaufman and Greenberg, Washington, D.C., 1991). His book has inspired a number of discussions. I've used material from Will Goldston, *Sensational Tales of Mystery Men;* Jean Hugard, *Houdini's Unmasking: Fact versus Fiction* (Magicana, York, Pennsylvania, 1989); Maurice Sardina, *Where Houdini Was Wrong* (George Armstrong, London, 1950); and S.H. Sharpe, *Salutations to Robert-Houdin.*

Chapter 8: Stealing Secrets

Harry Kellar's quote is from the introduction to the American edition of Ottokar Fischer, *Illustrated Magic* (Macmillan, New York, 1931). Devant's quote is from David Devant, *Lessons in Conjuring* (Routledge and Sons, London, 1922). DeKolta's flowers were described by Will Goldston, *Exclusive Magical Secrets,* and LeRoy's Garden of Sleep was from Mike Caveney and William Raucher, *Servais LeRoy, Monarch of Mystery.*

The Maskelyne effects were described in S.H. Sharpe, *The Magic Play;* George Jenness, *Maskelyne and Cooke, Egyptian Hall;* and in Bruce Armstrong, *The Encyclopedia of Suspensions and Levitations* (Mickey Hades International, Calgary, 1976), and in the appendix to David Devant, *My Magic Life.*

The story of the Bambergs' visit was recounted in David Bamberg and Robert Parrish, *Okito on Magic.*

Kellar's story has been recounted in Milbourne Christopher, *The Illustrated History of Magic,* and Harry Kellar, *A Magician's Tour, Revisited* (Phil

Temple, San Raphael, California, 2000). I've also had a chance to read his unpublished biography, written by Harry Houdini, which was in the Mulholland Library in Los Angeles.

The Kellar review is from John Northern Hilliard in *The Sphinx* magazine. Smashing the box was described in S.H. Sharpe, *The Magic Play*. John A. McKinven had a correspondence with Will Stone, Valadon's assistant, in the early 1960s and shared a letter explaining how Kellar acquired his illusions. I saw a letter in a private collection from Houdini to Kellar, explaining how Devant had told Houdini about Teague. Devant wrote about Valadon's leaving in David Devant, *My Magic Life*.

The levitation was first described in Will Goldston, *Exclusive Magical Secrets*. The full explanation of the Kellar prop was explained in Maurine Christopher and Jim Steinmeyer, *Howard Thurston's Illusion Show Work Book*. The story about setting it up, including stalling and going out for beer, is from Guy Jarrett, *Magic and Stagecraft* (by the author, New York, 1936), and is reproduced in Guy Jarrett and Jim Steinmeyer, *The Complete Jarrett* (Hahne, Burbank, California, 2001). I'm indebted to John A. McKinven and John Gaughan for their interest in this illusion and their careful research and reconstructions. Gaughan presented Carter's version of the apparatus—the only surviving complete apparatus for this illusion—at the 1991 Los Angeles Conference on Magic History. I spoke on the science and evolution of the illusion at the 1999 Los Angeles Conference.

I recounted the Valadon and Kellar show from Houdini's *The Conjurer's Magazine* and *The Sphinx* magazine. Devant described the ball trick in David Devant, *Secrets of My Magic*. Kellar's patter for the trick is quoted from Neil Foster, *The Tops Treasury of Illusions* (Abbott's Magic, Colon, Michigan, 1965).

Chapter 9: Special Effects

Méliès's quote is from Paolo Cherchi Usai, *Lo schermo incanto* (International Musuem of Photography at George Eastman House, Rochester, New York, 1991).

The story of St. George's Hall has been based on information from Anne Davenport and John Salisse, *A Candid View of the Maskelynes* (John Davenport, Leicester, England, 1995); Anne Davenport and John Salisse, *St. George's Hall* (Mike Caveney's Magic Words, Pasadena, California, 2001); David Devant, *My Magic Life;* and David Devant, *Secrets of My Magic*. The Devant quotes are taken from these two books. I also wrote about the transition to St. George's Hall and the Maskelynes' attempt at special effects in Jim Steinmeyer, *Art & Artifice*.

The dimensions of Egyptian Hall were assembled from Richard Altick, *Shows of London* and Anne Davenport and John Salisse, *St. George's Hall.* Devant's address was noted in Edwin A. Dawes, *Stanley Collins: Conjurer, Collector and Iconoclast* (Kaufman and Company, Washington, D.C., 2002), and his presentations explained in S.H. Sharpe, *Devant's Delightful Delusions* (Magical Publications, Pasadena, California, 1990). Programs from Egyptian Hall are in my collection and reproduced in George Jenness, *Maskelyne and Cooke, Egyptian Hall.*

The fashion for spectacle shows is noted in Michael R. Booth, *Victorian Spectacular Theatre, 1850–1910* (Routledge & Kegan Paul, Boston, 1981); Dennis Castle, *Sensation Smith of Drury Lane* (Charles Skilton Ltd., London, 1984); and George Rowell, *Theatre in the Age of Irving* (Rowman and Little-field, Totowa, New Jersey, 1981). The story behind Peter Pan is from Roger Lancelyn Green, *Fifty Years of Peter Pan* (Peter Davies, London, 1954).

"The Mascot Moth" was described in David Devant, *Secrets of My Magic* and S.H. Sharpe, *Devant's Delightful Delusions*. A draft of his script is an appendix in *My Magic Life*. We recreated the Mascot Moth—the illusion and the play—at the 1999 Los Angeles Conference on Magic History. Our cast consisted of John Carney, Jim Piper, Roger Cox, Craig Dickens, T.C. Tahoe, Kate Walker, and Revital; the Moth was played by Tina Lenert. Patrick Albanese, in Devant's role, played Bob. John Gaughan built the apparatus, which needed some very ingenious revisions for our stage, seventeen years after he had first rebuilt the Moth illusion for "Merlin." The play is a wonderful, effective setting for the illusion. I wrote about the history of the effect and our production for the January 2000 issue of *Magic*, which included William Stout's poster for the performance and photos of the production by Bill Taylor.

Devant's presentation for the Obliging Kettle is quoted in David Devant, *Secrets of My Magic.*

Chapter 10: Magic Words

Howard Thurston was famous for promising, "I wouldn't deceive you. . . ." He spoke the words onstage, and they were printed in his programs.

My clock trick was originally presented on a network television magic special and reproduced in Jim Steinmeyer, *Impuzzibilities* (Hahne, Burbank, California, 2002).

David Thompson's quote is from *Rosebud* (Alfred A. Knopf, New York, 1996). The story of the Valadons and "Will, the Witch and the Watchman" is assembled from the Will Stone letter in John McKinven's collection and Guy Jarrett and Jim Steinmeyer, *The Complete Jarrett*. The story is also told by Theo Bamberg and Robert Parrish, *Okito on Magic* and Harry Kellar, *A Magician's Tour Revisited*.

Thurston's story is based on Walter B. Gibson, *The Master Magicians* (Doubleday, Garden City, New York, 1966); Robert E. Olsen, *The Complete Life of Howard Franklin Thurston* (Hades Publications, Calgary, Alberta 1993); Grace Thurston, *The Thurston Scrapbook* (Phil Temple and Company, San Raphael, California, 1985); and Howard Thurston and Jane Thurston Shepard, *Our Life of Magic* (Phil Temple, San Raphael, California, 1989).

Bamberg's account is from Theo Bamberg and Robert Parrish, *Okito on Magic*.

Thurston's card sleights were described in a book he published, Howard Thurston, *Howard Thurston's Card Tricks* (London, 1901). The Back Palm is now a standard bit of sleight of hand described in many magic books. The story of Mark Schantz was revealed in John Braun, *Of Legierdemaine and Diverse Juggling Knacks*.

Selbit's quote is reproduced in Eric Lewis and Peter Warlock, *P.T. Selbit, Magical Innovator* (Magical Publications, Pasadena, California, 1989). The criticism of "cheap" British stage equipment is from Harry Leat, *U.S.A. Depot Magic* (by the author, London, 1925).

Thurston changed his presentation for the Levitation over the years. His patter here is assembled from a workbook routine in Maurine Christopher and Jim Steinmeyer, *Howard Thurston's Illusion Show Work Book*. Kellar's anger was recorded in Guy Jarrett and Jim Steinmeyer, *The Complete Jarrett*, and in *Genii* magazine, July 1970. Don Bice recounted the story of the man at the diner.

Carter and the Levitation is from Mike Caveney, *Carter the Great* (Magic Words, Pasadena, California, 1995). Carter later became the romantic lead in Glen David Gold's novel *Carter Beats the Devil*; Mike Caveney's research revealed a hard-boiled, commercial performer who had a successful career but was a thorn in the side of other professional magicians.

Jarrett's story is from Guy Jarrett and Jim Steinmeyer, *The Complete Jarrett*. For many years magicians assumed that the egg trick was a creation of Devant's, given to Thurston. The story of Thurston's origination of the egg trick was explained in Maurine Christopher and Jim Steinmeyer, *Howard Thurston's Illusion Show Work Book II*. Devant's version is from David Devant, *Secrets of My Magic*.

Chapter 11: Solomon

Devant's quote is from David Devant, *My Magic Life*.

"Merlin" ran at the Mark Hellenger Theatre in New York from December 10, 1982, to August 7, 1983. It was produced and directed by Ivan Reitman, written by Richard Levinson and William Link, with music by Elmer Bernstein and lyrics by Don Black. The show starred Doug Henning, Chita Rivera, Nathan Lane, and Michelle Nicastro. Steve Kirsner and William Kennedy operated the Moth apparatus beneath the stage. I described the onstage and beneath-stage coordination in Jim Steinmeyer, *Art & Artifice*.

Material is quoted from Nevil Maskelyne and David Devant, *Our Magic* (Routledge & Sons, London, 1911).

The story of Devant at St. George's Hall is from Anne Davenport and John Salisse, *St. George's Hall*; David Devant, *My Magic Life*; and S.H. Sharpe, *Devant's Delightful Delusions*. Devant's discovery of Morritt is from David Devant, *My Magic Life*.

I've reconstructed Morritt's trick from contemporary accounts. I first wrote about it in Jim Steinmeyer, *Art & Artifice*. Reviews appear in the September 1912 issue of *The Magic Wand* and the same month's *The Magician Monthly* as well as Anne Davenport and John Salisse's *A Candid View of the Maskelynes*. A drawing of the apparatus also appeared in the "To-day, 1914" issue of *The Magic Mirror*, a promotional paper from Devant, which was reproduced in the December 1944 issue of *The Sphinx* magazine. I'm also grateful to John Fisher for his assistance in the research and materials from his collection.

Edward Victor's story is from Rae Hammond, *The Magic of Edward Victor's Hands* (Kaufman and Greenberg, Washington, D.C., 1995). Devant's notebook presentation was shown to me in a private collection in London.

Beauty and the Beast was described in David Devant, *Secrets of My Magic*. Ragtime Magic was reconstructed from reviews and a photograph in the collection of John Salisse. It's interesting to note that Devant explained only his own illusions in his book, so he did not explain the Disappearing Donkey. But Beauty and the Beast, it is recorded, was a collaboration with Morritt and involved Morritt's principle.

Chapter 12: Houdini

Houdini's quote is from Patrick Culliton, *Houdini Unlocked*.

Houdini's Water Torture Cell was described by Milbourne Christopher, *Houdini: The Untold Story*, and Kenneth Silverman, *Houdini!!!* John

Gaughan restored the Water Torture Cell for its owner, Sid Radner, shortly before it was destroyed by fire. The audio recording of Houdini was noted by Patrick Culliton, *Houdini Unlocked,* and a segment from it was played on an A&E Network documentary that I produced with Rick Davis, a history of magic titled *The Story of Magic.* Sharpe's comments are from S.H. Sharpe, *Conjurer's Psychological Secrets,* and S.H. Sharpe, *Devant's Delightful Delusions.* When Sharpe was a boy, he saw Devant perform and was disappointed. Devant later refused to write an introduction to one of Sharpe's books. Sharpe held his grudges for many years.

Information on Goldston is from Edwin A. Dawes, *Glimpses of Goldston* (Dane Hill, Ridgewood, New Jersey, 1999). Goldston described Houdini, the mysterious manuscript, and his suggestion of Morritt in Will Goldston, *Secrets of Famous Illusionists,* and Will Goldston, *Sensational Tales of Mystery Men.* I've also quoted from Will Goldston, *Who's Who in Magic,* as well as Will Goldston, *Tricks that Mystify* (Will Goldston, London, 1934). I've also used Morritt's letters in my collection. Houdini's letter to Kellar is from *Magicol* magazine, November 1993.

DeKolta's Die was long considered a strange pipedream, but in recent years it was recreated by John A. McKinven and John Gaughan. McKinven pointed out that the assemblage of springs, spreading rapidly in three dimensions at the same time, is technically a "mechanical bomb." It's a curious, difficult piece of apparatus, but it gives a surprising effect.

A bill for Houdini's show appeared in Milbourne Christopher, *Houdini: A Pictorial Life* (Thomas Y. Crowell, New York, 1976). The "primitive hunter" remark is from Kenneth Silverman, *Houdini!!!* LeRoy's remark is from Mike Caveney and William Raucher, *Servais LeRoy, Monarch of Mystery.*

Although the escape artist never actually admitted the source of the Vanishing Elephant, a number of Morritt's contemporaries recorded that it was his illusion, including Sidney W. Clarke, *The Annals of Conjuring.* I've reconstructed Morritt's conversation with Houdini.

Chapter 13: Jennie

Jarrett's quote is from Guy Jarrett and Jim Steinmeyer, *The Complete Jarrett,* as is the story of the model and Burnside. The Hippodrome and its productions were described in Norman Clarke, *The Mighty Hippodrome* (A.S. Barnes, Cranbury, New Jersey, 1968).

The Maskelyne and Devant disagreements are from Anne Davenport and

John Salisse, *St. George's Hall,* and David Devant, *My Magic Life.* The Morritt letter is in my collection. The Morritt and Hertz show is described in Anne Davenport and John Salisse, *A Candid View of the Maskelynes.* The story of Devant and the handkerchief is from an interview with John Salisse and *Genii* magazine, May 1974. The Lesson in Magic is described in Nevil Maskelyne and David Devant, *Our Magic.*

Houdini's version of the Vanishing Elephant is based on Patrick Culliton, *Houdini Unmasked;* Kenneth Silverman, *Houdini!!!;* and Jim Steinmeyer, *Art & Artifice.* Houdini's account is from the March 1918 issue of *The Sphinx* magazine.

A bill for the Times Square appearance is reproduced in Milbourne Christopher, *Houdini: A Pictorial Life,* as is the only sketch showing a part of the Houdini apparatus.

Jarrett's quote is from Guy Jarrett and Jim Steinmeyer, *The Complete Jarrett.*

In 1930, years after Houdini's illusion, Thurston planned to tour with an Appearing Elephant, using a baby animal. The illusion utilized a different cabinet trick invented by Gustave Fasola, a clever British magician, but it was never produced because of the difficulties in traveling with the elephant.

Chapter 14: Sensations

The Selbit quote is from Eric C. Lewis and Peter Warlock, *P.T. Selbit, Magical Innovator.*

Henry Hay's quote is from Henry Hay, *The Amateur Magician's Handbook* (Thomas Y. Crowell, New York, 1972).

My friend Mike Caveney is an expert on the history of the Sawing in Half illusion and has even presented it—using Jansen's original apparatus, as it was presented in the Dante show—for our 1993 Los Angeles Conference on Magic History. At Mike's performance, Dante's famous co-star, Moi-Yo Miller, reprised her role as victim. I'm grateful for his insights and assistance with my own research into the Sawing. I wrote about the illusion in Jim Steinmeyer, *Art & Artifice.*

George Facer related the audition story in *The Magic Circular* magazine, July–August 1956. I also used reviews of Selbit from the January 1921 issue of *The Magician Monthly* and the February 1921 issues of *The Magic Wand* and *The Magic Circular.*

Selbit's story is from Eric C. Lewis and Peter Warlock, *P.T. Selbit, Magical Innovator;* Milbourne Christopher, *The Illustrated History of Magic;* and

Anne Davenport and John Salisse, *St. George's Hall*. The story of the French and English productions of Grand Guignol are from Mel Gordon, *The Grand Guignol: Theatre of Fear and Terror* (Amok, New York, 1988), and David Skal, *The Monster Show* (Penguin, New York, 1993). Goldston's remarks are from Will Goldston, *A Magician's Swan Song*.

Goldin's claims are from Horace Goldin, *It's Fun to be Fooled* (Stanley Paul, London, 1937). Carl Rosini insisted that the idea came from news of Selbit's success, in Robert Olsen, *Carl Rosini: His Life and His Magic* (Magic Inc., Chicago, 1966), and also from Walter Gibson in a conversation with me. The review of Goldin's first performance is from the July 1921 issue of *The Sphinx* magazine.

Thurston wrote of Jansen's improvements in Howard Thurston, *Our Magic Life*. Mike Caveney has documents from Goldin privately disagreeing about the importance of Jansen's improvements. The road company story is from Milbourne Christopher, *The Illustrated History of Magic*. The Goldin publicity stunts are from a brochure in Mike Caveney's collection. Thurston's patter is from Maurine Christopher and Jim Steinmeyer, *Howard Thurston's Illusion Show Work Book II*, as well as accounts from John A. McKinven and Orson Welles.

In a conversation with me, Dornfield recalled seeing and speaking with Selbit. The *Variety* review is from the September 30, 1921, issue. Bamberg's account is from David Bamberg, *Illusion Show*. Ads for the Sawing are found in the November 1921 issue of *The Sphinx* magazine. The Torrini account is from Jean Eugene Robert-Houdin, *Memoirs of Robert-Houdin,* and the clown illusion is from A.A. Hopkins, *Magic* (Munn & Co., New York, 1897).

The Pankhurst publicity stunt is mentioned in Selbit's early British reviews. Selbit's later illusions were described in Milbourne Christopher, *The Illustrated History of Magic,* and Eric C. Lewis and Peter Warlock, *P.T. Selbit, Magical Innovator*. Jeffrey Atkins told me the story of the Crushing, which had been related to him from Oswald Rae.

Chapter 15: Keeping Secrets

David Bamberg described seeing the Kellar apparatus at Kellar's home. After Kellar died, Charles Carter, who had already stolen the secret of the Levitation and had it copied for his own show, petitioned the Kellar family for the Levitation. No doubt he wanted to keep it out of other hands. Eventually, it was sold to Harry Blackstone, a popular magician who worked in opposition to Thurston. Blackstone continued the tradition, proudly presenting the Levitation of Princess Karnac throughout his career, although the illusion was particularly difficult to install on each stage. George Johnstone, a former assistant to Blackstone, told me about working with the Levitation, explaining that the Blackstone crew sometimes got lucky, playing a theatre where Thurston had already performed, which meant that the trapdoor for the Levitation had already been cut.

Houdini's story is from Kenneth Silverman, *Houdini!!!* Jasper Maskelyne's quote is from Jasper Maskelyne, *White Magic.* The fate of the Maskelyne shows is from Anne Davenport and John Salisse, *St. George's Hall,* and Jim Steinmeyer, *Art & Artifice.*

The Man in the Trance was described in Jim Steinmeyer, *Art & Artifice.* The account of Morritt in Halifax is from local newspapers, researched by my friend David Britland. Various reports appear in 1928 issues of *The Magic Wand,* and I've quoted from Morritt letters in my collection.

Thurston's show is reconstructed from Maurine Christopher and Jim Steinmeyer, *Howard Thurston's Illusion Show Work Book II;* Robert Olsen, *The Complete Life of Howard Franklin Thurston;* and Thurston's souvenir programs from 1927 and 1928.

Jarrett is quoted from Guy Jarrett and Jim Steinmeyer, *The Complete Jarrett.*

The account of Devant is from Ian Keable, *The Writings of David Devant* (by the author, London, 1999); S.H. Sharpe, *Devant's Delightful Delusions;* and *Genii* magazine, May 1974.

Jarrett's account is from Guy Jarrett and Jim Steinmeyer, *The Complete Jarrett.* The analysis of the elephant trick is from Walter B. Gibson and Morris N. Young, *Houdini's Fabulous Magic* (Bell, New York, 1961). I had a chance to discuss the Morritt method with Walter Gibson years later, and I demonstrated it, using a large model, to a group of magic collectors at the 1983 convention for the Magic Collector's Association in Chicago.

The story of the Magic Circle show is from Francis White's recollections, *Genii* magazine, May 1974.

Chapter 16: Encore

I performed the Disappearing Donkey in November 1995 and discussed the principle in a talk, "Rediscovering Morritt," at the 1997 Magic Collector's Association convention in Chicago, and another talk, "Discovering Invisibility," for the 2001 Heritage Weekend at the Magic Circle in London. I've written about it in Jim Steinmeyer, *Art & Artifice*, and Jim Steinmeyer, *Two Lectures on Theatrical Illusion*.

Alan Wakeling's magic was described in Jim Steinmeyer, *The Magic of Alan Wakeling* (Hahne, Burbank, California, 1993). Jasper Maskelyne's anecdote is from Jasper Maskelyne, *White Magic*.

The French production was described in J.J. Moynet, *L'Envers du Théatre* (Hachette, Paris, 1875), and translated in Alan S. Jackson and M. Glen Wilson, *French Theatrical Production in the Nineteenth Century* (Max Reinhart Foundation, Binghamton, New York, 1976).

I couldn't have found a better collaborator and more willing trainer than Jerie Garbutt. She wrote her own account of the illusion in *The Brayer*, Spring 1996 issue, the publication of the American Donkey and Mule Association. Willie Kennedy built the apparatus with several modern mechanical improvements, which meant than I no longer needed assistants beneath the stage and could perform it without the clown assistants for the donkey. I was particularly proud that the magicians able to see the illusion included Jay Marshall, John Salisse, Alan Wakeling, and Elizabeth Warlock, the talented magician and daughter of the grand old man of British magic, Peter Warlock. Peter had been mystified by Morritt and the Disappearing Donkey many years earlier, and had kindly shared his recollections with me.

Index

About the Illustrator

Artist William Stout has been a designer on over thirty feature films, including the "Conan" films, "First Blood," "Masters of the Universe," "Dinosaur," Men In Black," and the cult favorite "Return of the Living Dead."

Stout's innovative look at prehistoric creatures, *The Dinosaurs: A Fantastic New View of a Lost Era* (first published in 1981 and recently updated as *The New Dinosaurs*), was followed by his work in Ray Bradbury's *Dinosaur Tales* and the award winning *The Little Blue Brontosaurus*, which won the 1984 Children's Choice Award, was the basis of the film, "The Land Before Time." His prehistoric murals are on display at the Houston Museum of Natural Science and Walt Disney's Animal Kingdom.

A recipient of the National Science Foundation's Antarctic Artists and Writers program grant, he first journeyed to Antarctica in 1989. The resulting one-man show of wildlife paintings, "Dinosaurs, Penguins and Whales—The Wildlife of Antarctica" has appeared at over 70 international museum exhibitions.

Stout recently illustrated Richard Matheson's award winning children's book, *Abu and the 7 Marvels*, which won the Benjamin Franklin Award for Best Young Adult Book, and Gold and Silver Medals from the Society of Illustrators. In addition, he is well known for his comic book art, album covers, movie posters and theme park designs for Walt Disney Imagineering, Universal, Steven Spielberg, and Lucasfilm. His company, Terra Nova Press, has published 26 books on art history. Stout has also been honored with three sets of trading cards devoted to his art.

He resides in Pasadena, California with his wife and their two sons.

About the Author

Jim Steinmeyer is well known among magicians for his designs and inventions. A recent profile noted that he is responsible for creating the "defining illusions in contemporary magic." He was the magic designer for Doug Henning for seven years and has created special material for the programs of many leading magicians around the world—including Harry Blackstone, Lance Burton, David Copperfield, Ricky Jay, Siegfried and Roy, and Orson Welles. He has also designed illusions for six Broadway shows and numerous Broadway, regional or off-Broadway productions—including *Ricky Jay and his 52 Assistants, Ricky Jay on the Stem, Into the Woods,* and Disney's *Beauty and the Beast.*

Jim has researched and rediscovered many great illusions of the past and has written numerous technical books on magic history and the techniques of illusions. He lectures on these subjects and is a contributing editor to *Magic* magazine, the leading independent magazine for magicians.

In addition, Steinmeyer has served as a consultant and producer for magic television specials in the United States and Great Britain, and was a writer and producer of the A&E network's four-hour history of the art, *The Story of Magic.* For several years, he served as a consultant and concept designer for Walt Disney Imagineering, developing theme park attractions for The Walt Disney Company.

Jim Steinmeyer lives in Los Angeles with his wife, Frankie Glass, an independent television producer.